Grail Child

LEONARD COMYN NOBLEMAN

authorHOUSE®

AuthorHouse™
1663 Liberty Drive
Bloomington, IN 47403
www.authorhouse.com
Phone: 1 (800) 839-8640

Published by AuthorHouse 01/23/2018

ISBN: 978-1-5462-2116-6 (sc)
ISBN: 978-1-5462-2114-2 (hc)
ISBN: 978-1-5462-2115-9 (e)

Library of Congress Control Number: 2017919062

Print information available on the last page.

Any people depicted in stock imagery provided by Thinkstock are models, and such images are being used for illustrative purposes only. Certain stock imagery © Thinkstock.

This book is printed on acid-free paper.

Dedication to Beloved Saint Germain

The Grail Child Portrait

CONTENTS

Introduction xix

Chapter 1   A Boy of Royal Blood Enters an Elite School 1
Chapter 2   The Roots of the Nobles 9
Chapter 3   My Mother's Family 11
Chapter 4   When Willy Comes Marching Home Again 23
Chapter 5   The Boy from Upper Canada 27
Chapter 6   The Sad Case of Louis Lippschitz 31
Chapter 7   Parkside Collegiate 34
Chapter 8   Indoctrination Camp 37
Chapter 9   Liberation from King George V Academy brings
             more woes 42
Chapter 10   The Paton Legacy 47
Chapter 11   The Return of the War Hero 52
Chapter 12   Major Duncan's Vision 62
Chapter 13   The Millionaire 64
Chapter 14   Academic Exccllence 73
Chapter 15   The Nisei 84
Chapter 16   A Little More about the Posnanskis 91
Chapter 17   And More on the Nobles 94
Chapter 18   Race Relations According to the Toronto Comet 98
Chapter 19   Justice at King George V Academy 103
Chapter 20   Some Communists are Disillusioned 106
Chapter 21   Deep Contemplation 110

Chapter 22 Renee in New York 117
Chapter 23 Vice Admiral Nelson at Trafalgar 120
Chapter 24 Final Years at Willington 123
Chapter 25 The Fledgling Professional 126
Chapter 26 Playing with the Members 133
Chapter 27 Playing with Good Players 137
Chapter 28 Renee's Triumphant Return 141
Chapter 29 A Promising Career Ends..160
Chapter 30 The Flight Cadet 170
Chapter 31 My Final Military Flight...181
Chapter 32 The Barkers and the Anders 189
Chapter 33 A Married Couple 196
Chapter 34 At Work in the Field of the Engineers....................202
Chapter 35 Unjust Dismissal..207
Chapter 36 Other Work Assignments...215
Chapter 37 Making the Change..218
Chapter 38 Hugh Watson Leaves "The Farm" 221
Chapter 39 The Farm is sold 226
Chapter 40 The Entrepreneur...230
Chapter 41 A Couple in Hibernation 242
Chapter 42 Return to Isolationism 248
Chapter 43 Teacher Training...250
Chapter 44 A More Responsible Position....................................264
Chapter 45 The Picket Line..267
Chapter 46 Agnes Finds True Love 272
Chapter 47 Yet another Career Begins...276
Chapter 48 The Executive Officer..281
Chapter 49 The New Principal 284
Chapter 50 My Final year in Teaching 285
Chapter 51 The Last Straw..289
Chapter 52 Total Commitment to the Light 293
Chapter 53 Robert and Renee are Old People............................296
Chapter 54 Alumni Reunion, the Same Old Shit 299

Glossary of Canadian Terms 301
Appendix 1 312
Appendix 2 – The House of Jesus 314
Appendix 3 -Car Payment Problem 317
Selected Reading 319
About the Author 322

INTRODUCTION

My mother's parents came from upper New York State. Have you ever wondered about your roots? Did your ancestors on both sides of their families come from Eastern Europe? Would a geneology search show their true roots? I always believed that was impossible because immigrants from Eastern Europe kept few records. At one time when I was about 34 years old I visited a psychic who said very little but for one thing. He said, "Mr. Nobleman, you should check your ancestry. You have Royal blood from the Scottish kings.

"Just how do I do that," I wondered. My mother's parents came from upper New York State. They crossed into Canada via the Niagara Frontier in 1898. They were looking for new opportunities. All their children were born in Toronto. At that time immigration laws were looser. The male spoke good English and the female spoke like she just got off the boat from Poland. I met this lady early in my life. The grandfather I never met. He died in 1934 before I came around. My mother, other than the fact that her parents came from the United States was never interested in her roots.

My father's roots were revealed to me earlier than my mother's. His family originated in the Ukraine. They came from Mogolov situated on The Dneiper River. Their ancestors didn't originate from that location. They came originally from Granada located in the Iberian Peninsula. They were expelled from Spain in 1492 when the United Kingdoms of Aragon and Castile finally ousted the remaining Arabs. Spain became a Catholic nation. Any Jews remaining could hold their properties if they became "Conversos." However if they relapsed they would come before the Spanish Inquisition. My ancestors left Iberia and migrated eastward. They ultimately settled in the Ukraine. In 1908 they arrived in Canada landing in Montreal, Quebec. All but the oldest two sons were born in Canada. In 1910 they moved to Toronto and settled in the slums. What I knew about my father's roots came from his mother Esther Perez. She kept an oral history of her people.

When I about 35 years old and working as a mathematics teacher I was compelled by Divine Light to look at certain Spiritual teachings. I was standing in the bedroom of my apartment when I was suddenly engulfed in a White Light. I then said out loud "What do you want me to do Lord." I never knew about the experiences of Saint Paul on the Road to Damascus. I was to be told in no uncertain terms. The book you are about to read is entirely true. I have changed the names and locations of things that I experienced. If they did not actually happen to me they happened to others I knew. Read about an almost 13 years old boy who discovers who he really is.

CHAPTER 1

A Boy of Royal Blood
Enters an Elite School

I was given the name of Robert MacAlpine Noble by my mother
Agnes Posnaski Noble when I was born in Toronto, Ontario, Canada
on December 1, 1932. It was Agnes's father Gabriel Posnanski who
requested that "MacAlpine" be my middle name. This was a tribute to
my mother's father's family who I discovered at 13 years of age were
MacAlpines and the lineal descendants of the first king of both the Picts
and Scots: Kenneth MacAlpine. Kenneth MacAlpine was the son of a
marriage between Alpine, King of Scots and the daughter of the King
of Picts. This marriage took place around 820 AD.

King Kenneth's foremost ancestor was Princess Tea Tempi. In 575
BC the Babylonians invaded what was left of King David's Kingdom
of Israel and killed off almost all of the successors to David. A great
many of the Israelites consisting of mostly the remnants of the tribes
of Judah, Benjamin and Levy were carried off to Babylon. There they
mixed with the various tribes of Persia and diluted and corrupted their
pure blood through intermarriage with gentiles. About 100 years later
they returned to Palestine. These returners were called "the remnant of
Judah" or "Jews." But even these people had Hebrew Blood. This blood
was somewhat corrupted from intermarriage with various non-Hebrew
tribes. The remaining sons of Judah and others of the Hebrews had
enough Hebrew Blood to consider themselves Israelites.

Recognizing the imminent peril to what was left of the Royal House the Prophet Jeramiah, ordained with the Divine Wisdom of the Ascended Masters, facilitated the escape of Princess Tea. He and the Princess travelled by sea and land and reached what is now Northern Ireland and today is called "Ulster." Princess Tea married into the Royal family. They knew who she was. This is a fantastic bloodline for me to have but it is only a small part of it. My mother had so much Royal Blood it makes the modern members of the remaining royal houses of Europe look like the peasants. This is the core of my mother's line but it is not the only important part. For I Am a "Grail Child;" a Scion of the Holy Grail and I will tell you what that means later. It is not pride that I have in this bloodline for pride is a negative thing. I do however feel extremely privileged. I first began to get an idea of who I was when I was 13 years old. Then I began to discover my Father's bloodline. It is my awakening that you are reading about.

My Mother and father lived in various locales in or near Toronto during my early years. I won't get into that now. Eventually, because my Father was earning good money at his trade my mother rented a fairly new house located in the Borough of York. It was located just outside the city limits of Toronto. This house was owned by her oldest brother George. When I was five years old I entered kindergarten and settled down. This occurred in September 1938. I spent five joyous years in that school and could never recall any thing shocking in my early schooling except the vaccination I had. Every kid the line started to cry after his injection but I remained silent. My arm ached for two days. I went to Humewood Avenue Public School. After this time I was placed in King George V Academy. This was at the request of my Mother's oldest brother who changed his name to George King. I thought the School was named after him. My Uncle George said that Humewood Public School was not a proper school for a boy of my blood. He being the eldest child of my grandparents knew and possessed a written history of his family going back hundreds of years. I attended, for two years, after being dragged out of a good school, the King George V Academy located on Eglinton Avenue west of Oakwood Avenue. It was situated on what was once a large estate owned by the Peckman Family, famous for being a great leader in the liquor industry. Sir Abraham Peckman served as a Liberal cabinet minister in Prime Minister Mackenzie King's wartime government. Peckman was the token Ashkenazi Jew in the Liberal Cabinet of the King government. In an earlier time he donated his estate to be used as a site for a Canadian version of a snooty English public school modeled on Eton or Harrow. King George V Academy was to have extensive multiracial clients. Even though Abraham Peckman, former bootlegger and champion of his people, was now a statesman and honored citizen. He had little formal education. He had become a philanthropist and a winner of the KBE for service to the British Empire. His father had made a small fortune recycling scrap metal and started to thrive during WWI. Abraham, his only son, took over the business in the early 1920's and used his capital to buy into the liquor and beer business which was not doing much trade due to the Temperance Act. When the Temperance Act was abandoned rumor had it that he shipped illegal liquor into the United States until the repeal of Prohibition put a stop to this. Prohibition, formally called the "Volstead Act" in the USA, had an equivalent law in Canada known as the "Temperance Act." The Temperance Act was done away with in the latter 1920's. The Volstead Act was repealed in the early 1930's. It died an overdue death during the administration of Franklin Roosevelt the 32nd president who was a fifth cousin of my mother Agnes through their common ancestor: Sarah Barney Belcher who lived in the mid 1700's in Massachusetts. This ancestral connection made me a 6th cousin of Roosevelt and also of General Douglas MacArthur and Winston Churchill!

Oddly enough though Prohibition proved to be the cause of the Peckman fortune it was a failure in its intention. It failed to cause temperance in America. Peckman's Breweries and Distilleries made a huge comeback in a short time, once the Volstead Act was scrubbed. The fortune was procured mostly in bootlegging. For a few short years they supplied the mobs with booze until it became legal again to manufacture it in the United States.

Work began on King George V Academy in the summer of 1937. The buildings were completed by the early summer of 1939. This was during the Great Depression and workmen and materials were inexpensive. After all, that great champion of the Jews: Conn Smythe, built Maple Leaf Gardens and financed it by getting the suppliers and builders to accept shares in the project. Two residences were built: one for junior school and one for the secondary school. The old mansion was to be used for the school masters' accommodations. School masters, were brought especially from England, to staff the new version of Upper Canada College soon to be established and soon to service the nouveau riche. Upper Canada College, which contrary to my knowledge at the time, did have a handful of Jewish clients. The new Head Master for King George V Academy was one "Percival Adams Proctor" who was supposed to have established a similar establishment for the upper-middle class in England and was that English school's first headmaster. He had enormous front teeth which made him look like Bugs Bunny. He was an all-around pedophile and homosexual sadist. He thrashed the innocent more often than the guilty. Perhaps his perversions were rooted in some way with his comical appearance. More will be discussed on this later. He recruited the staff of King George V Academy so that they would be available the final week of August 1939. Most of them, English to the core, had poor clothing, stooped stature and hideous large yellow teeth. They looked similar to Proctor. This no doubt, made them relatives of Bugs. They never saw a toothbrush. They claimed to be entirely dedicated the upbringing of the upper middle class boys. Most were failures as teachers and anxious to leave their motherland for one reason or another. There was not, except for the maintenance staff, cooks, and school nurse, one native born English-speaking Canadian amongst them. They all spoke English as if they were constipated. They strained to get every word from their mouths as if they were ejecting a large piece of stool. Passing crap is pure animal pleasure but these people had bowel problems.

I originally started there in September, 1943 at 10 years of age. I was a week late getting there because I was sick with some sort of malady no allopathic doctor seemed to understand. Agnes took me to a regular MD for examination.

"Now young man," the medico said, "jump up on my examining table so I can look you over." The doctor sounded extremely unctuous.

The medical creep wanted to do a thorough examination and made me lie on the examining table. Then he removed my short pants and underwear with Agnes present in the room and began to inspect my genitals. He spent a good five minutes squeezing the penis and feeling the testicles. I noticed he was salivating.

"Sometimes these childhood ailments are the result of problems in the genitals," he told Agnes. Agnes swallowed completely the excuse to fondle my nether regions. At that time I did not know what the word "genitals" meant nor did Agnes when she was asked to explain it to me later. I had a viral cold. Anyhow, the cold passed by itself at the end of the first school week and Agnes took me on the streetcar from Oakwood and St. Clair to the school grounds for the processing of my admission. At least the ride was on a small Peter Witt streetcar. I already had my uniform, a blue suit with ridiculous looking too short, short pants which the majority of the English private school boys seemed to wear with black Oxford shoes, lighter blue stockings, a blue shirt and the school "clip on" tie. In fact, I possessed two of these outfits all paid for by fabulous Uncle George. After all, I had to look the part of a proper British school boy. George also paid the tuition fees. This kit also included the TTC Scholars' tickets and TTC identity card. In fact, I owned a whole school year's supply of them. On the way to the school I felt like a freak in my school getup. I felt relieved there were not too many people around. I was ashamed of the way I looked. I wanted to hide.

Agnes and I entered the front gate of this school and tread the 100 yards to the large building that Agnes was told was used for the administration of the school. To me the administration building seemed to be larger than the school. I followed my mother into the building, where we traveled along the corridor and found the sign that said "Head Master's Office." Inside we found a small reception office. The sign on the receptionist's desk read "Miss Snowball." Miss Snowball would send Agnes home when I entered Proctor's office. I would be alone and defenseless.

"Head Master Proctor will see you at 9:00 A.M. just sit there for the next five minutes," Miss Snowball said, pointing to a chair immediately beside the entrance to Proctor's office. I noticed three other older boys, possibly 12 or 13 years of age, all dressed in their school uniforms. They looked equally ridiculous in their school togs. They were standing beside me and because they were larger than me I thought they might be even look more ridiculous. Miss Snowball got up from her desk and the three boys followed her in. I had seen frightened kids enough to recognize fear in the face of each boy. Miss Snowball came out after a minute and asked me to come in. I was led to a seat beside the head master's desk. The three boys were standing in front of the desk. Mr. Proctor, a man about average height, was also standing up. He looked old by my standards, late 40s or early 50s. Mr. Proctor opened a cabinet beside his desk and removed a long cane. He laid it on his desk. Mr. Proctor spent the next minute writing something in the large black-covered book that he took from his desk top. The three boys were nervously eying the cane.

"You all know the routine. Remove your jackets. I will start with you." Proctor said, pointing at the biggest of the three boys. They did as they were told. It seemed as if they had been through this routine at an earlier time. Mr. Proctor picked up the cane. He pointed the cane at the biggest of the three. He pushed his cane into the chest of the biggest boy. "You know what to do." The tall boy walked up to the desk and bent over it. I was now terrified. "May you learn from this experience," Proctor said as he laid into his first victim's rear end six times. He paused for a few seconds after each stroke. Proctor called this "letting it sink in," The biggest boy stood up from the desk obviously in great pain and fighting to hold back his tears, while Proctor pointed into the middle sized boy and repeated the whole action that had occurred with the first boy. When this was over, he beckoned to the third and smallest boy.

Weeks later I figured out that this blatant act of sadism was purposely designed and staged in front of me with the unhappy cooperation of the three other boys to terrorize me and perhaps the other three boys into absolute obedience. To tell the truth, in my case, it had its effect and I tried hard to avoid any situation that would place me in a position where I would need private counseling in Proctor's office. This need for private counseling allowed Proctor to frequently speak of the sound education that every boy should have. He said: "it should begin from the bottom up." I would have occasion to be privately counseled twice.

"Go to the detention room and wait for your next class," ordered Proctor. The three boys picked up their jackets and left. Proctor turned and looked at me. "Now young man let us see what I can do to you." Actually Miss Snowball later told me that Mr. Proctor said: "What can I do for you?" With the misheard remark I reacted like any brave boy. I got very dizzy and fainted. I came around in a few minutes while lying on the couch in Proctor's office. From then till I left Proctor's office I remained in a state of supreme fear. When I entered Miss Snowball's office, she informed me that Agnes had been sent away.

In the September 1944, I was inside the school buildings coming back from the washroom when three boys flew by me going the other way. Somebody had pitched a firecracker into Miss Snowball's office. This office preceded Mr. Proctor's office. The pyrotechnical device scared the crap out of Miss Snowball. Proctor saw the three boys in the corridor because the door to his office was open. He screamed out: "Halt," at the top of his voice. So loud was Proctor's drill sergeant command that I often imagined all the boys at King George V Academy suspended in animation when they heard it. Proctor hurried out of his office in hot pursuit. The boys took off and as they rounded the adjacent corridor at the end of the hall they knocked me down. I got back on my feet just as Proctor rounded the corner. The three boys were out of sight. Proctor grabbed me by the left ear and dragged me back to his office. Once inside a short interrogation began. Proctor asked me for the names of my two accomplices. I could not answer because I honestly didn't know who the miscreants were.

"Liar," shouted Proctor. "Liars get beaten, you know." I removed my school jacket. This is but one of two incidents at King George V Academy where I got into "trouble." There was a second, when a kid in grade seven admitted he was responsible for some antic and when asked for his name by a new teacher to the school replied "Bobby Noble." This resulted in additional bottom up counseling. This happened in April 1945. Innocent or guilty punishment was inevitable. You simply couldn't reason with Proctor. I was in grades seven and eight. The experienced boys at the Academy referred to it as "Caning College."

When I had ceased to attend King George V Academy I had read about a famous doctor who had invented a medical instrument for examining patients' rectums. It was called a "proctoscope." I chucked as I thought of Percival Proctor who was certainly in need of some sort of examination in that region. He was so full of it. But in my view he was dangerous.

I thought both of my parents hated me. Why else would they send me to King George V Academy. After all, it was an establishment school or at least pretended to be.

CHAPTER 2

The Roots of the Nobles

M y paternal Grandfather whose ancestors were originally from Iberia was born in Eastern Europe about 1884. He listed his birthplace as "Mogolov on the Dneiper River." As a young man he served in the Tsar's army in 1906 during the Russo-Japanese war. The Tsar lost that war. When war broke out between Britain and Germany, Maximilian Noble, whose real name was "Maximillian de Leon Hombre Noble" was a landed immigrant in Canada and living in Toronto. During August of 1914, he enlisted in the Canadian army at 32 years of age. It was with the Toronto Scottish-Irish Regiment. He was gassed during an attack on Canadian troops somewhere along the Western Front. When he returned to Canada in early 1919, although showing no signs physically of war wounds, he was not right mentally and began to change from the hard-working husband and father into a brutish lout who would fly off into a murderous rage in an instant. By the 21st century this ailment my grandfather had would be known as "PTSD" or "post-traumatic stress disorder." He would abuse his wife and children savagely. He lived until 1932 and expired ultimately from war wounds. He was 48 years old.

My father, Lemuel Noble, born in 1906, was the oldest son of Maximilian. My father was a man filled with bullshit. Because of this he could recognize it in other people with ease. He would also dispense it with ease. He would often relate how he and his father and his younger brother Al were working in an automotive plant in Detroit in the mid

1920's when they stopped in after work at a pool room. They began a game of Boston (at least that's what Canadians called pocket billiards) in a room full of Colored people. They were called "Colored" rather than Negroes, Blacks or African Americans. He recalled that Max Noble had his cue ball wind up behind the black ball (eight ball). These stories stuck with me down through the years and I could recall them vividly.

"Get away from there, you black bastard," the grandfather said. A remark immediately picked up by the many Colored people in the room. Slowly they approached the old man. Apparently my father Lemuel wanted to beat a hasty retreat. The second oldest child Al and the old man were armed with pool cues. The old man loved a fight and so did Al. My father fled to a corner to shrivel up and cower. Within two minutes there were five Colored men on the floor with severe wounds. Four others scooted out the front door.

When the police came to take information from the black owner of the pool room he said it was a white gang of 20 or so that caused the problem. Max, Al and Lem had calmly departed before the police came. I thought the whole tale was bullshit, which typically came from Lem, until my uncle Al showed me newspaper clippings from two Detroit papers describing the incident. Yellowed with age they had an air of authenticity. It took me some time to fully accept that Lem and his siblings were also Grail children. They behaved like wild animals. If they knew you had a nickel in your pocket they would murder you to get it. I spent many years trying to figure out how they could be so rotten and yet when I first became a teenager also discovered they were the descendants of a man with the purest blood ever to walk the earth. They suffered from the Archon infection. The Archons were those who gave down from the heavens and bred with the daughters of Man. My mother also suffered this malady. Both parents had royal blood. Most royalty suffers from this disease. Their spiritual vibration ranged from 20 up to 150 on Dr. Hawkins scale. (see Power versus Force)

CHAPTER 3

My Mother's Family

I had a half-brother Bill and a full sister Marion. Back in my early years my mother, my father, Marion, Bill and I resided in the Borough of York just north of the City limits near Oakwood Avenue at 77 Rimsdale Road. This was a pleasant street with two story brick houses built in the mid 1920's. Agnes rented the house for a pittance from her oldest brother George. He was known as the "king of the newsboys." He even changed his surname to "King." For him the name King sounded better than Posnanksy. It was an attempt to deny his Jewish roots. He owned several houses in Toronto and its suburbs. He was a wealthy man, but how he made his money after he graduated from selling newspapers no one exactly knew. Strangely enough, even though my mother Agnes called him her "favorite brother," and George referred to her as his "favorite sister," so my mother often said, I never found out his occupation. I never met my uncle George and I wasn't interested in meeting him. Once, when I was 10 years old George King showed up for a visit at 77 Rimsdale Road but I was out all day. When George visited Agnes was ecstatic. Her older brother George had dropped by for a day! She had advance notice he would be there but never told me.

When I was in grade 3 my inept elementary teacher Miss Fielder told us many times in class that she was overjoyed when King George VI and his wife Elizabeth Bowles Lyon visited Canada in 1939. Miss Fielder oozed saliva when she spoke of the British royals. Agnes oozed in a similar fashion about George King. Thus I lost the only chance I ever had to meet my fabulous uncle. George had seven children from two wives giving me seven first cousins whom I never would meet. All of these cousins were older than me. George King was 12 years older than Agnes.

There were two other boys in Agnes's family. There was Uncle Eddie, a strange little man who used the name "Walker" as his surname. Street people who knew him called him "Whoopee." He was a bachelor and in 1945 was about 40 years old. He earned his living by taking bets. When he volunteered for military service during War II the recruiting officer questioned him as to what he did for a living and where he lived. Eddie answered the officer by saying: "I gamble for a living and stay with my mother." The recruiting officer wrote: "he toils not either does he reap," on the forms he was filling out.

Ultimately we had to move out the House on Rimsdale Road. I will get back to this momentarily. We moved into a slum apartment building. This happened in late June 1945. This place was called the "Peel Apartments." After this move Agnes took on tenants. The second tenant was her brother Eddie. Eddie had a rupture and had to go about his daily business wearing a truss. I did not know what a truss was when Uncle Eddie came to live with his younger sister Agnes in late August, 1945, after the departure of Joe Noble, her first tenant who occupied the living room. The living room now became Eddie's bed room. Joe Noble was the youngest of Lem's siblings. Joe Noble, who for about one month, had lived in the apartment. Joe was on his first wife: "Olga" who was a shiksa. As far as I could observe this young lady was always in a state of tears. They occupied a spare room in the Peale apartment for a few weeks then moved out. Joe eventually married another woman. This woman was of German background. I never did learn what became of Olga.

I Am writing about these people to show that not every Grail Child is a saint. There was much ado about Eddie's truss made by Agnes. Eddie's favorite snack was to chew on a bulbous raw onion while partaking of an entire tin of sardines. He had to be one of the most miserable bookies in Toronto. One early summer day in 1945, Eddie was arrested for criminal activities by the Toronto Police. It wasn't a violent affair that these things usually became when it involved the Toronto Police. When cuffed, Eddie diligently, and feeling deep shame, shuffled along to the cruiser and was gently tossed into the back seat of the unmarked vehicle. There was no safety barrier between the back seat of the cruiser and the policemen who sat in the front. Thus they were always in danger from the felon in the back seat but in Eddie's case the police were in no peril. Eddie could not raise payment on the $100 fine levied against him by the magistrate presiding in Police Court the afternoon of his arrest. This is when Spike, Eddie's younger brother, stepped in and paid the fine. Of course, Spike now had the opportunity of being the hero and he played his part to the maximum.

Spike, whose given name was Erle, was a child born between the births of Eddie and Agnes. He had a dangerous habit of shoving people. Most of these people were much larger than him. Despite his name, Spike was very tiny standing about 5'1" tall and weighing perhaps 110 pounds. Spike made his living running a "boiler room," an enterprise in which several shady characters sitting behind desks sold advertising over the telephone for sports programs designed for athletic events. Spike was very successful. The boiler room employed young teenagers, usually working after school, running about collecting the fees for the advertisements from the various clients. The drawback to all of this was there never a program issued for any of the athletic organizations or events being staged. Spike's wife, Lilly, was visiting with Agnes at the Peale Apartments when she remarked to Agnes that Spike had spent six months in the Guelph Reformatory for "business fraud." Lilly said, "the time did him good because it got him out of the foul air in the boiler room," which reeked of cigarette smoke. Spike smoked cigars. Lilly was a good cook so at least Spike had that going for him.

Spike's older sister Minnie had red hair. She might have been 5'3" tall but called Spike: "Midget." I considered this insulting to Spike. Spike showed no reaction to this derogatory nickname. Agnes's family was composed of compassionate, loving people. They loved the white Christians with great passion. To the Posnanskis, which was Agnes's family's last name, they were "goyim." A term which taken in the proper context, was equal in odium to "Kike, Nigger, Jap or Packi" or whatever derogatory name the Posnanskis frowned upon when the goyim used derogatory names to describe the Jews as "kikes" and other ethnic peoples equally odiously.

While Spike was in the reformatory Lilly ran off to New York City to visit one of her relatives. When Spike was released from jail, Lilly was not there to greet him. So Spike found out from Lem that his wife was in New York shacked up with 22 years old colored buck. So off he went to chase up his wife down in New York City. Spike and Lilly reconciled and they came back to the Peale Apartments. Spike felt that he was exposed to "real life" when he found out that his sister Agnes moved into the Peale Apartments. So he moved in with his wife Lilly two months later. This was after Eddie and Joe Noble left. Spike and Lilly took what was the living room of the three-bedroom flat as their quarters. Joe Noble had left Peale Street Apartment a few weeks earlier. Then Eddie moved out about a month after that. Then finally Spike and Lilly moved in and occupied the living room.

Eddy had moved out shortly after his fine was paid. He only lived on Peale Street for about one month. I noticed that something strange was occurring in Uncle Eddie's life. He was seeing a woman. Eddy was, on occasion, living at her house. A few months later he married this woman. She began to clean him up. Even before the marriage she had an influence on him. No longer were there days he didn't shave. He started to bathe. He dropped the raw onions and the bookmaking. He even dropped the sardines. He took a job running the stockroom in the large market his wife owned. Then one day in late November 1945 Eddie's wife phoned Agnes. There was distress in her voice. "My Eddie is dead," she said. "He had a heart attack." So Eddie "Whoopee" Walker, a loser most of his life, but now slowly climbing out of the latrine his circumstances and ethnic background had dug for him was becoming a winner. This was but for a short interval. Then came a great defeat or was it a great relief, a relief from the physical body as many advanced life streams consider death.

One of Agnes's sisters, Bertie married a young man named Jack Haynes. He was working as a baggage clerk for one of Canada's two national railroads when he married Bertie. Jack would be constantly promoted, usually because of the sudden death of his immediate superior. That as time passed, by 1945, he was the superintendent of a large area consisting of stations, freight yards and rolling stock. He would eventually retire as a vice president of his railway. Bertie had married a winner. Jack Haynes had grade 10 education!

I often wondered if societal attitudes of that time forced most of Agnes's siblings to be losers. Was there some circumstance of life that could change this? Agnes' family surname "Posnansky" meant a person from the city of Posnan in Poland. Agnes said her father Gabe wanted me to be named "MacAlpine" after Gabriel Posnanski's family. So I would have the name "MacAlpine" as a middle name. This puzzled me for a few years until I discovered more about my mother's family. How could they be Polish and have a Scottish history at the same time? Worst of all they were Polish Jews or Ashkenazi or at least, claimed to be. Ashkenazis who originated in Eastern Europe were lowly regarded by Esther Perez de Leon Hombre Noble, Lem's mother. Esther Perez was a Sephardim. In her mind she was a real Hebrew.

"The Sephardim people are very close," Esther would often say. "We don't mix with those other Jews." At least here Esther admitted the Ashkenzsis were Jews "but never Hebrews. We are true Hebrews," she would often say. "My grandmother was my great grand-uncle's niece." She also told me of "too close" marriages between other of her family members. Some of these arranged marriages were almost incestuous but all marriages in her immediate family were with outsiders. These outsiders were all true Hebrews. According to Esther, my mother's family was Scots or Deutsche. The Posnanskis were fair skinned blue eyed blonds with the exception of Minnie, Agnes's second oldest sister. She had flaming red hair. They came from Poland to the USA in 1847. Then they spread out all over America but a majority settled in Charleston, South Carolina. My maternal grandparents settled in Elmira, New York. I later discovered their ancestors fled Scotland in 1746 to escape the English when the Great Rebellion of 1745 also referred to as the Jacobite Rebellion failed. They bore the surname of "Graham." The tribes of Scotland were called clans. Oddly, Graham was the smallest percentage of my Scottish bloodline This ancestor lived in a ghetto in Warsaw and posed as a Jew. Esther seemed to know a great deal about both sides of my family. Many escapees of the Jacobite Rebellion wound up in Germany, France or Poland. Bonnie Prince Charlie whose real Name was Charles Edward Stewart the leader of the Rebellion escaped capture by the English by masquerading as a woman. He ultimately wound up living in the tenements of Paris and died abusing his wife and drinking too much. It is said by the English that the Stewart line died out. This is not true. Remember that the victors write the history.

My father Lemuel Noble was a loser. He had no interest in his children. He was about 5'7" tall and overweight at near 200 pounds. He had little respect for anyone and would describe his sexual exploits to his friends in front of his two boys. The conversion could be about any important thing, even the Second Coming, but he would divert it away with a dirty joke and then brag about all the women he had; but never in front of his wife. He had disgusting habits. During meals while sitting at the dinner table he would lift his right leg and fart. This was a natural and regular event. He smoked "Black Cat" cigarettes consuming about four and one half packs each containing 20 cigarettes per pack. He smoked in bed and often fell asleep with a cigarette in his mouth which on at least two occasions set fire to the mattress. This was his major vice apart from sex. He didn't drink alcoholic beverages. He didn't steal unless he was certain he could get away with it. I found out he did time in an Ontario reformatory called "Langstaff Prison Farm" for petty theft and that gave him fear of being sent back if he got caught again. He was a natural "schzlub" who littered the house with cigarette butts and ashes. He often confessed that his main ambition in life was "to take a bath in a tub of Coca Cola but because it was scarce in wartime Canada, Pepsi, would have to do." He went to the end of grade five in a Toronto public school. Agnes completed grade eight.

Lemuel was very good at languages and spoke fluent English as his first language and German, Italian and Spanish and some Ukranian and Russian all well, but ask him to add two and two and he would get three. He was, in all aspects of his life, a real achiever! He was especially astute with his comments displaying great insight. This made him an excellent role model for his children not to imitate! Two days after the Pearl Harbor attack the Toronto Comet printed some quotations from Franklin Roosevelt's Wartime Speech asking the American Congress for a vote to declare war on the Empire of Japan.

"If there is anything worse than American bullshit" Lem said, "it's British bullshit. We will fight to the last Canadian to defend the States." He didn't like Roosevelt. Frequent references were made to Churchill as "Weinstein Churchill. After all," he said, "He and Franklin Roosevelt were fifth cousins," Lem pointed out. Roosevelt's real name was "Rosenfeld." "The War was also planned by the Rothschild bankers!" He made this comment and then started to talk about the Royal visit to Canada of King VI and Queen Elizabeth in 1939. This royal visit was to drum up Canadian support for the coming war in Europe. Lem talked about WW II as it were planned. "This royal visit" was considered to be "British bullshit" according to Lem. I did not believe this when I first heard it. When I became an adult I believed it.

Lem could not accept the truth about anything. Irving Berlin never really composed any of the 100 or so songs he published, they were written by aspiring composers who sent them to Berlin for his approval. He then published them under his own name. Abraham Lincoln never wrote the *Gettysburg Address*, he had a speech writer. And of course Shakespeare never wrote those plays. Possibly he was correct in some of these remarks. There are many scholars who think people like Francis Bacon or Christopher Marlowe were the true authors of work credited to Shakespeare. According to Lem they were done by a Jewish writer from London called "Moise Shakesberg!"

Lem's bosom buddy was Hal Summers who showed up for the first time at the Peale apartment block in the summer of 1945. Agnes said he had been in a "rest home" for three years and was finally discharged from the hospital because he was cured. This was the story told concerning the mysterious absence of Hal for three years. It had a false ring to it as far as I was concerned and one afternoon when no one was home I saw a yellowed open letter lying on the kitchen table. I picked it up and began to read it. The letter was addressed to Agnes and dated May 1942. It was from the Summers' Detective Agency.

Dear Mrs. Noble,

It has come to my attention that my wife Faye has gone with you for several evenings to residences where games of chance are played. The most commonly played game is poker. I do not want my wife to be corrupted by such behavior and I must ask that you to stop trying to corrupt her immediately. If not, it can result in serious consequences. Yours sincerely, Hal Summers.

The way the letter read I wanted to know how Faye's "immediately" was corrupted. And what was an "immediately" anyway? I put the yellowed letter back in the envelope and left it on the kitchen table; went into the living room and turned on the radio. Agnes came into the room. Agnes asked me if I had seen the letter and I said "no." Agnes then noticed the letter, now back in its envelope, and picked it up. Later on, I questioned my mother and asked why Hal no longer ran a detective agency. Agnes, not realizing that I had read the letter, related how Hal had a very successful detective agency dealing mostly with divorce cases. In Ontario, in 1942, the only grounds for divorce were infidelity and to prove it private investigators were hired to dig up evidence of misconduct. Hal created his own evidence. Hal had lied in court about a case. He committed perjury, just to service his client. It says in the Bible: "Thou will not bear false witness." This resulted in a jail sentence for perjury. The exact prison where Hal Summers served his sentence was not told to me. Agnes did not like Hal Summers. When he came to the Peale Apartment to pick up Lem, who was Hal's fellow traveler in sin, I was polite but Hal would put his head up in a snooty fashion and not return the greeting. After all, Hal was all class. It was the first time Agnes ever answered a query from me honestly.

In time, Lem introduced Hal to the members of his club: "The Manning Club." Its membership consisted of the most degenerate lot in Toronto. They all smoked, they all drank they all gambled, and they all cheated on their wives. It was officially chartered in 1935 by the Province of Ontario. Within a year of Hal being nominated and accepted as a member of the Manning Club, he had screwed and swindled several members out of thousands of dollars. The members, all of who were deviants themselves, were furious and wanted to "work" Hal over. They were not too happy with Lem either. Hal left the Manning Club shortly thereafter and was not seen anywhere in Toronto until the spring of 1947. Agnes said he was working for his father's furniture factory as a manufacturer's agent. The Summers' furniture factory was a big small business employing 500 people. Worst of all Agnes invested $1500 of her savings into one of Hal's businesses. She would never see that money again. At that time, the summer of 1945 Agnes was financially badly off.

Lem's brothers and sisters were all like my father with the exception of the younger sons: Joe and Lonny. The second youngest: Lonny was about two years older than Joe. Lonny was drafted into the Canadian Army in 1944. Lonny didn't like being a "zombie" and changed his status to a volunteer and stayed in the army after V-J Day serving more than 30 years and retiring with something called a "Classified Commission" having achieved the rank of major and the Canadian Armed Forces Decoration. He took his army pension out in cash and bought a GM dealership and started a Canadian Tire Store. He rapidly became wealthy. His oldest son wound up a full professor at a western Canadian University. I later in life would win an AFC. Unlike my half-brother Bill, Lonny never saw overseas duty.

Joe Noble became a diamond setter apprenticing diligently from the age of 17 years to 22. He earned a good living at his trade. He would ultimately have three wives and the third would survive him. He had no children because he was sterile. They attempted to do open heart surgery on him when he was past 70 to repair a hole in his heart that he had all his life. He died on the operating table. The heart defect kept Joe out of the War. His third wife Yetta survived him. Yetta was a Sephardim. The first two wives were gentiles. One wife, Joe's second, was surnamed "von Beckstein." Was she a Nazi?

There was Willy Noble, a brother of Lem and the third youngest of Lem's family. He served about one year in the Canadian Army but never got overseas. He had already been married when he joined the Army but the marriage ended late in 1944. The other Nobles referred to Willy's wife as "Ant Eater Alice." They were such loving people. I never met her. Bill not to be confused with my half-brother married a second time to a woman called "Pat." Bill could not hold down a steady job. He purchased his home under the Veterans' Benefits Act. It would develop into his only asset. Eventually, he learned the business of spray painting. This too turned into failure until one fateful day he made a bid to the Province of Ontario to paint the newly constructed highways with markings in white and yellow paint. He started to build a successful business. Then in the mid-1950s he was cheated out of his business by some wise guys. He could never financially recover from that. He had a quick temper. He once procured employment with a large industrial bakery, called "Canada Bread." When one of the other employees made a remark about Jews Bill hauled off and slugged him. He was quickly dismissed.

There was Al Noble, the second oldest child of Maximilian. With the exception of the patriarch Maximilian, Al could lick any man in the world. He reversed the last two letters of his surname and became "Nobel." He entered the garment industry as a teenager. He was talented at it but was never properly compensated for most of his working life. In his youth he was a brawler. There was a race riot at Christie Pits in Toronto during the 1930's. Al beat up several goyim in that escapade. When I got to know him, Al was opposed to violence. Al married Rita and the marriage produced a daughter Phyllis. She was developmentally disabled which is why Al and Rita never had more children.

When Rita died of a ruptured brain aneurism in the early 1960s Al Nobel married a second time. This marriage was to an ambitious woman. As a result of this marriage Al began to get due compensation for his work in the garment industry. When he passed on in 1980, he left a fortune of $4 000 000! He left $2 000 000 to Phyllis and the remainder to his second wife. Then the vulture circled. Phyllis could now not be located and Al's second wife wanted all of the estate. Phyllis was now married to a developmentally disabled man. Eventually the lawyers, who employed competent investigators, located Phyllis. Al's second wife had to settle for her fair share of Al Nobel's Estate but not after she put up a determined fight to become Phyllis' guardian. After all, Phyllis was only 46 years old at the time! Al's second wife's lawyer assessed a fee of $19 000 for work mostly done by secretaries and private detectives when he already knew the case was a lemon. He did not want to oppose the Legal Firm of Walter Abercromby KC. This was the lawyer for Phyllis. The courts would see through Al's second wife's intentions. Phyllis was effectively given custody of her own money. It was the Abercromby Law Office that managed Phyllis's Portfolio! This company was to play a vital part in my life. Oddly enough, they were Lonny's lawyers as well. They seemed to look out for some of the Noble's. I never met Al's second wife.

Finally there were three sisters of Lem: Dorothy, Sally and Rose. Dorothy was originally married to an orchestra leader and was fairly prosperous during the era of big bands. She had a child by him, a girl name "Rosalind." The marriage was failing. When the big band leader passed on she married Benny Seltzer and had a boy with him. A boy they called "Michael." Benny worked for Borden's Dairy, a large North American enterprise. Eventually, he accumulated so many debts that he fled Canada moving to Florida where he found employment with the same large dairy he worked for in Toronto.

Rose married a failed businessman who eventually purchased a farm in eastern Ontario and failed equally well at that venture. The sister Rose wed a man called "Rose." So Rose Noble became Rose Rose. She had four children. I knew little about them. When Lem died I met Rose at his funeral service. She did not know who I was.

Sally married a man in show business. This man used to be a song and dance man. Other than seeing him on television on local RBC shows I knew little about him. I met the ex-vaudevillian at Lem's funeral. All I could remember was that he spoke with a Limey accent. I felt my cousins were all degenerates. After all I had 26 first cousins.

Things picked up in Toronto after V-E Day. Gasoline rationing ceased. Rationing for butter and milk ceased. Six and one half ounce iced bottles of coke reappeared in the stores. Two hot dogs, a cold Pepsi in a 12 ounce bottle and a slice of apple pie cost 20 cents at the local diner near Bathurst and St. Clair. The place was called "Let's Stop In." The quality of the hotdogs was terrible. They had no taste. Lem said: "they are made from 'scrape the kitchen.'" Lem admonished: "Never eat a hamburger there." After a pause he continued: "You'll get ptomaine poisoning." Money was becoming available. Agnes, Lem, Marian and

I were now left to occupy the house at 77 Rimsdale Road. We would survive there till June 1945. Then George, Agnes's oldest sibling put the house up for sale. Our family had to find new place to live. The Noble clan had to vacant. Agnes had found new quarters. She had rented a "prime" three bed room flat in the Peale Apartments. To Agnes it was like moving into Buckingham Palace.

The Nobles were fairly well off in mid-1941. My older brother William was my half-brother from a failed first marriage of my father. I never met my half-brother's mother. She was a non-Jew and could not take Lem's abuse. One day, a few years before I was born, she packed her baggage and simply disappeared. I never found out what happened to her. If fact I never knew her maiden name or her first name. Bill grew up without the nurturing of a woman until Agnes came on the scene. Lem neglected his first born. He ran around molesting women and gambling. When Agnes arrived Bill was four years old. My father Lemuel never cared for any of his children. He eventually would have two boys and one girl, the girl born in 1942. I was about seven and a half years old when the girl, his youngest child was born. Her name was Marion.

Agnes took an afternoon off while I was attending the ritzy the King George V Academy. She left Marion with a baby sitter while Lem was at work and went apartment hunting. Agnes unearthed the treasure of the Peale Street Apartments.

CHAPTER 4

When Willy Comes Marching Home Again

Things ran smoothly for all of us until disaster struck our family. My older sibling Bill, or "Willy" as Agnes called him, was caught stealing tools and merchandise from the factory where he was employed and Bill's employer leveled charges against him with the police. Bill decided to run away and he joined the Royal Winnipeg Grenadiers in July, 1941. He was 17 years old. The employer dropped the charges in the face of the looming war. Bill went to Winnipeg and received training in the infantry. He was then was posted with his regiment to Hong Kong late in 1941. He was 18 years old when this happened. After that no word came about him until January 1942. It wasn't from Bill at all but from the Department of Defense. Agnes was told by the army that Bill might have surrendered with his regiment when Hong Kong fell to the Japs or perhaps had been killed. They didn't know.

Nothing more was learned of Bill until October 1945 a few weeks after VJ Day. I was now attending Parkside Collegiate and in the first form. The army sent a statement that Bill survived almost four years in Japanese POW camps, finally being liberated in September, 1945. When he returned from the War in October 1945, he had lost 70 pounds during his captivity and was in terrible shape. He was discharged from Sunnydale Military Hospital in November 1945. To consolidate his requirement of rest and pleasant surroundings Lem and Agnes were going to provide him with a room of his own in the Peale Apartment. In his early 20's he was nearly blind and shuffled like an old man. I did not recognize him when I first saw him after he was discharged from the military hospital. Other than a few weeks spent recovering in Sunnydale Military Hospital in the Toronto suburbs he had to have permanent accommodation and care. It was apparent at that time that he would ever be able to work at a semi or fully responsible position. This is what the army doctors thought.

Bill was able to prove them wrong. As the years passed he regained his health. When my half-brother Bill went to Hong Kong in late 1941 his regiment was poorly trained but was good at playing softball. This did not help them against the Japs unless of course they determined to hurl fastballs at them. Winston Churchill had asked Mackenzie King, the Canadian Prime minister at that time, for soldiers to help the garrison in Hong Kong. Mackenzie King, without caring a damn about Canadian lives was willing to sacrifice any Canadian. He wanted to show Roosevelt and Churchill that Canada was committed to the War. I was much later in life to discover that Churchill and Roosevelt were 5th cousins of Agnes via their common ancestor "Sarah Barney Belcher." King foolishly exposed two regiments of Canadian Youth to torture and privation for nearly four years. They never had a chance.

In time Bill recovered most of his strength and health. He would never be properly compensated for his war service. He did however become self-reliant after the War and became a successful businessman. Every member of his regiment was branded as a coward in early 1942 by the British, buffoon generals who ran the show in south-east Asia. The unfortunate Bill paid dearly for his voluntary war service to Canada. It was doubtful that the Canadian government appreciated it.

I was often told by my various elementary school teachers: "the War was being fought to save the British Empire." After dedicating their classes to this noble cause these twits would then fetch out a globe and show how nearly one quarter of the land was colored red. "Those red areas are the British Empire and we have to defend it," so said Miss Fielder, my grade four teacher at Humewood Elementary School. The woman teachers were all spinsters except Mrs. MacCutcheon. She was hired by the York Board of Education even though she was not a spinster because many younger male teachers were away serving with the armed forces. She did the same job as the male she replaced but received half the male's pay. Is it any wonder Women's Liberation arose?

With Bill gone the income to our household fell off almost to the point of 50% and the upkeep of the Rimsdale Road house was becoming almost too much. However we survived until early June 1945 and stayed on in the house. Agnes found a job in a War plant serving in a canteen. She would always recollect that she was a "good sandwich maker." In time, cheaper quarters had to be found. Besides, Fabulous Uncle George put the house up for sale. So ultimately, in the first days of the summer 1945, the house was sold and our family moved into Agnes's old area of Toronto called "Niagara" where Agnes found an apartment on Peale Street west of Bathurst and North of Queen Street. The area was so dilapidated it made the scenes depicting the Lower East Side of New York in the movies look like Park Avenue. It was usually Warner Brothers that made this type of film. Movies such as *Angels with Dirty Faces*, stared James Cagney and Pat O'Brien. The Bowery Boys provided the gang of Juvenile delinquents.

What was it like to be a 12 years old boy to living in a pleasant house in a clean neighbourhood to be rooted up and deported to the slums? I would always remember the lonely weekday morning trip through Toronto via Rimsdale Road, East on St. Clair Avenue to Bathurst Street, south on Bathurst and West on Queen Street to Peale Street. It seemed to drag on forever, like waiting in Head Master Proctor's office; waiting for doom. I tell you more about Headmaster Procter in a while.

Later I learned that Mackenzie King, stalwart Canadian prime minister, had worked for the Rockefellers before entering politics. He was responsible, during World War I, for selling rotten meat, army boots made of cardboard and many other shoddy products to the Canadian Army. When he was prime minister of Canada in the late 1930's, he refused to allow entry to Jews fleeing from the Nazis into Canada just prior to World War II! He was in every way a humanitarian! King received excellent advice on political matters from his mother. Strange, though, the mother had died many years earlier! The story goes that King had "a message from mother" in April 1945. So important was the message that he telephoned Franklin Delano Roosevelt. "Franklin," he said," I have had a message from mother." Roosevelt, it was rumored, died on the spot.

CHAPTER 5

The Boy from
Upper Canada

S outh of the Peale Apartments about one half block was situated the
Peale House, a tavern which rented rooms and operated something
called a "beverage room." The entrance was located on Peale Street.
It was quiet then but near the end of 1945 it got steadily busier. The
last part of World War II ended in August and the Japanese formally
surrendered in September. On V-J Day there was a massive crowd
taking in the Triple A baseball game at Maple Leaf Stadium at the foot
of Bathurst Street on the South side of Fleet Street. You could see Lake
Ontario from the higher seats of the stadium. More importantly you
could also see aircraft taking off and landing on Prince George Island
Airport.

I was told by my aunt Binnie, at 12 years of age, that I was, possibly,
the most beautiful boy in Canada. I now stood 5'6" tall, weighed about
125 pounds, had curly light brown hair, a fair complexion, penetrating
deep blue eyes, a small pointed nose, and the face of an angel. I did not
resemble a Sephardic Jew. I walked and stood with extreme erectness.
My walk was described as "catlike." My voice although not yet changed
was strong and distinct. I spoke with a derivative of the United Empire
Loyalist accent typical of some of the first settlers in Toronto. They
entered the area from the newly formed United States around 1794.
These settlers were called "United Empire Loyalists." These were granted

land if they would clear it and build roads. My round blue eyes and extreme beauty made heads turn when I walked along a street or entered a crowded room. I soon learned to dismiss peoples' stares. "There was something wrong with them," I would think. I thought I was ugly! My sense of nobility like my name was born in me. I was utterly incapable of cheating, stealing or doing the petty criminal acts so many of the boys of my age did.

I rapidly became familiar with the numerous yellow painted twin engine Avro Ansons flying in and out of the Island Airport that were manned by students and their instructors and used by the Royal Norwegian Air Force and in all probability sponsored by the British Commonwealth Air Training Plan! The entire location was known as "Little Norway." This perked up my interest in airplanes and I began to contemplate a career as a pilot. By the end of World War II in September 1945 that training facility no longer existed. Now it is a commercial airport called "Billy Bishop."

There was a barn behind the Peale Apartments that was converted from a stable to a car park sometime in the 1920s and was rented by the two butchers from Slovakia who had a shop next to the Peale Hotel. It was rarely used, except for storage by them. One day on my way home I found the door open on the old barn. The Goldberg brothers owned the apartment building but rented the barn to the meat market owners because not one of the Goldberg brothers could drive. I went into the barn but nobody was in there. I climbed the stairs to the loft when I heard snoring. Looking around I discovered a man in a dark khaki suit sleeping on an old trashed mattress. He was dirty and unshaven. I guessed him to be about 35 years old. I knew he was a "rubbydub," after all I had seen a handful staggering out of the Peale House but none of them ever reached the half block north where the barn was located.

I began to shake the man in an effort to rouse him and eventually he stirred. "What the fuck do you want?" the man said.

I noticed that it was not a suit the man wore but a uniform. "You're on our property," I replied, "you can't sleep here."

"I am Major Alastair Duncan," the man replied.

My interest immediately peaked. "Was this man a war hero?" I thought. The dirty khaki uniform was now fully displayed. The man had two and a half rows of campaign ribbons on his chest and I spotted the crowns on the shoulders indicating the man was indeed a major. I had learned to tell rank while in the pseudo cadet corps at King George V Academy. But he didn't have a great coat, just a battlefield uniform and a pair a black boots. It was getting cold in early November 1945. There was black beret lying beside Major Duncan. I had heard war tales of how the Canadians fought hard in Italy and the black beret was a sign of a tank man. Just who was Major Duncan and why was he lying up in the hay loft of a semi-used barn? He was obviously sleeping one off.

Major Duncan opened a billfold that he pulled from his pocket and removed a fresh $10 Canadian bill with the portrait of King George VI and handed it to me. "Get me something good to eat and come back here pronto." So I left the veteran and went down to Queen Street West and into Goldberg's Delicatessen. The deli was run by a man called "Tarzan." This Goldberg was a first cousin of the three brothers who managed the Peale House. He had the unsanitary habit of picking his nose while serving his customers. I found the mining of Tarzan's nose to be fascinating. I ordered a corned beef sandwich on rye bread with mustard, a cold 12 ounce bottle of Pepsi-Cola, some coleslaw and a large kosher dill pickle. I returned pronto with the food. Major Duncan was still in the barn but was out cold so I deposited the food beside him, left the $9.60 change and went out of the barn. I didn't see Major Duncan for the next two days. I figured the "war hero" was out of my life.

So it was back to the usual things! The incessant boredom of Parkside Collegiate was getting to me. There was one boy in particular, a "Gerry Zaretsky," that liked to hassle me. One day in wood working shop, Zaretsky, who must have been watching a *Three Stooges* movie, started to poke some of the boys in their eyes. Eventually this fun loving "schzlub" worked his way around to me. His made a gesture to poke me in the eyes but jabbed me in the mouth as I moved to avoid the poke. Zaretsky poked again but I lost my willingness to let it pass. Calmly and deliberately I reached across the work table and grabbed Zaretsky by his ears. Oh how this must have hurt. Then Zaretsky was quickly placed in a neck lock. "Get him by the balls," a few of Zaretsky's victims shouted. As Zaretsky slowly reached out for the balls, I ran him face first into a steel column. Zaretsky fell backwards out of the neck lock. He needed eight stitches to close the head wound. So severely did blood gush from the wound while the bully lie there a one inch deep pool of blood formed.

I was not punished for this assault. I felt odd that the victims were rooting for Zaretsky all during the melee. The shop instructor, Mr. Helmer, approached me after the fight collaring me at dismissal.

"You did a good job on that fart, young man. I have talked to the administration of this school twice about Zaretsky. They kept dumping the lout back into my class. The administration of our school is locked away behind their office doors. They don't care what happens in the classroom."

"If I did such a good job on him, how come his victims were all cheering for him?"

Mr. Helmer answered: "They are weak, cowardly kids, more cowardly than Zaretsky. If you beat up on Zaretsky, whom they are afraid of, it confirms their weakness to everyone. You had to lose that fight to justify their cowardly submission to him. You beat the crap out of him. Therefore you proved their weakness was worse than his.

For about two weeks friends of Zaretsky would stop me in the hall or on the school grounds outside the building. "You think you are tough Noble," they would say. "Well don't try anything with me. I can take you anytime." I would make a fist and they would, without waiting for a reply, walk away at a very rapid pace. They did not want a real confrontation.

CHAPTER 6

The Sad Case of
Louis Lippschitz

Early in July 1945 I was exploring the neighborhood north of Queen Street a hundred meters or so away. There I discovered a huge man sitting on the sidewalk with his legs straddling the curb. When he stood up for a few seconds I noticed he was a man, perhaps 6'4" or more in height and weighing well over 200 pounds. The man rose to scratch himself in his genital region and adjust the manner in which his pants lay on his bum. While doing this, three kids from the neighborhood about 12 years of age began to taunt the huge man. From their mouths suitable mocking phrases such as: "Hey Louie you dirty piece of Lippschitz, why don't you scratch your head instead of your balls; that's where your brains are." Or alternately: "Only horses shit Lippschitz and drop it in the street." Louie began to chase the three boys but they split up and Louie would stop unable to decide upon which individual boy to pursue. Alternatively one of the boys would get the closest in proximity to the hapless man. Then from the mouth of Louie spewed the filth of the gutter: "you dirty cocksuckers, wait till I catch you." These boys raised the anger in Louie easily. He would then chase them for a few minutes then sit down again on the curb when his pursuit of the boys became futile. Presently an elderly woman barely five feet tall would come out of the house. She would walk haltingly to the curb and fetch the big man and lead him into the house. Louis and the small woman would leave the street walking together while she led him by the hand into the house. That evening I questioned Agnes on the subject of Louie. I asked about why the kids picked on him.

"He's simple," Agnes answered. "His mother told me he has an IQ of 50. I suppose that means he's stupid." Agnes possessed a niece from her older brother George King, a woman who was also "simple." For Agnes the word "simple" was the euphemism for "mentally retarded." By the 1980's it would be "developmentally handicapped." This was a replacement of the euphemism with another euphemism. Thus political correctness was taking its roots in North American English. After all, the world by 1973 was becoming steeped in politically correct language. The honesty and integrity of Toronto English was rapidly declining. George King handled the problem of having the middle child of his brood, who was retarded, in a kindly way. He "boarded" her in a special school to "train" her to adapt in the outer world. Or to be more precise: to train her to disappear when company showed up. The girl was named "Helen." Agnes showed compassion for Helen, the only one of her family that gave a damn about this undesirable relative. The same thing happened to Phyllis who was Al and Rita's daughter. She also was neglected by her stepmother when Al Nobel died. When Al Nobel passed away Phyllis' foster mom could not bear the thought of her step daughter coming into a small fortune. She wanted Phyllis institutionalized. As for Louie, his mother did not want him in an institution. So she looked after him. But now that mother was becoming infirm. Her house was not kept clean and Louie could not be kept clinically hygienic. Soon the social workers would be feasting upon Louie's mother. They wanted Louis placed in a home for retarded adults. Louis' mother was a widow. She inherited some insurance money when the father died plus a paid for house and furnishings. This kept her going. Things were getting worse for what was left of the Lippschitz dynasty. I reflected on Louie's last name. Not only was Louie untrainable in the simplest of job skills; his last name sounded like a curse from the bully god I was coming to detest. The city run school system let him go at 16 years of age while he was in grade 3. They felt it was best for the other students. I would attempt to talk with Louie but his attention span was

limited. Louie was easily distracted. Besides my short talks with Louie
I found the other kids in the neighborhood loved taunting Louie. Then
one day they noticed I was talking with Louie.

"Hey Louie," they began "He must be a dummy like you else why
would he talk with you?" They came too close to me one day and I
kicked one of the local boys in the rear end. More days passed. Louis
didn't seem to be around. Then about one month after I last saw him the
Toronto Police discovered the bodies of Louie and his mother inside the
1939 Packard sedan the old lady owned that was parked in the garage
at the back of her house. It had belonged to her husband. The car was a
token reminder of the prosperity the small family once had. The police
had been told by Mrs. Lippshitz's friend, an equally elderly woman
confined to a wheel chair. The friend's name I never knew but she was
a double amputee with both legs missing below the knee.

"She had 'sugar,'" Agnes answered when I asked why she lost her
lower legs. The quacks didn't know this until an infection had set
in. I shuddered when I heard this. This friend of the survivors of the
Lippshitz family was told not to contact the authorities for 30 days.
This request she obeyed. When the police looked over the property
they found the bodies of Mrs. Lippschitz and Louie inside the Packard.
The car had run for a time then ran out of gasoline and shut down.
The engine of the old Packard idled inside a closed garage subsequently
doing in both Louie Lippshitz his elderly mother. The last survivors of
the Lippshitz family had ended their burden on society. I never knew
what became of her property. My own fortune was in a few months
to change drastically. For the rest of my life I would grow up to fear
diabetes and mental retardation.

CHAPTER 7

Parkside Collegiate

On a cool Friday at 4:30 P.M. in mid-November, 1945 I returned from Parkside Collegiate Institute, a dull place, where I had been enrolled in September 1945. After June 1945, Uncle George abruptly stopped the tuition fees at the ritzy independent school: "King George V Academy." I loved this idea. I considered the Academy: the "shits." The Nobles had relocated in the slum district of Niagara by then. No doubt, when it was first settled in the decade of the 1820s, Niagara was a pleasant area, a rural village just outside the town of York which was the original name of Toronto but a succession of wave after wave of impoverished immigrants and greedy landlords had run the area into a slum. Those land lords did not do their jobs maintaining the properties. The area was no longer inhabited by Orangemen and Scots but by Irish Catholics and Slavs. Just the owners were Orangemen or the Scots-Irish. They didn't like their tenants. They only liked their rent money.

My mother Agnes was ecstatic that she was finally out of the "sticks" where she had lived in York Township. She was back in her old neighborhood where she grew up as a child. She loved the new flat even though it was infested with rats and cockroaches. The Goldberg brothers owned the apartment building.

By the 1890s, Toronto had moved its boundaries westward and absorbed the Village of Parkdale about two miles down the road. Earlier the old village of Niagara was absorbed into the city when the western boundary was set at Dufferin Street. This occurred in 1832.

It was my daily job to fish out at least one dead rat from the toilet bowl and dispose of it. Agnes could not do his. She was afraid of all living animals and even some dead ones. The manner in which she prepared meat dishes indicated this apprehension of all living and dead animals. She overcooked everything. Her first husband was Lemuel and she was his second wife. They tolerated each other. He worked during the war at a factory which manufactured knapsacks and other military gear not only for the Canadian Armed Forces but for any other allied forces training in Canada and that included the Royal Norwegian Air Force. The Canadian taxpayers undoubtedly footed the bill for every ally.

The Peale apartment block was built in 1885. Gas vents for lights were present in every room but by early 1890s hydroelectric power would quickly replace the gas lights. Then coal replaced the wood furnace. The apartment had hot water heating using cast iron radiators. Along the Queen Street streetcar line half the cars were old TTC Peter Witt steel street cars. These were the first new vehicles ordered by the TTC. They were built in Canada from 1921 to 1923. They ran along with the almost new PCC streamliners. The PCC's had their parts manufactured in St Louis and their final assembly was done in Canada at the Canadian Car and Foundry located in Montreal. They were painted in the maroon and cream livery the TTC employed.

The Peter Witt made an unusual noise when it ran at or near full speed and you could distinguish them from other vehicular traffic from blocks away. I loved the TTC, especially the Peter Witts and had ridden every single route they traveled going to all parts within the City Limits. However they were underpowered. A small Peter Witt with a full load of passengers could be outpaced by a healthy man on foot when both were climbing the Bathurst Street hill just north of Davenport Road! The four 35 HP, DC motors simply didn't have it. The empty weight of nearly 50 000 pounds exceeded the PCC car by 13 000 pounds. The PCC car with the same load could make double the pace up the hill. The PCC car had four 55 HP motors with an empty weight of 37 000 pounds.

When I lay in bed in the late evening I would listen for streetcars and would always pick out the Peter Witt when it approached. This is how I spent my spare time: going on various voyages of discovery; learning about the different, former villages, that once lay outside the city but now were part of it. I was so interested in Toronto that I often visited the main library of College Street to study its history. I also visited the John Ross Roberson photographic and art collection depicting Toronto's earlier moments.

CHAPTER 8

Indoctrination Camp

As a reprieve I was enrolled in summer camp to commence after Dominion Day in 1944. The camp, called the "The Young People's Camp," was located near Hamilton, Ontario. I found out I was to go there at the end of grade 6 as a reward for my good work at King George V Academy. After all I had only been caned one time that year. I had survived that clone of Doutheboys Hall for an entire school year. On a Monday Morning, in early July of 1944, I was taken by Agnes to the YMHA near Bathurst and College Streets. When we got there a large crowd of parents and some children, all boys, were mingling at the corner of the residential streets: Baldwin and Major where the YMHA was located. A bearded man with a generally messy appearance was talking to parents while writing at a bridge table, one of those folding contraptions with four legs that folded up neatly inside the table. There were two vacant folding chairs in front of the bridge table. These chairs were obviously originally sold with the table. Nobody was busy with the messy man so Agnes and I went up to the table.

"Is this little 'mensch' going to camp?" the man asked, in a broken accent. "Vat is his name?"

"This is my son Bobby," Agnes responded. "He is going to Camp Young People." Agnes had gotten the name of the camp wrong.

"Das is goot," the man replied. "How old is the mensch?"

Agnes responded with the usual replies, giving my medical immunization record and my age.

"Vait here for one of the buses," the messy man ordered. "You may go," the man said waving Agnes off with a flap of his hand. Agnes resented the wave-off. She stayed with me for five minutes when a "Gray Coach" bus showed up at the side of the street followed quickly by a second bus. The boys boarded the two coaches along with some older boys, who were obviously councillors and two middle-aged men. The luggage was placed in the baggage compartments of the buses. Off the buses went toward Bathurst Street and turned south on Bathurst motoring along until they reached Fleet Street along the shore of Lake Ontario, and then turned west traveling, in time, onto Lake Shore Road. Eventually we came to the entrance of the Queen Elizabeth Way. We passed the sculpted monument of lions depicting the entrance of the four lane road and headed west. We eventually took a side road off the QEW and traveling up the graveled country road and reached the camp. The motor coaches arrived at the camp and we boys retrieved our gear. Names were called out and each boy was designated to a different cabin. This took about 30 minutes. Every boy was assigned a bunk and stowed his baggage on the bed. Then we went off to lunch.

The lunch which consisted of boiled beef and kasha with hot cocoa for a drink was not bad. The cocoa had no dairy product in it. This kept faith with the dietary laws of the Torah. When the lunch was over another bearded man went to the front of the dining hall. A microphone was rigged up so that he could speak to the 130 or so people in the room.

"Velcome to the Young Peoples' Camp," he began. "Our glorious world socialist movement has made this camp possible. My dear hearts, we vill show you here how our glorious comrades in Russia are beating the savage fascists. These are the dedicated Socialists who forced the Germans out of Spain." I thought it was the other way around. Didn't the fascists kick out the Commies by 1939? "The Germans are animals. Soon our courageous army shall walk the streets of Berlin."

The man was called "Daniel Breck." I would have to endure three weeks of indoctrination at the camp. They were daily horrors stories of Nazi brutality related by Daniel Breck. One day, after lunch, he told the story of how the Nazis invaded a small Russian village in The

Autumn of 1941. The dirty rotten Nazi bastards looted the village and raped the women. It was a fine matter for young kids to hear about. One brutal Nazi, after raping an old lady, saw an expensive ring on her finger and started to remove it. But the ring wouldn't come off so the filthy German Nazi bastard took out his bayonet and chopped off her finger! Then in March 1943, the victorious Red army recaptured the village. The old lady was so grateful for her liberation she went to her jewelry box and found another ring and gave it to the Russian commander of the liberation force. This actually had occurred, so spoke Daniel Breck. These types of talks went on every day for two hours after lunch. It was story after story of the glorious Red army fighting off the dirty rotten Nazi bastards at great cost to the Soviet Union. Never was a word mentioned about any other participant in the War. The allied airmen that died in bombing raids over Germany were none existent and so were all the other Allied Armies except for the Russians. Daniel Breck seemed totally ignorant of the Allied landings in Normandy that occurred earlier in June 1944. The opposition to the Nazis was provided solely by the Soviet Union. Never mind the notorious brutality suffered under the Communists. Never mind the millions of Kulaks that starved to death in the late 1930's. Never mind the slaughter by Stalin of millions of Russian peasants that occurred during and before the War. Never mind the millions suffering in gulags. Never mind the starvation of Leningrad. Communism was achieved in Russia. Now it had to be spread over the world. The campers were needed to defend and propagate communism. Communism was the only righteous cause. To Daniel Breck the words "world peace" meant no resistance to communism. I saw Daniel Breck clap his hands together in joy as he said: "so what if millions die, we will have world communism!"

Every morning at 7:30 A.M. the Union Jack was raised. All the boys attended this ceremony. They sang "God Save the King" like good British subjects and then they sang the "International" like the best of communists! There was no real recreation in the camp. Daniel Breck and his cohorts would only prefer hikes. These hikes were frequently interrupted for lectures on communism. So it was: getting up in the morning, shitting and washing, then doing a flag ceremony. Sometimes at the flag ceremony Daniel Breck would lead the boys with a song sang in Russian. It was total insanity. Strangely, many of the boys seem to understand these songs but poor me, ignorant of Russian seemed only to hear babbles: "Koseekoosah, kooseekoosay, kosciqueque, and dosvidonya." They seemed to speak complete babble as well. I spoke no Yiddish or Russian but was becoming fluent in Spanish thanks to my paternal grandmother Esther Perez de Leon Hombre Noble.

On "visitors' day" Spike used one of his cars to drive his wife and Agnes to the site of the Young Peoples' Camp. The chauffeur was "Ship Wreck Kelly." This was a pseudonym for one Joe Pritzker, a little man five feet tall who weighed in at 200 pounds. He resembled a beach ball with legs and arms. He was notorious as a lady's man, and his sexual exploits were well documented in the sub journalistic papers known as the "Whisper" and the "Slush Weekly." I often wondered how Joe Pritzker, unusually short and unusually fat could ever engage in sex. Surely, such acts were academic in my opinion. These "journals" always reported the doings of the sexually perverted souls that lived life on the streets of Toronto to the darkest. Of course the rags never used Joe Pritzker's real name. That could possibly be considered libel. He was always referred to as "Ship Wreck." Pritzker loved the attention. Everyone knew there was only one "Shipwreck." He smoked more cigarettes in two hours than Lem did in one day. There was always a lighted cigarette on his presence. I wondered if he ever breathed fresh air. He lunched on two sandwiches per day, one pastrami sandwich and one corned beef. Then he ate two knishes, one liver and one beef. He drank two bottles of 12 ounces Pepsi Cola and finished off with a kosher dill pickle. When I was a meat eater, could barely finish one sandwich. Ship Wreck actually had a peculiar odor about him. It stayed with him even if he bathed three times a day which he regularly did.

Ship Wreck was very interested in me. "Do you 'masturbate?" he asked when he talked to me at camp. "I used to do it three times a day!" I did not know what "masturbate" meant. I later read an article saying that Hitler became a vegetarian because he thought meat eating made his sweat smell. Ship Wreck's lady lovers often complained about his smell.

Agnes arrived on a Sunday three weeks after I had first bunked down at camp. "Take me home," I pleaded. "This place is driving me nuts."

"Why dear?" Agnes answered, "I thought, you were having fun."

"If you don't take me home now, I will come home by myself. I will hitchhike. Why did you so send me here anyway? The boys call me a 'goy.' They said I don't look Jewish. I don't have a Jewish name!" I was later in life to find out I was not Jewish this came as a shock.

"It was free," Agnes answered.

There was no room for me in Spike's car. Agnes went off and left me at 4 PM. I packed my duffel bag, walked a mile to Highway 2 and flagged a Grey Coach Bus. The fare was $1:30. I rode the bus to the terminal at Bay and Dundas Streets and boarded a Bay Street "Brill Peter Witt Street Car" that took me to St. Clair Avenue, along St Clair and stopped at Rimsdale Road. I had come home by myself in three hours. I schlepped my duffle bag over my shoulder. I fetched the key from the mailbox, went in the house and waited. Nobody was home. Agnes went from work at the canteen to a Poker Game. Lem was at the Manning Club and Marion was being looked after by the next door neighbor. The sun was just setting. I had left a note on the pillow of my cot at the camp. It said: "To hell with communism, I have gone home." The morons running the camp did not bother contacting Agnes for two additional days. They didn't even know I was missing. They thought my bunk was unoccupied. They never apologized to Agnes for their misplacement of her son. Communists lose everything. In the Soviet Union and the post war occupied countries all human rights were lost!

CHAPTER 9

Liberation from King George V Academy brings more woes

I was to spend one year in grades five and six as they were combined on my transcript and shown as done in one school year. The same thing happened again in taking grades seven and eight. I passed the Ontario High School Entrance Examinations easily at the end of Grade Eight. I was 12 years seven months old when I completed my year and was dismissed from King George V Academy in mid-June. I tried to roll with the punches at King George V. I often thought of Teddy Cash a boy about the same age as me. Teddy wasn't a bad kid but he seemed to be Proctor's whipping boy. The creepy Proctor was always after him. Proctor patrolled the halls of the Academy with cane in hand. It was always displayed prominently and every boy noticed it. By the time I was 12 years old I shared a class with Teddy Cash. Proctor entered the room armed with his rod of correction. Everybody froze. He began an assault on Teddy for not showing at his office before school for counseling. I suppose Proctor wanted Teddy to get settled in. One day Teddy never showed up at the school the day after this last beating. The period Proctor had entered the class was immediately before lunch. Rumors circulated that Teddy was committed to "999 Queen Street West" for psychiatric assessment. He refused to return to the academy. He ran off the street car transporting him to school while with his mother and disappeared. The police found him hiding under the front porch of his house. During his last week in school he was caned on three different occasions. Nobody in authority outside the Academy ever investigated; while I was in attendance at King George V Academy; any complaint uttered by any boy about the excessive use of corporal punishment made to any parent. Teddy was examined by a quack that the police took him to and the wounded bottom was discovered. The remedy for all this in juvenile court was to commit Teddy to a mental hospital. These bad practices at the academy were to surface when much more serious goings on were to be unearthed after I had permanently left the school.

The summer break had begun for the older boys. I was to return in September 1945 to start secondary education in the collegiate part of King George V. Oh how I dreaded this. In late June of that year Uncle George sold the house at 77 Rimsdale Road. He did not want to pay my expenses at King George V Academy any longer and told Agnes to enroll me in a public high school. This was like an answer to my prayers. I made these prayers to the only Ascended Being I knew, the Beloved Jesus. I wanted Jesus' help to escape from the brutality of King George V Academy and my prayers were going to be answered in a highly unusual manner.

Liberation from King George V Academy came with a new slavery of a different sort. There were my music lessons. Agnes decided to make me study the piano. She engaged as a piano teacher, a Miss Hollowly, a short fat spinster who lived in a small house on the east side of Bathurst Street between Queen Street and Dundas Street. This woman was in her late 50's or early 60's. There was another old lady living in the house called Miss Ryder. Now Miss Ryder must have been at least 80 years old. She was emaciated, and I never saw her when she wasn't sitting in the kitchen of the dilapidated dwelling. Miss Ryder was the violin teacher. But all she ever played on the instrument was one note, an "A" or something by which she tuned up her violin while Miss Hollowly played the "A" on the piano. Miss Ryder was always surrounded by two large Doberman Pinscher dogs which I thought were insane animals. When she stirred in the slightest, the creatures would circle her like the

Indians would circle the wagons in a wild western movie. The whole scene was macabre. I had three months of music lessons from the pudgy Miss Hollowly. Finally, I summoned up the nerve to ask her to play something she was trying to teach me.

"Oh I can't do that," she replied, "People standing over me make me nervous." Reluctantly she played the Grade two-piece, an oversimplified version of a Bach composition. It didn't sound too bad. At least I had a vague idea of what I was trying to achieve. As time passed I advanced from grade one to grade two. Miss Hollowly taught using the Royal Conservatory of Toronto music books. This consumed about three months, from the early summer in August 1945 until November 1945. "Play these 'longapeggios'" Miss Hollowly commanded me to do. It took me three months to determine she meant "arpeggios."

Miss Hollowly fees were half the recommended rate that the Royal Conservatory spelled out. Twice a week I had to return from Parkside Collegiate but didn't exit the streetcar at Peale Street but instead at Bathurst. From there I walked the two blocks to the Hollowly house. Before each piano lesson was to begin, I would run my finger over the top of the old Steinway Upright. The dust was so thick you could plant cucumbers in it. With water they would probably grow. Miss Hollowly complained frequently about how housekeeping would get her down! There was, after all, so much of it. For all the dust there was also gardening to do. Her lawn was a jungle.

Miss Hollowly often grumbled to me about the outrageous salaries paid to movie stars. She was a devout socialist and made her views known to all her students. "Did Betty Grable get $100 000 for making her last movie?" she commented. "They don't give an honest plumber or electrician that kind of money for a year's wage. And they really help people. If I were in charge of the government nobody would make more than $50 a week. It's ungodly." Dorothy Hollowly's altruism was entirely misplaced. In her world everybody would be paid the same wage.

One time while I was leaving the house a parent was waiting in the living room. The parent offered the spinster a cigarette which the chubby one accepted. "Oh I feel so wicked when I smoke!" she commented as she dragged on the "Virginia Oval." Miss Hollowly never inhaled. She wasn't that wicked.

The final time I attended the Hollowly house for a piano lesson the spinster asked me to stop inside the kitchen to see Miss Ryder. I approached the door of the kitchen. I did not want to enter because the dogs were prowling in circles about the old woman's rocking chair.

"Here sonny," Miss Ryder said. "Come in the kitchen and get the money. I want you to pick up a loaf of Christie's White Bread and a bottle of homogenized white milk from the grocery store next door." No doubt Miss Ryder loved being a white woman.

"White milk as opposed to colored milk," I thought. I had made a big racist joke in my mind. I was wary about entering the kitchen but approached the old lady cautiously. I picked up the empty milk bottle from the counter. Then as I started to approach the old lady one of the Dobermans ran at me with his teeth bared. I, out of reflex reaction, swung at the animal with the empty milk bottle striking the animal directly on the muzzle. The animal dropped like a sack of flour at my feet. The other animal started to whine while prowling around in circles about Miss Ryder's rocking chair. I left the kitchen in a big hurry after I dropped Miss Ryder's money on the floor. Later that evening a large police constable called on my mother and me at the Peale Street apartment.

"We had a complaint that your son Bobby has assaulted Miss Ryder's dog, and broke its jaw. We had to have the animal destroyed," the large policeman told Agnes. Agnes took all this in with her usually calm hysterics. She was glaring at me with intense anger. Of course, anger was her steady state mood.

"What kind of trouble have you gotten yourself into?" she screamed.

"Nothing, the dog attacked me, I hit it in the face with a milk bottle."

"This is the third complaint the police have had about those dogs," the constable said. We will have an order drawn up to put the remaining dog down. Those are two queer old women."

Nothing more was heard about Miss Ryder or Miss Hollowly after that for some time. I had ceased to be a piano student. The two spinsters did not want that "vicious boy" near their dogs.

It is interesting to note that about two years later while at "The Farm" where I was after a few months relocated to and taking both grade 11 and grade 12 subjects at the Willington Academy; I read an article in the Toronto Evening Telegraph about an old lady who passed on from natural causes.

> *Two starved Dobermans feed on the decaying corpse of 92-years old spinster found dead by her companion Dorothy Hollowly a 65-years old music teacher and spinster. Police are probing the incident. Police report that the Humane Society had destroyed two previous Dobermans the women owned.*

CHAPTER 10

The Paton Legacy

I returned to the Peale Street apartment house in mid-November 1945, after riding the PCC red and maroon air-electric streetcar from Parkside Collegiate to the corner of Peale and Queen Streets. It was 4:15 P.M. and the one hour ride was not entirely boring. The front and center doors hissed when they opened and closed because of their air induced operation. When I departed the PCC I crossed the street car tracks and headed north up Peale passing the Peale Hotel. I examined the brewery truck unloading kegs onto the chute that went into the cellar under the beverage room. Then they unloaded several cases containing 24 bottles of beer and or ale directly onto a cart and began taking them inside.

The Peale House as it was formally known; was opened in 1872 by a family man called "Paton." He was an Irish Protestant, who came to the city in 1830; when it was called "York." He started the family's fortune. This was a man who had scruples and the son from a family of innkeepers. These people even before they left Ulster were Orangemen to the core. They were also enterprising people. Before long, in Orange Toronto, they had made connections with members of the Family Compact, themselves Scots-Irish and Orange men, and acquired a large tract of land west of the muddy York town limits. It was an original plot laid out in 1796 by surveyors acting on behalf of Lieutenant Governor John Graves Simcoe. Sean Paton bought the 160-acre property in 1831 for 300 pounds and began to farm. In 1832, the town limits of York were extended. The western boundary was now at Dufferin Street and Sean

Paton's homestead now fell within the boundaries of an expanded city area. York also went east to the Don River, and north to Bloor Street. Its southern boundary was Lake Ontario. In 1837 York became Toronto, reverting back to its original Indian name. The Paton prosperity began around 1832 and went on throughout his lifetime until he died 45 years later. Sean Paton, the original patriarch was 25 when he arrived in York in June 1830, a young married man with a robust wife and a small daughter. He was lacking a place to set up his own inn keeping business and decided to borrow funds from Family Compact members and risked all his worldly goods, which were not much in establishing the farm. He borrowed using his family name and other nonmaterial heirlooms as collateral.

By 1840, Sean Paton had sold off several parcels of land bordering on Lot Street, soon to be called "Queen Street." The sale of these lots provided enough funds to repay the loans from the Family Compact. By 1842, the now thriving family decided to re-enter the hotel business and plans were drawn up by Toronto architect R. J. Bennett to build a hotel at the corner of Peale and Queen Streets. Paton now built a frame building on the northeast corner of Peale and Queen. In 1870, his sons had the old building razed and a modern brick, three floors, hotel with a dining room was started. Sean Paton, an immigrant from Ulster, at the age of 53 years, in 1868, had made it big in Toronto. His children, three boys and a girl were now also thriving, and the girl had three children of her own, so Sean Paton was now a grandfather.

During the First World War, Sean Paton's grandchildren sold the property to Moise Goldberg, an immigrant from Russia, who landed in Toronto, at age 18 years, in 1913. He worked as a rag peddler, scrimped and saved and also began to prosper. He had a lame right leg, a trait his three sons would inherit. This kept him out of World War I. When the Paton heirs decided to sell the hotel Moise Goldberg had the funds to make the down payment. He lived until 1978 and died at the age of 83. The hotel passed on to his three loser sons, none of whom could hold down a real job and each of whom failed in every business venture and job they tried. They had no useable job skills and didn't want to acquire them. Each of the three boys was about 5'8" tall and weighed about 200 pounds. Somehow they had neither their father's nobility nor his work ethic and inevitably, when a business venture failed, they returned to the Peale House for monetary support. By late 1945, the Peale House no longer had the postcard picture condition it possessed when Moise first purchased it. The sickening vibratory action of the three sons had debased it thoroughly. It had become a "beer parlor" with a true "spit and saw dust" atmosphere. It was beneath the dusty saloons portrayed in the low cost Bob Steele Westerns made by Republic Pictures.

The true character of the Goldberg boys soon began to become apparent to me. One early evening in November 1945, Agnes wanted me to run down to the local "Toronto Store" and pick up some milk and a few groceries. It was about 8:00 P.M. when I approached the opposite corner to the Peale House on the north side of Queen Street. There was a crowd of people standing about all seemingly looking at a fight of some sort. But it wasn't a fight. There were the three Goldberg boys assaulting a drunk outside the entrance to the beverage room. While they were kicking the helpless drunk in the head and upper body a City of Toronto Cop, in uniform, stood by watching. The cop made no visible effort to stop this assault. The cop must have been at least 6'4" and 220+ pounds. Instead, when the Goldbergs tired because they were in poor physical shape they went off through the entrance to the beverage room and disappeared. The onlookers disappeared and the cop went over to the victim and handcuffed him. Then a police paddy wagon arrived a few minutes later. The coppers staffing the wagon lifted the victim into the back of the wagon and drove off. There didn't seem to be any medical attention given. The side walk was a pool of blood. I had nothing but contempt for the Toronto Police for years after that.

I later found out the victim was a man called "Johnny Bunyon," a veteran, and chronic alcoholic who was jobless. Agnes called him a "schicker." On two occasions he passed out on the main entrance to the Peale Street Apartments. This necessitated fetching one of the Czech butchers to come to the main door and move the drunk. Bunyon hung around the beverage room panhandling for nickels and dimes and occasionally scored enough to purchase sufficient draft beer to plaster himself. It was that time in 1945 when veterans, primarily those from

Europe or those who never left Canada were being discharged from the Canadian Forces and when they arrived in Toronto the Peale House was waiting for them. Of course, in every ward of Toronto, there were cousins to the Peale House. After a few drafts Johnny Bunyon would then sleep it off in a storage shed behind the Peale House. Draft beer, in 1945, was five cents a glass! The glass held about eight ounces.

Johnny Bunyon disappeared from Peale Street for several months in late 1945. I found out from Lem that Johnny had re-joined the Canadian Army. Lem had seen him walking around the Peale House in an army uniform. About two months after reenlisting he was back on the streets. Apparently his alcoholism had hastened his second discharge. I was getting a large lesson in the sin of drink. My thoughts also reflected on Major Duncan, surely he wouldn't be treated like Johnny Bunyon. Major Duncan had commando training and was proficient in self defense and after all was an officer. I later on, was to perform a few acts of kindness for Major Duncan and these spontaneous doings were to change my life dramatically.

Not everything that occurred at the Peale House was tragic. There was a colored prostitute named Pearl that serviced "tricks" in her third floor flat in the Peale House. One evening about 9:00 P.M. a commotion erupted outside the "Ladies Entrance" Two rubbydubs were quarreling about some fattish woman outside the entrance to this room. All three were noisy. All sorts of profanities were spoken. The two men and the fat lady had too much to drink and showed it. The two quarreling men suddenly ceased their arguing, shook hands, and returned to the Ladies' Room. Both men were too cowardly and too drunk to start a physical fight. The fat lady was left outside. The crowd quickly dispersed. The fat lady crouched down on the sidewalk like a baseball catcher and lifted her skirt and started to pee. Like a draft horse gallons of liquid came from her. "Skipper" a German shepherd, belonging to the two Czech butchers wandered onto the scene. The dog never was tied up. He began to sniff the urine of the fat lady. He then began to bark. This drew the attention of a few straggling spectators who resumed walking when they observed the fat lady. In the meantime, Pearl, the prostitute, had crawled from her apartment out onto the window ledge and was observing the whole scene. She sat down with her legs draped over the ledge and her back resting against the window. How she didn't fall off the ledge, amazed me. The sidewalk immediately below Pearl was a sea of piss. Skipper was now howling. Pearl was actively cheering on the urinating woman.

"Deary," she hollered down to the fat lady, "Dem men are all death. Dey is all bastards." She owned a Caribbean accent.

Possibly the weirdest spectacle I would witness was put on by the Salvation Army. At 7:00 PM early during a July evening they gathered at the corner of Peale and Queen Street directly opposite the Peale House. They had a small trio of three musicians. One played the violin and each of the other two played a trumpet and an accordion. There was also an Army Captain. The army captain was the preacher.

"Friends of humanity," the captain began. "We are gathered here near the Peale House. I will talk about the sins of drink." There was a momentary pause while the captain fetched out a rubbydub that was surrounded the other Army personnel. The rubbydub was escorted to a position at the head of the gathering. "Look at this poor soul," the captain went on. "His hard earned wages have already been wasted in the Peale House on beer. What a shame! This poor wretched soul has drank those earnings away; earnings that his poor wife and children will need for food and rent."

Of course with draft beer selling for 5 cents a serving this would have been hard to do. The man could have easily plastered himself for less than one dollar. At this point the rubbydub started to cry. "Let us repent and sing." The crowd began to sing *What a Friend we have in Jesus*. The rubbydub sobbed noticeably while the spectators watched. Then the Salvation Army Captain dismissed the crowd while the three Goldberg brothers looked on. They were visibly angered with the Salvation Army. The Army workers marched down Peale Street with music played by their small orchestra and turned west on Queen heading toward their building. When it was all over and the spectators departed the scene and the Goldberg brothers went back into the beer parlor followed by the rubbydub. Such is life in the outer world!

CHAPTER 11

The Return of the War Hero

In late November 1945, I was on my way home from Parkside Collegiate Institute. I had spent nearly 45 minutes traveling on an old Peter Witt streetcar. I was fascinated watching the motorman "wind up" the streetcar. I got off the Witt at the corner of Peale and Queen and walked up the west side of Peale to avoid any proximity to the Peale House. At 4:20 P.M. the sun was far down in the sky and strangely enough my thoughts turned to Major Duncan. When I reached the apartment block I went behind the building to have a look inside the barn. Major Duncan was there, lying on the old mattress, but he was out of uniform. He was wearing a dark-blue business suit but no overcoat. Everything he wore had a scruffy look. Beside him were some old blankets that Agnes discarded. He sported a white shirt and tie but wore army boots. The too large boots combined with the scruffy blue suit gave Major Duncan a circus clown look. Beside Major Duncan lay an almost empty bottle of "Newfoundland Screech." Major Duncan seemed to be out, for how long I didn't know. I thought about whether the man had eaten for I knew that most rubbydubs hardly ever ate. I looked around for anyone else. If Agnes found out he was laying in the old barn she would have thrown a fit. I had to rouse him and send him home. Major Duncan was soon awake.

Major Duncan opened his wallet and handed me a $20:00 bill.

"Give this to your mother and tell her not to disturb me for the rest of the night. Bring me something to eat but no more delicatessen food. It nearly killed me the last time. That stuff you bought lay on my stomach like a rusty piece of shit."

I went inside to my apartment, explained the $20 bill, gave it to Agnes and took a plate of her beef stew for the man and a thermos of coffee and brought it back to the barn. Major Duncan looked a little more sober that I had last seen him. He was sitting up and accepted the bowl of stew.

"This doesn't look that bad," Duncan remarked.

I replied, "You haven't tasted my mother's cooking. She burns water. This is tolerable."

Major Duncan wondered about me more than I did about him. He said I appeared to talk like an adult and not a 12-year-old. A conversation soon began between us.

"My name is Robert MacAlpine Noble. I am 12 and three quarters years old, almost 13 and was born in York Township on December 1, 1932." I could never give my birth place as Toronto. I thought Toronto sounded so much like a slum. I was always a precise person. I continued on. "I am now at Parkside Collegiate Institute in the first form. I speak some Spanish to satisfy my paternal grandmother whose ancestors came from Leon, a part of Iberia. I hate Parkside Collegiate. Everything they teach is British bullshit. Did we really fight World War II to save the British Empire? For all their glory they are still starving. We still send them 'Bundles for Britain.' We are not Limeys. We are Canadians. I am a Canadian and I will always be proud to be one."

"Well I am Major Alistair Duncan recently acting battalion commander of the 5th Suffolk Canadian Tank Regiment. I graduated from the Royal Military College in 1934 at the age of 22. My great-great-great-grandfather was Alan Duncan, one of the first settlers in Upper Canada. In 1796, he left his regiment stationed in the Niagara Peninsula and settled in what is now Kingston where he got a land grant. He was a major also."

Duncan went on to describe to me how he was schooled at Victoria College, a snooty equivalent of King George V Academy but more favorable to parents with "old money." Trying to enroll a non-Anglo-Saxon or non-Scot, or non-Orange Irish boy was almost impossible at this school. He told me that by early 1939, he had become a Captain and after a course at the Staff College in England, was assigned to a British tank regiment in early 1940 to observe and study tank tactics. During his assignment with the British army he studied under a Major General Bernhard Law Montgomery. In the early 1940's they went to North Africa to fight the Italians and the Germans. Later in the war Canadians began to see action in North Western Europe and Duncan now a Major began a command of a tank battalion. With the gradual retreat of the Germans back toward Germany in late 1944 Major Duncan, MC was now a highly respected tactics officer with the third Canadian Division and slated for promotion to Lt. Colonel. There was one drawback, however: Duncan was becoming a lush.

Alistair's dad drank too much and so did his two older sisters. Alistair was known to his troops as "drunken Duncan." I would meet the Major Duncan's older sisters at a later time. Alistair knew he could have the bad genes in him that could affect him as they did his father and sisters so he made a secret vow to never drink. The stress of the campaign in Holland was undermining his resolve. He could no longer sleep, even for a small time, and by late 1944 was in a state of chronic fatigue. Besides that, Canadian armor consisted mainly of the Sherman tank which was affectionately known as the "Tommy Cooker" and the "Ronson" after the cigarette lighter that lit up at all times. "Tommy" referred to the British soldier who inside the tank could be incinerated if the Sherman sustained a direct hit. It was inferior to the German tanks in every way except speed and range and the ability to be manufactured at a phenomenal rate. The Sherman was outgunned and lacked good armor. It was a mobile death trap.

Duncan became seriously concerned about his men and tried only to enter a combat situation only when he and his command had at least a 50% chance of success. Once in the mid-Autumn of 1944, his company entered a wooded area where a freshly equipped Panzer brigade lay in ambush. He was under strict orders to take the town on the other side of the woods. The attempt cost him 50% his command. On top of this, the British general in charge of the division called him and his men "cowards." My how those senior British commanders could judge courage. It seemed strange to me that every engagement the British ran failed primarily because of Canadian incompetence and cowardice. In some cases it failed because American allies were not up to it. This was it for Duncan and for the first time in his life he had a drink, which led to many more. The onset of the disease called "alcoholism" had him by the throat. He would enjoy few days of sobriety thereafter. He was relieved of command in January 1945 and sent back to Canada and by March, 1945 was in Sunnydale Veterans' Hospital. A later inquiry cleared Duncan of misconduct and decided that he acted bravely and wisely as the commanding officer. He was awarded the DSO for this action. They could have awarded it posthumously for Major Duncan was a walking dead man.

By October 1945, Duncan was considered fit for release from the Canadian Army and from Sunnydale. He had dried out at Sunnydale. But his craving was overwhelming. The army medics, not familiar with treating alcoholics, released him to the custody of his oldest sister, Anne Duncan, a secret alcoholic. She and her younger sister Carol never visited him for the nearly three months he was at Sunnydale. They knew he was there but they didn't give a shit. For reasons I did not dream of at that time I was to have an encounter with these two disturbed women in a short time later that would give me a huge look at depravity.

Anne Duncan was a drunk. From a pleasant looking young girl in her early teens she had become a bone rake by the time she was 40. At age 14 she discovered her father's hidden cache of liquor and decided to sample it. The old Chinese proverb says: "a journey of a thousand miles begins with the first step." And with Anne Duncan the journey would begin at the Duncan Mansion in Rosedale and was only interrupted by numerous stays in sanatoriums while she was drying out. When she left the sanatorium, she would resume drinking once back in the mansion. She had a permanent maid who looked after her from the age she left Yorkton Hall, the exclusive and prime Toronto School for the young ladies of Upper Canada. She had completed second form or grade 10 as they now call it at 15 years of age but that summer, at the Duncan cottage in Muskoka, the hidden drinking had reached a zenith. Anne passed out in a canoe and drifted 100 yards from the cottage. It was totally dark by the time the family missed her. They couldn't locate her for several hours. They found her the next morning laid out in the canoe. Anne Duncan had violated the First Commandment: "I Am almighty God, thou shalt have no other gods before me." Drink was now her god and that god had to be worshiped.

The army had made a mistake allowing her custody over her younger brother. The Canadian Army didn't do its homework. Alistair knew this and after arriving at the mansion being delivered by an Army jeep he wanted to reconcile with her. He secured entrance from Anne's maid. The maid led Alistair to her drunken form laying on a large sofa in the study.

Anne heard him enter and looked up. She was not totally out of it. "Give me a drinky-winky," she called out. A half empty bottle of scotch lay beside her. Alistair left the mansion immediately. He was still sober. He never saw Anne Duncan or her younger sister Carol again,

Major Alistair Duncan DSO., MC., B.A. made his way fully uniformed, over to Yonge Street and grabbed the trolley near the Glen Echo Loop, asked for a transfer, and road downtown. He transferred to a Queen West Car and for some reason got off at Bathurst Street. Alistair had no definite plans. He stopped in front of a wine store: "Parkwood Wines" about 100 yards north from Queen Street up Bathurst and bought two bottles of "Newfoundland screech." The clerk placed them in a brown paper bag, accepted the money and didn't ask for ID, after all Alistair was in uniform. Then he wandered aimlessly along Queen heading west until he came to Peale Street. He walked up Peale and found the apartment block. He walked around to the back and found the barn and wandered in. He lay down on the dirty mattress and began to consume the screech. He didn't want to drink but the craving overwhelmed him. This occurred at 1 P.M. I found him later for the first time.

I was to have many encounters with Major Alistair MacLeod Duncan during mid-November to early December 1945. They went on nearly every day. Each day Duncan would open his wallet and give me a $10 or $20 note and I would go into the apartment, turn over the bill to Agnes who prepared a plate of food, usually hot and a thermos of coffee. Agnes prepared beef steak which was so tender you could cut it with a spoon, the bottom of the spoon! Occasionally she baked cookies. Had these cookies been available during the recent War they would have functioned as deadly missiles in the hands of the Allies. They were so hard they could penetrate anything, especially a Sherman tank. Uncle Eddie demonstrated their unique ordinance qualities by nailing one sample to the kitchen wall. When he did that act the nail had bent.

Agnes was curious about the former soldier lying in the barn but was afraid to go and have a look see. After I delivered Duncan's evening meal, I began to get into conversations with Major Duncan but Duncan seemed more interested in me than in talking about himself. He wanted to know more about me. I was nearly 13-years old. What was my schooling, what interested me, what was my career ambition, what did my father do and so on? I felt an enormous desire to tell what I really felt strongly about. To these questions I would answer: "that I went to Parkside Collegiate and was in First Form; that I wanted to find the Holy Grail, that I wanted to be a professional pilot; and that my father was a professional loser." But why find the Holy Grail, I couldn't say? I didn't even know what it was!

I took an old electric space heater that was still functioning from the apartment and an extension cord so that Major Duncan would not freeze to death during the ever increasing colder evenings. Agnes did not complain much as long as those frequent $10 and $20 notes kept coming. The $20 notes represented almost one half of Lem's weekly pay. Major Duncan had a strong chance of remaining undiscovered so long as he remained in the loft and so he remained undiscovered. He seemed to venture out only to buy booze.

The first snow felt in Toronto in early December, 1945. It was slight, a sharp contrast to the swamping the city took a year before on December 11, 1944. Schools were closed for two days while the city shoveled out. For me there were two days of peace providing time to read my borrowed library books. These were books about King Arthur and the Knights of the Round Table. I also perused the King James Version of the New Testament when I could find a copy.

Alistair Duncan was well read. He asked me what he thought of those tales. I would answer that I wanted to know what the Grail was. I said: "I will find out what it is or die trying." The need to find out was programmed into my DNA although I did not know that at that time. It was also written into the DNA of Agnes and Lem but they subverted it.

A few days passed with more questions and more answers. Answers which I would never attempt to tell my parents or anybody else. That I was supposed to be a Sephardic Jew but had never been in a synagogue or a church of any type. Sections of the Scriptures were of unlimited interest to me. I purloined a bible from my English class at Parkside Collegiate to study during my leisure and I went through it. I could not stomach the "bully" god who could flood the entire earth if people did not fall down and kiss his ass. Why grant those people free will? This god was a god who could and would destroy a whole city like Sodom if no one who was righteous could be found living in it sounded like a" prick." I could not grasp this god's divine right to vengeance.

I thought about Mrs. Kerry our dilapidated next door neighbor. Her husband was the caretaker at a local elementary Catholic school. I never saw him come home from work sober. He too had a problem with drinking. The Kerry's had three sons, the youngest, also called Bobby was 12 years old as well but he lacked all ambition. He was interested in becoming a working man, nothing more. The middle son Freddie had a lame leg, seemed to be about 17 years of age and was skinny and tallish. He didn't seem to attend any school or work at any job but spent hours every day hanging around "Tremblay's Billiard Hall," next door to the Czech Meat Market. At the front of the pool room Mike Cohen had a barber shop. I would visit him once a month for a haircut and Mike, a man of about 50 years, would talk my ears off. But it was somewhat enjoyable to me that Mike Cohen was interested in what I had to say. I never ventured inside the poolroom because those guys in there looked pretty rough. Besides, you had to be 18 years old to enter. It was during his first visit to Cohen's Shop that I noticed Freddy Kerry, never playing pool, but keeping company with bad dudes.

The Kerry's oldest son, Johnny Kerry, was in the RCAF and worked as a radio technician. When he first enlisted he was selected for Air Crew training but opted out in favor of ground crew duties. He never got overseas spending nearly three years stationed in the Maritimes. The highest rank he reached was LAC. "I would never go up in one of those things," I heard him often say, after he returned home, "they're made of string and paper." Johnny was the only one of the three boys with any semblance of ambition. His first job after discharge from the service was in the factory where Lem worked as a lead hand. He got Johnny the job, but Johnny would leave after a few months finding employment with a radio and electronics manufacturer. Johnny was a whiz at building electronic gizmos from scratch using "discarded parts." When Johnny was last heard about 10 years after securing the job he was in charge of a large manufacturing division of this company and doing well.

Although the Kerry family were close to starvation, Mrs. Kerry a woman about 45 years of age worked hard scrubbing floors for the Peale House. She would then donate her hard earned pennies to the local Roman Catholic Church, called "St Mary's," which they willingly accepted even though the local priest knew the Kerry family financial state was unhealthy.

Things were the usual bore during history class at Parkside Collegiate. Grade nine history class consisted mostly of the history of England. Canadian History was considered not important. The teacher was a Mister Albert Holmes B.A., M.A. who could be flustered by his scholars with the greatest of ease. He had two favorite expressions. One was: "great Caesar's ghost" and the other: "great balls of fire." Well one day during his dramatic recreation of what led up to English King Charles I's beheading at the hands of Parliament and while he was putting his scholars to sleep he got angry. "Great Caesar's balls" he shouted, "don't you people ever pay attention?" There was silence for a few seconds then loud laughter. Mister Holmes did not have a clue as to what he said.

Mr. Holmes, like Tarzan of Goldberg's delicatessen, had the unpleasant habit of cleaning out his nose at his desk when the kids were doing seat work. A few pupils like me studied this venture in nasal mining. Methodically, "melekas" were removed and rolled up in his handkerchief. Holmes was a study in classic manners. He was a lay preacher in a Baptist Church and I overheard other teachers referring to him as "Reverend Holmes."

One day, in the mid-December of 1945, I returned to the barn to check on Major Duncan but he wasn't there. There was none of his clothing and no trace that he had ever been there. I was worried. Agnes expected the $10 or $20 bill but I had nothing for her. There was a minor tiff when she didn't get her usual $20 fee for providing food and shelter to her unwanted guest. Duncan was unwanted but his money was not. Besides she never met the man! I challenged her to come to the barn and see for herself that Duncan was absent. Agnes refused and grew silent. Secretly, she hoped he would retake up residence in the barn but he never returned. She did spend the money on the family but withheld a few dollars to indulge in her passion for poker. On these occasions Bill and I had to stay home and look after Marion our younger sister.

Then in late December, just before the Christmas Break, while I was in mathematics class sitting through a poor lesson on polynomials, the principal of Parkside appeared at the door with a grownup dressed in a gray suit partially covered by darker gray overcoat. The principal of Parkside Collegiate, Mr. Stanley Bigelow, B.A., B.Ed. seldom ever seemed to leave his office. He was a firm believer in promoting quality education by remaining soundly locked behind his office door. He would appear occasionally walking the halls. He rarely visited a classroom. At least he didn't patrol the halls of Parkside like Proctor with cane in hand looking for some poor boy to assault. I thought I was in trouble when Bigelow asked me to step out of the room, "but pack up your books first." There was a pause while I packed my gear. "Come with us," Bigelow said. We went to Bigelow's office on the main floor.

"Oh God," I thought, "Are they sending me back to King George V Academy?"

The gray suited man and I went in and Bigelow stayed outside. We didn't bother to sit down. "Bobby, I have some grim news to report to you," the gray suited man said. "My name is Walter Abercromby, and I am - or was Alistair Duncan's friend and also his lawyer. Alistair is dead. He was walking along Queen Street near Bathurst at 5:00 P.M. and stepped off the sidewalk directly into the path of a streetcar. It wasn't the streetcar driver's fault. Alistair just walked in front of street car. He was killed instantly."

"Was it a new PCC streetcar?" I asked. "Major Duncan deserved to be killed by that rather than one of the older ones. It had to be a streamliner. Was it a new Red Rocket?" Walter Abercromby smiled.

I was dumbfounded. How could a man like Major Alistair Duncan DSO, MC, BA, bring an end his life in such an inglorious manner?

Walter Abercromby continued, "About 20 days ago Alistair came to my office on Bay Street. He wanted to discuss his will. I don't know if you can understand it but he was well off financially. Alcohol destroyed him but when I saw him last he was sober, probably for the last time in his life. What an effort it must have been for him to remain sober for almost a day. I want you to know that you are Alistair's sole heir. He had no sons or daughters. He had no wife. He did not want his sisters to have anything that was his. They have their own resources. A trust fund has been set up for you. Some potentially valuable property north of the city has been left to you as well. Believe me if money has a fraction of the value in 50 years as it has now you will not be poor. Tomorrow instead of coming to school you will stay home and be driven to my office along with your mother and father. We will discuss Alistair's will then. It has already passed probate court."

I left with Mr. Walter Abercromby and was driven back to the Peale apartment in Walter's blue, 1941 Cadillac Sedan. Mr. Abercromby left me at the door of the apartment building.

Later that evening I lay in bed about 8:00 PM reading the New Testament. I came to the chapter and verses that described the disciples caught in a storm. Jesus calmed the storm. One disciple remarked: "what manner of man is this that even the winds and seas obey him?"

I thought out loud: "Oh how do I become like that?" From that instant on Life would direct me on a definite path that would lead me to raising my spiritual energy no matter what obstacles were thrown across my path.

CHAPTER 12

Major Duncan's Vision

Major Duncan was desperate to shake off his alcoholism. For the first time he prayed to God in order to attain help. As he lay there in the barn behind the Peele Apartments he began to sob. He reflected on his failures in the War and why he had to use liquor as an anesthetic. "Please God," he said, "why can't I lick this problem?" Suddenly, an angelic being had appeared in front of him. Major Duncan was not frightened. Instead he grew extremely sober. The Being was quiet. Duncan relaxed.

"I Am one of the Lords of Karma," the being said. "I Am come to help you through these final days of your embodiment. Do you know who this boy is who helps you?"

Duncan did not answer. The being continued his conversation. "He was your son in a previous life. Now you have a chance to make amends for that lifetime when you neglected him. If you do the right thing your miseries will be lifted off of you. You know what to do. Your will be sober for the next three days. Do what you must do."

So Major Duncan contacted his friend and lawyer Walter Abercrombie. Dressed up in one his good suits, after he showered and shaved at his estate he attended an appointment the next day. He rode in a taxi all the way from Vaughan town ship north of Toronto to Downtown Bay Street in Toronto. It would be the final time he would be clean and sober. He would be dead shortly after that. At that time I thought Major Duncan committed suicide. Later Walter Abercrombie requisitioned the police report. Major Duncan had three times the legal limit of alcohol in his blood stream. This was determined by an autopsy. He literally was out of it. The coroner and police ruled it was an accidental death.

CHAPTER 13

The Millionaire

Agnes was giddy at the thought of my inheritance although she wasn't informed of any of the details. Lem was sleeping in a bed having been home from work since 2:00 P.M. A lit cigarette hung from his lips. Mr. Abercromby had briefed Lem at his workplace and went home with Lem to the apartment where Agnes was briefed. Mr Abercromby had covered all bases but would give none of the details to either of my parents. He also paid out two days of Lem's wages to Agnes. It was going to be a very interesting the next day.

A car came by the apartment at 10 AM. It was Abercromby's 1941 Cadillac, driven by a young employee. The car picked up Agnes, Lem and me at 10:00 A.M. and drove us downtown to Walter Abercromby's Office near King and Bay Streets. I had on my formal suit and wore a white shirt and blue tie. The family departed the Cadillac as it stopped on Bay Street, entered the building at 127 Bay and went through the lobby to the elevator and rode up to the fifth floor. A man dressed in a blue suit took possession of Walter Abercromby's Cadillac to park it. We entered directly into the reception area. A sign overhead said "Walter Abercromby KC and Associates." The receptionist sent us directly into Abercromby's Office. He was there waiting at the doorway. He said nothing. He just motioned us in. We entered the office and sat down where Walter Abercromby motioned for us to sit. There were two other women also in the office; one looked about 40 and the other about 38 years old. Walter Abercromby pointed to the older one and said: "this is Anne Duncan and this is Mrs. Walton, nee Carol Duncan, pointing to the younger lady."

When everybody was seated Walter Abercromby seated himself and began to speak. "This is a meeting to discuss the final will of Major Alistair Duncan, formerly a career soldier of the Canadian Army who passed away from a vehicle accident that occurred in Toronto this December, 1945. It reads as follows:

> *This final will is to instruct my lawyer Walter Abercromby KC of how to dispose of my estate. My property is located in Vaughan Township. The funds all my bank accounts are to pass to Robert MacAlpine Noble, a youth of 13 years of age. He resides at the Peale Apartments with his parents. The youth was born on December 1, 1932 in Toronto and now currently attends Parkside Collegiate Institute in Toronto. Control of the estate will be held by Walter Abercromby and will remain in his hands until my heir reaches the age of majority. Robert's parents are not under any circumstances to participate in the management of the estate. Robert's father Lemuel Noble shall be paid $7500 in upfront cash and a stipend of $5000 annually for life. His mother Agnes shall receive $10 000 annually to cover her living expenses and that of her children. She may reside at my property in Vaughan Township if she chooses but I hope her and her stepson William and her two natural children will take up residence at my rural estate as soon as possible.*
>
> *Roberts's parents cannot have access to Robert's inheritance in any form, other than the allowances provided for them in this will. This allowance will be provided for Agnes whether she lives with Robert or not. When he is of legal age, the contents of the estate will pass directly to him. The estate is now maintained by Hugh and Margaret Watson who live in the small bungalow that sites on the property and are provided with funds from my estate*

to support them. Unless they wish to leave the estate of their own accord, they will continue to live in the smaller house. Hugh and Margaret Watson are to receive $20 000 immediately after the reading of my will. If they leave the employment of my estate, they will still receive an additional $20 000. My two sisters, Anne and Carol Duncan are not to share in the wealth of my estate in any manner. They were amply provided for by our father. With regards to Bobby's schooling: I believe that this should be Willington Academy, a school near my estate in Vaughan Township. This facility will best meet his special needs.

Abercromby produced legal papers and Agnes signed them without reading them. Abercromby called two secretaries into his office and made them sign as witnesses. Then Lem, as well, signed papers without reading them. Nothing was presented to Alistair Duncan's two sisters. They were doing a slow burn in the corner of Abercromby's office. "After all" a sister said, "this was our own brother!"

The will was negative black mail. Agnes and Lem were being bribed to allow me to live in the country. I was to be supported by the inherited estate, attend a unique school that would meet my needs and yet have no real say in anything until I turned 21 years old. The other papers Agnes and Lem signed were carefully designed to ward off the negative influences they seemed to foist on their children whether they intended to or not. It never became apparent to either one that both Agnes and Lem had signed away control of Marion and me as well as the responsibility for our half-brother William who by this time was of legal age. In 1945, the $10 000 Agnes was going to receive awed her. This was after all more than four times what Lem earned and there was no rent to pay. Income tax was paid on the estate earnings but Agnes and Lem were provided with tax-free incomes.

"We are going to see our lawyer," Anne Duncan shouted. "Imagine leaving a fortune to a complete stranger." Anne Duncan's righteous indignation would even make the famous movie and radio comedian: Jack Benny feel shame. But before they could leave the office Walter

Abercromby warned them they had no case, this will had already passed through Probate Court, thanks largely to Abercromby's connections. Abercromby had affidavits from the visitors' book of Sunnydale Hospital showing no records of visits from either sister to see their "beloved brother." He had written statements from her maid that Anne Duncan had been drunk when Alistair last visited the Rosedale mansion.

The next day the Duncan sisters visited a lawyer they selected from the telephone directory. This lawyer knew Abercromby well and refused the case but first he charged a $20 consulting fee for the sisters' first visit. Abercromby had done his homework. The day after the will was read the Duncan sisters visited a second new lawyer. This lawyer explained that under the terms of the will of the father of Alistair and his sisters all were provided for equally. He also mentioned the proof Walter Abercromby had showing Alistair was estranged from the two sisters. All the time he was in service overseas during the war they had not sent him one bit of correspondence. He had not been invited to the younger sister's wedding in 1934. It was apparent they did not want any part of Alistair, they just wanted his assets. For them Alistair was a nonentity. His money wasn't. At least the Duncan sisters had an honest lawyer. He advised them strongly to drop the case charging them an additional $100 for his fees. This fee they bitterly griped about. "Why that lawyer did nothing for us," Anne Duncan commented. In time, the sisters consulted other lawyers not knowing that Walter Abercromby was a friend and a mentor to every lawyer the sisters contacted. None would represent her. Those lawyers were not "ambulance chasers."

The younger Duncan sister Carol married in June 1934, to a medical doctor who had a newly established practice in Rosedale, now part of Toronto. During the early years of the marriage she bore two boys, smart young boys. The children were then assigned to the care of a nanny. Carol acquired a French poodle after assigning the mothering of her second son away to another nanny. The physician husband of Carol was away serving in the RCAF. He willingly volunteered to be away from his wife. This nanny kept the children apart from their drunken mother. Carol then proceeded to lavish her undying affection on a French poodle she overpaid for when she purchased it from a swanky kennel. She named her dog "Pierre" and she became totally enamored with the pooch. It was eerie that Pierre received more love that either of her two children and her husband. The dog regularly did its business on her best carpets or on her hardwood floors. Sometime Pierre liked the mountain air and mounted her sofas for his business. It was almost as if the pet had contempt for his mistress. She doted on the pet and totally neglected her husband and children when that husband and his children tried to visit with her. By the War's end, she lived a companionless existence, except of course for Pierre. Her husband had legally separated from her. He then gained custody of his children. As she entered Abercromby's office for the reading of her brother's will, she engaged in a brief conversation with her sister.

"Pierre was constipated this morning so I rushed him to the vet and he gave Pierre an enema!"

"Oh dear," the older sister Anne, replied.

Lem was more than happy to abandon his family for steady income which he didn't have to earn. He walked out on Agnes and took up residence with a strange woman a few months later. One afternoon he fell asleep in their bedroom with a cigarette dangling from his lips and set fire to the mattress. He received some minor burns but his new woman quickly threw him out. I saw Lem only one more time. He died of a heart attack in late December, 1947, almost two years to the date of his departure from his family. When he became alert shortly after his heart attack he was in the Toronto General Hospital. He looked up and uttered the words: "am I still here;" turned his head to the side and perished right then and there. I did attend the funeral with Agnes and my half-brother Bill and my younger sister Marion. A Sephardic Rabbi spoke about Lem's life for a few moments. The rabbi said how he was: "a wonderful father and husband," but avoided the talk of his two wives. And the rabbi continued, "he left the world its most precious gift of all: his jewels, his three children. These are his precious jewels."

While standing for the services I felt a nudge in my side. While the funeral attendees were leaving my older brother Bill said: "open the coffin and let's see if we buried the right person."

Agnes fumed about not gaining access to the three and one half million plus of Alistair's estate. She did not want to move to the Vaughan Township property and ranted about "really living really out in the sticks." She could have accepted $10 000 as a payment and remained in the Peale Street Apartment. Besides the rent would come out of her own pocket if she found her own quarters. If she did that I might have to board at my next school which was to be The Willington Academy. This school was recommended to my parents by Walter Abercromby as one which would best suit my special needs. She relented, took the money, which was an annual salary just to be around, and moved into the estate in Vaughan Township after arrangements had been made with the transfer company to move her furniture and other belongings. Agnes had now become a "remittance woman." When she got to the Vaughan Township estate, she found the large house was fully furnished and kept in immaculate condition by Margaret and Hugh Watson. There was no place for her poor furniture so it was stored in one of the two outbuildings by the movers. Hugh Watson showed them where to store it. Secretly, Hugh felt Agnes's furniture was junk and wanted to burn it. It took up too much storage space.

When Alistair stayed at the estate before the War, the Watson couple always kept house for him. Now they would do the same for the Nobles. They were an "elderly" couple in their middle 50's. Hugh was a Canadian by birth while Margaret, judging from her midlands English accent, was, at one time, a landed immigrant from the British Isles. They were both good cooks. The estate had 160 acres of which 10 acres were reserved for the main house and the smaller house occupied by Hugh and Margaret Watson. An additional 10 acres had a warehouse on it. The building was owned by an appliance manufacturer. The land under the building was rented. A huge lawn surrounded the residences. The structures, all produced from scratch, were in excellent shape. There were two outbuildings housing two farm tractors, one equipped with a tow behind a rotary grass mower that cut a six-foot swath. The Watsons had a prewar De Soto sedan at their disposal that belonged to Alistair but was left in the will for the exclusive use of Hugh and Margaret. They washed it every day and used it to shop with. They kept a daily log of travel expenses and what else they were using the car for. The local

Chrysler dealer gave the vehicle regular maintenance. The car had been undercoated with a coating of oil to prevent rusting in the winter. The house and motor vehicle data and receipts for the estate's expenses were picked up monthly by someone from Abercromby's office where cash from the Abercromby employee who collected the bills and receipts was paid back to Hugh Watson for his outlay. Hugh and Margaret Watson never farmed the property, instead that was done by tenants. Their transactions were handled by Walter Abercromby's office. There was a prewar Chevy pickup truck also kept in good running order and was used for heavier work on The Farm.

I was enchanted with the farm. I named it "The Farm." Alistair Duncan had called The Farm "Kingston." I had never lived in a rural setting. It was quiet during the late evening and early mornings and sleep was easier to come by. I was a chronic insomniac ever since I could remember. I became worse with the two year sentence to George V Academy which I was sentenced to after I completed grade 4. It was a reward for doing well at the local elementary school: Humewood Heights. I seldom slept more than four hours a night. Agnes frequently visited her children's rooms when they lived at Rimsdale Road. When she found me awake she would scream at me: "Why aren't you asleep?" Having discovered my insomnia Agnes took me to a local M.D. who prescribed sleeping pills. The local druggist told Agnes not to give me the pills because they were strong enough to knock out an elephant. They were forced on me twice but didn't help. After that at bedtime I would hold them in my mouth and secretly spit them out.

The Farm was the best Christmas break I had ever experienced. After settling at The Farm two school weeks had passed from the moment I was taken out of math class at Parkside collegiate. I was to start at Willington Academy and finish first form. Memories of King George V Academy began to frighten me. Was I in for another brutalizing at the hands of the head master at this new alien school?

Well at least Bill, my half-brother was healing up from his almost four year ordeal as a POW of the Japs. I hated the Japs. They were dirty yellow bellied bastards. After meeting Margaret Watson I lost a lot of anger against the British. This anger was flung at me by Canadians using such phrases such as "loyal British subjects." I was losing the habit of rendering extreme judgment against the British after I met Margaret. It was to my advantage to do so. Bill had gained back some of the weight he lost. Margaret Watson was patient in feeding him and complied with what the army doctors requested. He began to regain some of the vision he lost during the war. He went with Margaret to shop in the small town of Richmond Hill. Later he got his own license and began driving Margaret Watson to the local market. But he only had grade 10 education having completed his last year of high school at the end of second form when he just passed his 16th birthday. He went to work in a factory during the summer of 1940 and never returned to school. I talked with Walter Abercromby about Bill at least completing his Junior Matriculation and Walter was looking into to it.

When Agnes would eventually leave The Farm for her new apartment in Niagara, Bill remained on The Farm. He was making himself useful. In time, Bill opened a small hobby shop in North York with funds he received from the Veterans' Benefits Act. He spent a year in Rehab school, applied himself, and earned his junior matric. Later on he would become a mature student and take night courses at a Toronto University and earn a BA. The hobby shop after a year grew ever busier. This venture needed additional space and expanded into a second vacant store next to the original location. Bill liked to build balsa wood model airplanes and was getting into model trains. Bill married in the summer of 1950. By this time he was on his way to becoming financially independent. He had three children making me an uncle. Bill had married a young high school teacher name Dorothy Wadsworth. Bill would show excellent business sense as the years progressed. He was a partner in a company that purchased old buildings near Bay and Queen Streets in the early 1950's. They also bought abandoned farm lands on the extreme northern boundaries of North York. The steady expansion of the population of Toronto made the properties ever more valuable. It was the beginning of Bill's fortune. When the newer City Hall was being planned in the late 1950's a rundown area suddenly became desirable. Bill was on his way to becoming a millionaire many times over.

My full sister Marion displayed signs of creativity early in her high school years. She would leave The Farm at 16 years of age with her Junior Matric and venture to the British Isles at the age of 16 and one half years. She began to appear in summer stock and minor TV shows for the RBC and then started writing novels. She was to become world renowned a few years later.

CHAPTER 14

Academic Excellence

In very early January 1946, Hugh Watson drove me to the Willington Academy. I was just six weeks past my thirteenth birthday. It was about two miles north of the Farm and not too far from Yonge Street. It could easily be walked to from the Farm. I was dressed in decent blue pants, a clean blue shirt and black, casual shoes with galoshes over them. I wore a gray sweater over my long sleeved blue shirt. This was a long way removed from the ridiculous outfit I wore my first day to King George V Academy. Over all this I wore a new blue parka. I also had a blue scarf. The parka, the sweater and the tie had a school crest sewn on them. The sweater and parka were crested on the right side of the chest. I also had a wool toque to repel the January cold. This was my new school uniform which Margaret Watson had obtained for me from McCardle's School Uniforms Company, a venture that sold the independent schools their supply of costumes for both girls and boys. Margaret had picked the two sets of clothing from McCardle's and my current clothes and she had done a good job. They fit perfectly. I had thought my new school togs would somehow resemble the ridiculous garb I wore to the King George V Academy. I almost felt proud to wear the getup.

The trip seemed short and the prewar De Soto ran well. Hugh kept the car in one of the out buildings to protect it from the elements. Willington was located on a working sod farm and had two main buildings: a school house, with two gyms and five classrooms, some washrooms, and a principal's office. The other house seemed to be a residence. The unusual uses that the sod-farm was put to would soon become apparent to me in time. Hugh took me to the principal's office. There was no secretary but the name plate on the door said "Kenneth MacAlpine B.A., M.A." This name really got my attention. I wondered if the new principal was related to me. After all, "MacAlpine" was my middle-name.

Kenneth MacAlpine was a tall, husky fellow who spoke with a delightful Scottish burr. He was about 50 years old. He was too old to have served in the military during WW II unless he was a professional soldier and a senior officer. When I entered his office, along with Hugh Watson, Kenneth MacAlpine rose from behind his desk and said: "This is young Mr. Noble I presume."

"It is," I replied.

Principal MacAlpine motioned for me to sit down at the front of his desk. MacAlpine had a folder with my formal name on the cover in prominent letters. Hugh Watson never sat down but turned around exited the room without a sound and returned to the farm. MacAlpine looked at me with a hint of admiration and said: "So you're the lad that wants to find the Holy Grail. Why do you suppose you want to find it? Is it some sort of Cup? Will it give you wealth?" There was a pause of several seconds. "Why is it a boy barely 13 years old walks into my office and I upon examining him finds that he has the spiritual vibrations of a person who has spent his last 10 reincarnations looking for Illumination. Who seeks the Holy Grail?" I felt a flash of energy run through me "Well," MacAlpine went on, "We will help you find it. But first let us attend to some academic matters." He handed me a thin booklet, printed on 8.5" by 11" white paper and covered with a cream white cardboard cover with the "Willington" printed on it in one inch blue letters. I read it rapidly. It had some pictures of the school grounds upon it and a mission statement: *To lead them to the Divine truth.* The rest of the text was a summary of school rules. Below the title was a portrait of a strange bird.

"That is the Phoenix," MacAlpine, answered anticipating my question. "It cannot die but rises always from its own ashes. You have risen from your own ashes several times in your quest to find the Truth. And this is over a few lifetimes. May I answer any questions you have?"

I felt much easier than I did at my first encounter with Percival Proctor but I felt compelled to ask: "do you cane the boys here?"

"We are not savages. We can deal any situation here with compassion and respect for our students and for our faculty. This is not King George V Academy. That type of school was created by dark forces to molest the minds and bodies of the unfortunate inmates who attend there. This molestation occurs in King George V Academy by terror and force and in Parkside Collegiate by boredom. These young people 'need' this abuse to become the leaders in politics, industry, finance, and whatever. When they are thoroughly molested and firmly terrorized they are ready to join the elite ruling class as upper class slaves. They are slaves of the 'dark forces.' Such is the state of the world today. A change in the power structure of the world is long overdue. Their institutions are not what schools should be. Most of their students sense this and either succumb to their blackmail or drop out to escape indoctrination. Conform or perish but don't explore your own Divinity. Don't think things out for yourself. That is the nature of these schools."

I noticed that Principal MacAlpine had to stop and catch his breath. I found the short rant intoxicating. After the tirade MacAlpine escorted me down the corridor to the First Form Algebra class. "This is Jack MacKay's class; he is the finest teacher at nearly all levels and branches of mathematics I know of. Just sit in the back and watch him in action. By the way you and I are kin. I am, a cousin of your mother's father. Some day you will understand that this is not some idle coincidence; you and I meeting like this."

I sat down in the back of MacKay's classroom. There were only 10 students in the room. I was the 11th. MacKay was a powerful life force in the room. All the boys followed his every word. He was talking about factoring trinomials and when he stopped to question a boy, the boy seemed eager to answer. Everybody was paying attention. MacKay went on questioning the boys, correcting their answers, and involving them in the lesson. He wrote the polynomial: "$x^2 - x - 6$" on the blackboard, and looking at me said: "Robert give us a start on factoring this one." I looked at it for a moment, wondered how he knew my name, and then I picked up on MacKay's radiation and answered. "Two numbers when multiplied together must be '-6' but when added must be '-1'. The answer must be: '(x-3) (x+2)'." MacKay smiled and wrote it on the board. I examined the board. I had been only a fair student in mathematics since I could recall in my earlier days at George V Academy. All of a sudden I could factor polynomials instantly. What had MacKay done? Such was MacKay's power that it automatically turned on the right or creative brains of the boys, and when they processed mathematics that way, they became very smart. Learning algebra, trigonometry, and analytical geometry by the time the boys studied it in fifth form (grade 13) would prove to be easy. Right brain learning made all matter of subjects easily learned. Most of the boys started writing their senior matriculation exams in grade 10. But, according to the learning scientists, grade 13 mathematics and sciences were supposed to be linear subjects, that is to say, they were supposed to be learned by mastering one logical step at a time. The boys in Mackay's class seemed to master topics all at once. Mackay called it "intuitive learning." There was a gramophone that played some sort of special music that sounded like it originated from a fine church organ.

School inspectors from the Ontario Department of Education used to stop and visit his classroom at every opportunity trying to fathom his technique. This technique was also employed by all the other teachers. As a result, Willington Academy earned ultra-high ratings from the Ministry. The Ministry disliked giving them. Inspectors were primarily in schools to enforce Ontario Curriculum standards. Many of those standards were copied from Prussian system of education. History was the exception. It was entirely British bullshit.

The boys' exams, for Willington in grades 9, 10, 11, and 12 were set by the local secondary school nearest the site of Willington grounds and graded, for a fee, by the teachers at that local school. The class averages always came out near 90%. Principal MacAlpine insisted in not knowing what the exams were, only that they conformed to the Ontario Curriculum. The exams had to be the same as those written at the local secondary school and conducted with a local secondary school teacher supervising them for a fee of course. The boys wrote the Ontario Department of Education Grade 13 examinations also in that local school also. These were graded by the Ministry who contracted certified secondary teachers to grade eight papers per day during the summer vacation period in the Department of Education office buildings. No candidate signed his name to a paper. Instead they wrote a Candidates' identification number on a special location and only once the exam was completed and the grade recorded was the name and number matched and the candidate's results sent out, usually to the home address.

In all of Willington's history till June 1945 there was never a hint of impropriety. But in late August of 1945, one on Willington's boys received a minimal passing grade in Physics while the principal's son, at the local high school received a first class honor grade. This rankled the grade 13 student at Willington who wrote that exam. He didn't even know the local secondary student that was assigned his grade in physics. Principal MacAlpine requested that all grade 13 results were to be photo-stated after he received them and then sent on to his students. After studying the results of the year 1945 candidates he initiated an investigation of the results by the Department of Education. He had good contacts with the Department and they got right on it. They examined the hand writing of the Willington candidate and the other candidates in physics at the local secondary school and found the principal's son's candidate number was assigned to the Willington student and vice versa. The Department of Education said: "mistakes happen." The grades were reassigned to their rightful owners. The whole incident was reported by the Toronto Comet, the Telegraph and the World and Post "It was all a clerical error," they printed. The Department of Education was not about to tarnish the career of a "public educator." MacAlpine demanded that all future grade 13 exams should be held at Willington under Department of Education supervision. He got his wish. By the late spring 1967 all Ministry of Education common subject examinations for all grade 13 students had stopped. Thus began "grade inflation." A "67" in a grade 13 Ontario Examination would ultimately become an "85" in later years. By the year 2000 an average grade of 70% in upper school mathematics and sciences had inflated to 90%!

Universities began to keep records of where the students earned their grades. It was not enough to have good grades; they also has to be from a respectable school.

It was not until the spring of 1946 that I had an outdoor class at Willington. My final year examinations were scheduled for mid-June. One afternoon at 1:30 P.M. the 12 boys in his class were led outside by Kenneth MacAlpine where a yellow unmarked training plane in RCAF colors was parked outside the large storage shed alongside the classroom building.

"This is the new Royal Air Force basic trainer now coming into service with the RAF and later with the Royal Canadian Air Force. It is called the "Chipmunk." It has a 150-HP air cooled in line engine and is capable of a top speed of 150 miles per hour. It is completely stressed for aerobatics. Had this type of craft been available in the recent war perhaps we would not have had as many training accidents as we had. We will have the airplane for the next three months. It is my hope that each of you in this school will have at least 10 hours of instruction in it."

MacAlpine seemed quite pleased with this little speech and introduced the strange RAF officer who stood beside him. He was a shortish, very slim man of about 25 years of age dressed in a winter RAF uniform. He wore the insignia of a Squadron Leader and had several decorations. "This is Squadron Leader Abraham Warshawsky of the RAF now assigned to waiting, as his discharge from the RAF is being completed. The RAF is reluctant to do this but it respects the Squadron Leader's wishes. He came to Canada along with the plans and this early production model of the Chipmunk to train and instruct our flight cadets of the RCAF and their instructors. His assignment is now over." While MacAlpine was talking, Squadron Leader Warshawsky took off his officer's cap and put on an old leather head warmer.

The squadron leader walked over to me and said: "Now young man, I was only slightly older than you are now when I first began to fly in the summer of 1934. I was 14 years old."

Abraham Warshawsky had graduated out of the top Gymnasium of Poland in the late-Spring of 1934 at the age of 14 years, two months. His father Simon Warshawsky had owned a large brick and block factory.

He started this industry in 1919, immediately after the Armistice was signed by the belligerents ending World War I.

"Wait, within 20 years and there will be another war," Simon used to tell his wife and children. "Within 20 years it will come and 10 times more people will be slaughtered. Our leaders are fools. They are dupes of the big bankers and munitions makers."

Abraham headed back to England in the summer of 1936 for his third year at Cambridge. The boy had done well finishing at or near the top of every class he took. In the summer it was Polish National Aircraft test flying everything his father could get his hands on. Polish National did not have the large financial resources necessary to develop a modern fighter aircraft on its own that were even moderately capable of matching the Bf 109C it purchased from the German aircraft manufacturer. Abraham, when not in Poland, spent the rest of the time at Cambridge. This was the year, 1937, his father sent with him two escorts and several small chests of gold bullion valued at almost 1 000 000 pounds! Simon Warshawsky knew a war was coming after the Germans re occupied the Rhine land in 1936. He sent his only son to England with a fortune in gold and made him promise to never return to Poland but to remain in England, complete his studies at Cambridge and possibly go to America.

Despite Simon's repeated warnings in September, 1939 the Polish Air Force had to oppose the Luftwaffe in obsolete craft. They were no match. Several of the Polish Air Force pilots escaped to England and flew with the RAF.

At the age of 17 years Abraham joined the Reserve squadron of the RAF that flew out of Cambridge. The recruiting officer did not want him as he was a foreigner and under aged but Abraham told Professor Banting and again strings were pulled. Abraham was accepted as a pilot trainee and at the age of 18 years of age in his last and final year at Cambridge and was commissioned a Pilot Officer. During training his instructors quickly advanced him and by early 1940 he was flying a Spitfire. He was one of a few pilots to fly a Spitfire in 1940, during the intense Battle of Britain, who possessed sufficient hours to be completely competent with the machine. It was the original Mark I. In September

1939, when war was finally declared he was frequently sought out to advise other pilots on aerobatics and tactics. At 19 years of age he was one of the most experienced flyers in the RAF. He also held the temporary rank of Flying Officer. During the Battle of Britain he was assigned to assist in the training of Polish Air Force pilots flying with the Royal Air Force. Later while with the Polish squadron, during the most intense part of the air war they engaged more than 100 German fighters and bombers. Abraham disposed of two bombers in that exchange. He soon had a DFC and was to win a second DFC in July 1941, while leading a flight of six Spitfire Vs in a raid on France. Then he was promoted to Flight Lieutenant in late 1941 and assigned to a training unit. He spent the rest of the war with training units. He was also a test pilot discovering the quirks of ever improving newer models of the Spitfire as it matched the steadily improving BF 109s during the war. In February 1945, with the Pacific War still raging Abraham was transferred to Canada and assigned to a training station for pilots near Toronto. In March 1945, he was promoted to Squadron Leader. Shortly after this advancement the British Commonwealth Air Training plan ceased to operate. Abraham was now assigned to flying a desk in Toronto. Then he received an assignment to familiarize himself with the new Chipmunk. He was formerly instructing young pilots in training in the intricacies of flying the North American Harvard Trainer and was to be second in Command of the training school. But in the peace time RAF, he felt he had a more important calling and future RAF service would hold him back so he decided to resign from the RAF as soon as the war with Japan was over. The RAF didn't want this to happen. On V-J Day he attempted to resign from the RAF. The RAF offered him a permanent commission at just about the same time. Abraham stayed on for a few more months assigned to mostly administrative duties. With his permanent commission his rank would ultimately be reduced to flight lieutenant. It might take him three or more years to regain his current rank of squadron leader.

Then it all changed. Abraham was approached by some Zionists who were working to establish the new state of Israel. They were older men, many who fought during the war with the American and British forces.

To go back to Poland was out of the question. The Communists had taken over. What happened to his father remained a mystery? He had not heard from him since August 1939. Abraham was never a Zionist. His father's fortune of one million pounds sterling if converted to USA or Canadian dollars was about $4 000 000. It was originally intended to start the young Abraham out in some venture that was constructive and would support the Warshawsky family. In fact, Abraham did not know what happened to his two younger sisters. They succeeded in contacting him in early 1947 through the RAF. They had been sent to the United States in the summer of 1939 and were sponsored by Simon's two existing first cousins who lived in some weird country called "Alabama." The exact location was a small city called "Dothan."

So when the war with Japan was over for a few months when I met young Abraham Warshawsky. I found out the young Squadron Leader was highly respected by both Kenneth MacAlpine and other staff of Willington. In the late spring of 1947, he would leave the RAF and began to embark on nation building. The future Israelis wanted Squadron Leader Warshawsky to help train a new air force for the new state of Israel. The new state would start out with gifts from American and Canadian Jews. What the new nation sorely needed were good fighter aircraft and people skilled in using them. In time, Squadron Leader Warshawsky became committed to finding them.

My first flight with Abraham Warshawsky indicated that I would be a mediocre pilot. My saving grace was my unusual ability to pick up navigational skills and the squadron leader was a skilled air navigator as well as pilot. "Young man," he said. "Give up this ambition to fly and learn to navigate, this is better for you." With that I only took one more ride in the Chipmunk. The squadron leader assigned my time in the Chipmunk to more promising students. I would regret this decision for a short time, a very short time. I had the uncanny ability to rebound from Life's setbacks with alarming speed. I was producing wind diagrams and solving elementary navigation problems. The other boys seemed less adept at this. I was a natural at it.

The summer of 1946 was passing. I was 13 years, 9 months was according to young ladies becoming a handsome youth so Margaret

Watson told me. I was now 5'8" tall and weighed 130 pounds. While I was not on the Willington grounds after 1:00 P.M. during the summer vacation, I preferred the solitude of The Farm and asked Hugh Watson to pick me up from the school in the early afternoon so that I could explore more deeply the wooded areas. There were about 15 acres of maples and evergreens on the property. There was, I soon discovered, a secretive, secluded area in a small clearing, in a heavenly spot. When I sat down on one of the large rocks located in the spot, I felt a calmness and peace I had never felt before. Time and again I felt like relaxing, to more fully absorb the things around me and to love them. I found everything Divine, even the scat of the frequent deer that wandered into the spot. It was a secret peace I began to feel, at first for a few seconds, and then for longer and longer intervals. My ever busy mind became quiet, questions ceased and I wanted to let things be. "I want to let the World pass by and love it no matter what," I often thought.

In late September 1947, Squadron Leader Abraham Warshawsky, late of the Royal Air Force. left his apartment at the Willington Academy, took a train to Montreal and boarded a steamer heading to the Middle East. The ship, aptly name "The Journey," was a former steam powered Canadian Merchant Marine cargo vessel built in 1938. The captain was an American who served in the U.S. Merchant Marine in WW II. His crew consisted of mostly WW II US naval veterans. There were three veterans of the Royal Canadian Naval Voluntary Reserve, all of whom served on Corvettes. The medical officer was Dr. Joseph Winehouse, formerly a shipboard medic with the Royal Navy. If tightly organized, the ship could carry about 60 adult passengers. The vessel, bound for Marseilles, took on final food stores, supplies of coal at Montreal and sailed down the St. Lawrence and on into the Atlantic. It reached the Mediterranean in about 10 days, then stopped at its French port of destination and picked up 55 people of all ages bound for Palestine. Most of these passengers did not speak English. They were survivors of the Holocaust, unwelcome in Europe and not really able to reach Canada or the USA. They were stateless. They were heading to the Promised Land. That land was Palestine. The crew members called that land "Israel."

I discovered a letter for me The Farm. Hugh Watson had picked it up at the Vaughan Post Office.

Dear Robert:

I am leaving for Montreal at 2:00 P.M. today. In Montreal I will board a steamer which after a few stops will take me to Palestine. I am going there to help start a new nation which will be called "Israel." I am going there to help these people build an air force to defend that nation in the war that is soon to break out there. I have enjoyed my posting in Canada and working with the youth of Willington but I feel that at this time of my life my work in this world remains incomplete. I will write you again when I can. I have left a gift for you. Abraham Warshawsky.

Hugh Watson offered me a small package. It was from the Squadron Leader. When I opened it I found that it contained Abraham Warshawsky's medals, including his DFC and DSO, The citations were also included. I could not have received a finer gift. Nothing further was ever heard about Squadron Leader Abraham Warshawsky until I was contacted by one of Abraham's sisters living in Dothan, Alabama. She had my address at The Farm. It was in late 1948. I received a short letter stating that:

Brigadier General Abraham Warshawsky, DSO, DFC, B.Sc., formerly of the RAF, now of Israeli Air Force has been killed in a plane crash. He thought highly of you.

He was 28 years old. I had just turned 16 years old.

CHAPTER 15

The Nisei

In the late autumn of 1946, Kenneth MacAlpine, the principal of the Willington Academy entered my grade 10 geometry class while Mr. Jack MacKay, wearing his tartan tie and a blue business suit, was helping the boys at his desk. MacAlpine's entry into any room commanded immediate attention. He had a boy of about 14 years with him. The boy remained outside the classroom door in the hallway. MacAlpine closed the door and addressed the class.

"The boy waiting outside the door is Charles Sasaki. He has arrived here from an internment camp in British Columbia. His family was placed there in early 1942 when we first went to war with Japan. He is not a Japanese citizen but someone called a 'Nisei.' This is a person of Japanese descent born in Canada. He is as much a Canadian as anyone here. I know you will treat him well as he is now your school mate."

Charles Sasaki sat next to me near the back of the room. He had the provincially approved math text and some three ring binders loaded with lined paper. Charles seemed very quiet. He was almost as tall as me which sort of dispelled the myth of the Japanese being a short race. The period ended and the class went to the cafeteria for lunch. I wanted to meet Charles and while we were in line at the cafeteria counter asked Charles to sit with me. This whole action was against my prejudice of the Japanese people but I felt an inner compulsion to get to know Charles so I introduced myself.

"Is that oatmeal you are having?" Charles asked. "I hate oatmeal. I had it every day in BC for more than three years." Everything served in the cafeteria was nutritious. The oatmeal I was having along with some fresh fruit to me was a vast improvement on my mother's cooking. I wanted to stop eating all forms of meat but still believed the myth that it was necessary to consume it if you wanted to be strong. In a few more years I would become a total vegetarian. At this time, red meat and pork were not part of my diet. Charles went on,

"My dad was a physiotherapist but could not practice his profession during the war. My uncles owned a fishing fleet in Japan. They sold out and my dad and his brothers moved. They came to Canada and settled on the coast of BC in 1922. They were hard working and within five years owned a boat of their own. They became Canadians. When war broke out, they owned three boats and their own homes and cars. We had to practically give it away when we were shipped to the camp. One of my uncles died at the camp. I have two older brothers that volunteered to serve in the Canadian Army. The army wanted soldiers to interpret Japanese. My brothers only spoke English! Anyway, the war ended before they could see any action."

I was amazed that Charles sounded like any Canadian. He had a "western" accent. Charles seemed wary of the other boys. As I learned about internment camps I soon discovered the injustice perpetuated on Charles and his family and for that matter all Japanese Canadians during the recent war. I found out that Charles' parents, after VJ Day, moved to Toronto and lived in Leslieville. They didn't want to return to the west coast; so they came to Ontario. His dad found a job as a therapist and his mother set up housekeeping. The two older boys, barely in their twenties, were attending rehab school and completing their secondary schooling. They were entitled to this because they each served two years in the Canadian Army. After that the government would assist them while they attended engineering school. The Canadian Government at least awarded its veterans the schooling it had deprived some of them. Both the older brothers completed school and went on to build professional careers. They became highly successful professional engineers. As my friendship with Charles was growing I found out Charles was a judoka and asked him for some lessons.

"The martial arts are not to be used for evil purposes or they will destroy you," Charles said. "A proper Judoka uses Judo first as a sport and secondly as an art form. It is last of all a means of self defense." Charles and I were usually alone in the smaller of two gyms that the school possessed. We rolled out a small wrestling mat and began to practice. I was amazed at the physical condition of young Charles. He was strong, slim and wiry. He seemed to be made of steel. Charles would board at Willington during the week rather than take the radial car down Yonge Street to the Toronto City Limits at Glen Echo. It would then be over a half hour traveling the Yonge trolley to Queen and getting the Queen car travelling east to Leslieville would require another 30 minutes trip. It was easier to board and visit his parents biweekly.

By 1951, his two older brothers would graduate from the University of Toronto as engineers, one mechanical and one electrical. In order to qualify as Professional Engineers in Ontario they accepted low paying employment with H.G. Fields and Associates as junior engineers. These two jobs lasted for two years. They struck out on their own after qualifying as P. Engs. The Sasakis were winners. Most of their work consisted of small projects the larger firms ignored. Then they bid and received a large multimillion dollar project three years after founding their business. This project made their reputation.

During WWII, a spate of anti-Japanese movies was produced by Hollywood. There was *China Sky* with Randolph Scott playing an American missionary doctor in China and *God is my Co-pilot* starring Dennis Morgan as the valiant pilot flying with the American Volunteer Group in China. They were also called the "Flying Tigers." These are just two of these movies. An especially ludicrous movie was *Air force* starring John Garfield and John Ridgley. John Ridgley played a US Army Air Corps captain in charge of a B17 bomber. The Ridgley movie career slid ever downward after that starring role. By 1950's he was forced to accept parts in such quality movies as were made, for example, by the Bowery Boys. These movies portrayed the ever interesting thespian skills of Leo Gorcey and Huntz Hall. The main scenario in *Air Force* occurs about the time of the Pearl Harbor attack where Ridgley nearly crash lands his plane. One particular scene concocted by Hollywood shows the B17 under attack by many "zeros." The gunners of the B17 are destroying the entire Japanese attack force with ease. One of the gunners turns towards the camera and comments on how the Jap fighters break into little pieces as they are hit. The main Japanese villain in these movies was always Richard Loo, an American of Chinese descent, who always played the part of a treacherous Jap. He played that part in *God is My Co-pilot* and *Chinas Sky*. It seemed to me that "So sorry," was the main line Richard Loo always uttered as a brave American slumped over in the cockpit of his P40 to died gracefully as Loo shot him down. Richard Loo said: "Japanese do not scream when they die." I always secretly sympathized with Richard Loo. The Americans in their P40s could shoot down two or three Zeros in 30 seconds with one burst of their machine guns, which if one could believe these movies. This would cause the instantaneous consummation of a Zero in a huge ball of fire. During another movie *Bombardier* starring Pat O'Brien and Randolph Scott; O'Brien was in charge of a school training bombardiers and he meets some opposition from Scott whose character insists that some of the cadets were being wasted as bombardiers when they would make excellent pilots. Later in the movie Pat O' Brien's graduates are flying with a large formation of B17J bombers over a large Japanese city and Randolph Scott is one of the pilots. Scott's plane is shot down over this city and he is captured by the Japs. (that is what they were called during the war) He quickly escapes, steals a truck, and proceeds to set fire the center of the city to show the bombardiers the target. The B17Js fly off, with a job well done as the city is now a glorious blaze. On the way to the target the B17Js were intercepted by a formation of fighters which were quickly dispatched! Not a single B17 was lost except Randolph Scott's plane!

The scenarios lacked accuracy. After the war it was discovered that the average accuracy of a bomb dropped from high altitude was about 7 miles from the target. Later the US Army Air Corps would adopted "carpet bombing" to hit their target and everything else around it. The US Army Air Corps used the Norden Bomb Sight which was presumed to be the most advanced bombing device in the world. The Curtis P40 was a dog and vastly inferior to most Japanese fighters, especially the Zero. It was used in the European Theater for anything but dog fighting. The Japanese Zero, perhaps a development of Howard Hughes' H1 Racer, was developed into a shipboard fighter and quickly became the scourge of Allied fighters in the Pacific. Not until early 1944 when aircraft such as the Grumman Hellcat and the P51C Mustang were introduced did the Allied aircraft have any chance against the Zero. When Charles and I saw such movies right after the war Charles would always leave the theater midway through the movie. I would later read up on the various situations of WW II and discover the truth. It would always bother me that governments would lie to the people that they were supposed to serve and WW II movies were part of their propaganda. I began to believe that governments should not be believed but watched closely. It was the governments of nations that started wars; not the people they were supposed to serve. Perhaps the armament makers and big international bankers were also responsible for creating wars.

As winter approached I called spoke with Hugh Watson about having Charles Sasaki stay at The Farm while he completed his schooling at Willington. I brought Charles to the De Soto one Thursday afternoon so that Hugh Watson could meet him. I had talked to Hugh earlier and then to Charles. Charles agreed to the meeting but had made arrangements for me to visit his parents on a future weekend. So on this weekday Hugh drove us to The Farm. I showed young Charles as much of The Farm as we could take in. It was getting quite dark by 5:00 PM when we arrived back at the house. Margaret Watson was now doing the cooking, while Agnes barely did anything but complain about living in the sticks. The Watson couple did everything. Marion, my younger sister, was in grade 3 at the local elementary school. Margaret walked the quarter mile with her to the school. If the weather was poor they would always drop off Marion first then take me to Willington in the De Soto.

When Agnes joined me and Charles, Hugh Watson and Margaret at the supper table she openly did not approve of Charles. She didn't say anything but her body language gave her attitude away. When she cornered me alone and out of earshot of everybody else she asked: "Can't you pick better friends? After all he is a Chink?"

"Not so," I replied, unable to resist the temptation of correcting her, "he's not a Chink; he's a Nip!" Agnes was very tolerant of everybody as long as they did not come near her. She was getting tired of living at The Farm. She had sufficient income in January 1947, to live quite well independently; so one weekday when the weather was good she got Hugh Watson to drive her to the Glen Echo Loop. She went down Yonge Street, transferred to a west bound Queen Street streetcar and began to look for a flat. She found one right on Queen Street West, a mere two blocks from the Peale Apartments, and square in the center of the old village of Niagara where she grew up. She had come full circle.

Interestingly, as I discovered later in life, as I was approaching 80 years of age, land developers were quietly buying up every building in that section of Toronto for exclusive redevelopment. My half-brother Bill was in with the developers. I put up $1 000 000 as well. I would recover about 10% more than I invested. Several units were reserved in the new development for needy tenants. They were going to build luxury condominiums. A former slum was destined to become a ritzy place to live.

After Agnes's departure from The Farm she saw less and less of me and Marion. She must have come to some secret arrangement with Abercromby, the KC and overseer of The Farm. Her income was not affected by her departure from The Farm. In fact, funds were provided for her to furnish and paint her new flat. It seemed as if Abercromby and the Watson couple wanted her to go. At any rate Hugh had ordered a trash disposal company to cart off Agnes's old furniture. They were some legal papers to sign regarding the immediate care of me, now 14 years old and Marion now nine years of age.

All during my four and one half years at Willington I met and talked with almost every student. Nobody paid tuition fees to the school, and many of the 60 boarders lived there free of fees for food and lodgings. "How was this possible?" I wondered. While I had money I wasn't asked for fees. One day when I just turned 15 years old I asked to see Kenneth MacAlpine in private. I asked directly why I wasn't paying any fees to the school.

MacAlpine answered: "This school was endowed by a very wealthy man in the 1920's. He donated $10 000 000 and purchased the land to be used for a school which could bring out the Spiritual Worth of each student. The students here are handpicked for their 'Inner Light.' Take Charles Sasaki as an example. His people are not rich. Yet powers behind the scenes arranged to have his immediate family brought to Toronto right after V-J Day. Suitable housing was found for them and suitable employment for Mr. Sasaki. Great things will be expected of young Charles and his two older brothers. Great things are expected of you. Haven't you ever questioned why you came to this Earth?"

I answered: "yes."

"This world needs life streams like yours. Your very Presence on the globe raises everyone." MacAlpine continued. "Your Spiritual Energy is of enormous benefit even if you just do nothing. Of course it is utterly impossible for that to occur. What did John Milton say: 'They also serve who only stand and wait'"

Later that afternoon I telephoned Walter Abercromby KC, and asked him to prepare a donation for Willington Academy of $50 000. I decided that this sum would be given to the school on an annual basis. At this time my income from my assets barely exceeded my expenses but in a few years the donation to Willington became a drop in the bucket.

CHAPTER 16

A Little More about the Posnanskis

I pondered Agnes's family. I found out that Gabriel her father died at 54 years of age possibly from a massive heart attack in 1934. Of all Agnes's family Gabe was the only one that my father Lem spoke favorably about. He was built well, about 5'8" tall and weighed maybe 175 pounds. He and his wife Rose were married in Elmira, New York around 1898 and crossed into Canada as 20 year olds. He settled in the Niagara Village area of Toronto and opened an appliance store. It barely sustained itself. His wife Rose, from what I could put together, wanted to go places fast and constantly nagged Gabe about his failures and lack of ambition. Gabe was a loving father but he didn't love his wife. He supported his family. For Rose, it was not sufficient. I was to meet Rose a few times just after I started to attend King George V Academy. Once, in the summer of 1945, Rose's second youngest child Erle, also called "Spike," wanted my services as a "grandma sitter." Spike was a man who could have been in his late 30s. He martyred himself by taking on the psychologically sickening chore of looking after his mother when all the other children were content to abandon her. He did everything for her. He made certain she took her insulin, he kept her clean, and when she started losing her mobility he found her a second floor room in his older sister Minnie's house. Minnie never called in on her mother and her husband Jack made snide remarks about Rose.

They referred to her as "Rose Shuffles Tumpowsky" in reference to her manner of walking. It was slow and awkward. Once when I saw her outside walking away from me she was hardly shuffling but traveling at a three mile per hour clip. When Minnie came into view and Rose saw her, she reverted to her shuffle. Spike wanted me to "grandma sit" her whenever I had spare time. I suddenly never seemed to have any. But one occasion after I finished grade eight in the late summer of 1945, I caved in and made the streetcar voyage along Queen and north on Bathurst to Lippincott Street and to my Aunt Minnie's. I was escorted upstairs to Rose's "apartment." While Jack, his wife Minnie, and their two adult children were downstairs I was saddled with my grandma. The woman was about 65 years old when I for the first time laid eyes on her. She looked at least 10 years older. I sat in a rocking chair directly in front of her and facing her.

"Vat do you vant to be when you grow up?" the old lady asked. She sounded like she just got off the boat from Poland. Here was an old lady, born in the USA, who spent her last 50 years living in Toronto who sounded like a newly arrived immigrant fresh from some Slav country. There was a musty smell in the room. Rose "shuffles" Tumpowsky was an enigma. It was not until the early 1960s when I was watching a TV program featuring Lawrence Welk and his champagne music that I heard another American speak English with such a thick alien accent that it defied the fact that Welk was a native born American. Welk started his orchestra with the chant: "a vun, a two, a tree." When they finished Welk would respond: "vunderful, vunderful." What a couple Lawrence Welk and Rose "shuffles" Tumpowsky would have made.

"I want to be a pilot," I answered.

To which question Rose replied: "If you become a pilot you vill drown in the ocean." Rose decided to have chicken for dinner. The carcass, plucked by the butcher, was fed into a pot of steaming "vasser." The nude corpse was slowly scalded into becoming dinner while I, the spiritual seeking youth, watched and fought off my looming nausea. While loathing flesh foods and still believing the myth that meat eating was necessary to be strong, I became more determined to become a vegetarian than ever. Eventually I would.

Erle did not pay me for my time. He relieved me at 9:30 PM. I was released from "Grandma sitting." Erle did not drive so 12 year old me rode the streetcars home to the Peale Apartments. It was the only enjoyable part of the day. That evening when I got home it was too dark to do anything but go straight into the apartment. Lem upon seeing me remarked snidely: "look at my son, the grandma sitter!" Then he inquired: "did Spike give you any money?"

I replied in the negative. I said I didn't even receive carfare. "Don't worry" I said, "I won't do that again."

The Posnanskis were a close knit family. When Rose Tumposki Posnanski made the journey into that unknown land from which no traveler returns Erle told all of his siblings. He informed them of the date and place of the funeral but only Erle, his wife and Agnes attended. The mysterious Uncle George did not attend, or did Bertie, or did Faye or Minnie. Indeed they were a "close knit" family. This funeral occurred in 1952, during the summer. The old woman was approaching 75 years. When the fabulous George passed on in 1980, he had relocated out of Toronto and lived in Kingston, Ontario. He died and Agnes never heard about it. He was fabulous to the end. He even died a secret death.

Agnes the youngest child of her family was the last Posnanski sibling to die.

CHAPTER 17

And More on the Nobles

Maximilian Noble, formerly "Maximilian de Leon Hombre Noble," started to succumb to his mysterious maladies by the age of 54. Esther Perez de Leon Hombre Noble took him to the famous Mayo Clinic in Rochester, Minnesota but they could do nothing. He died shortly after this visit. His death occurred in 1932. I never knew him but I did receive an extensive oral history of my father's family tree from Esther when I was nine years old. By the time I was 14 years old I was bilingual; fluent in a corruption of Spanish called "Ladino Spanish" and English.

When I was 14, Esther's daughter Dorothy and her husband, Benny Selzer, now established in Miami Beach, Florida and running up debts that would soon surpass those left behind in Toronto, demanded that Esther sell her modest Crawford Street home and make the move down south with the proceeds of the sale. The house was sold and the matriarch of the Nobles was "transported" like an English convict going to Australia in the mid-1800's. She made the journeyed to her new home in Florida. In Florida, her desire to live decreased rapidly. She passed on in 1956. When they opened her trunk the Seltzers found several jars of mint state old coins, almost entirely Canadian large one cent pieces, and Max's World War I medals including a Military Medal, a high Canadian and British Army decoration. There were also a few medals Max had earned serving in the Tsar's army during the Russo-Japanese War. There were also mint state small one cent pieces from the reign of George V. There were many one cent pieces from the reign of George VI and none from Elizabeth II. These dated from 1920 to 1936 for George V and 1937 to 1952 for George VI. The matriarch was, in a way: a numismatist. The large Canadian pieces dated from 1906 to 1920 and there were several of each date. There were several old jam jars containing these items. The jars were cleaned out after the residue of the jam was used up and became a depository for the collection. This kept their condition brilliant uncirculated. I had examined the collection and Esther promised to leave them to me when she died. These coins Dorothy gave to her two young grandchildren to play with. All the medals were in mint condition. They also became toys. There was a substantial fortune in those jars, enough to cancel all the debts the Seltzers had. Undoubtedly, they could have then started all over and ran up a new collection of debts. Fools throw out what wise men dare not waste. The Seltzers would rather steal a penny than work for a dollar to paraphrase Washington Irving's comment on Rip Van Winkle. I suspected their thieving mannerisms were why they left Toronto.

One interesting story that Esther told was that when Columbus sailed west during 1492, on his first voyage, was that he had on board his ships six Sephardic Jews. Esther claimed two of them were her ancestors. I wanted to know if this was true. In the year 2010 I found out it was. In 1492, the expulsion of all Jews from Iberia who would not become "Conversos" also took place. The reigning monarchs of Castile and Aragon had to please the Papacy. The Sephardim were allowed very little to take with them. With the capture of Granada, also in 1492, all the Arabs were expelled. No one in the Noble family cared about their lineage but Esther and me. I tried to make notes when I spoke with Esther. She told me several Conversos became heretics after changing their faith. If caught they could be burned at the stake. I began to feel privileged that my ancestors became established in the Americas in the late 15th century. They came to America first; long before the Mayflower crowd.

These horror stories of the Inquisition reminded me of the tales the youngest of Mrs. Kerry's three sons, also called "Bobby" would tell stories about his local Catholic elementary school. "Did you hear" the youngest Kerry boy would say, "Brother Ralph found a kid wandering about the hall at school today and punched him and he fell down the stairs." Brother Ralph seemed to be the greatest offender. There was Brother Francis, "he kicked a boy in the ass." The nuns also seemed to be guilty of numerous offenses. Their local school, St. Mary's was attached to St. Mary's Roman Catholic Church. There was no Catholic public secondary school these poor souls could attend except St. Michael's College and that was for rich Catholics.

St. Mary's school also taught the Kowalski brothers. These were two underachievers, aged 14 years, old and were both nearly six feet tall and looked to weigh about 200 pounds each. They always hung out together. They walked to school and returned from school together. They bullied the neighborhood together. They held part time employment as ushers at the local Peale Theater. No, this was not owned by the Goldberg boys. The theater was owned by Marcus Levy and his brother Saul and it occasionally showed superior movies. One day, in July 1945, I took Marion to the Peale Theater. It was a Saturday matinee. It usually ran a news reel, a cartoon, hopefully a "Bugs Bunny" one, a short, and a double feature. One end of the double feature was *Lost Horizon*, the other a Bob Steele western. In any Bob Steele western he usually got into a fight in a saloon (not the Peale House) with some 250 pound bully usually called "Slade." The combatants would repeatedly slug each other until "Slade" went down. This was all implausible because Bob Steele was barely five feet tall. He wore a padded shirt to appear husky.

The movie playing, *Lost Horizon,* starred Ronald Coleman and Jane Wyatt. Thomas Mitchell, the great supporting actor, played an honest plumber turned criminal fleeing from the long arm of the law. There are other roles in the movie. John Howard plays Ronald Coleman's neurotic brother George. The characters all board a 1937 aircraft. I believe was a DC 3 and begin a flight to escape from war torn China. When aloft the passengers find that they are flying deeper into China and heading towards a mountain range. The DC3 flies on and lands in a crude air strip and is refueled. It takes off and flies higher and higher until it runs out of fuel and crashes high in the mountains. They examine the cockpit and discover that the pilot was not the white man they expected but an Asian. While high in the mountains a rescue party "discovers" the stranded passengers and dresses them so they can endure the short but treacherous trip to a mountain retreat. When they enter the retreat they are told it is "Shangri la" located in "the Valley of the Blue Moon." Shangri la has magical powers. The inhabitants live for 100s of years. Later in the movie Bob Conway, the part played by Ronald Coleman, is told by the High Lama, played by Sam Jaffe, that he was deliberately brought to Shangri la to succeed the High Lama as leader. The entire movie was based on the idea that man could live in a paradise on Earth. I was fascinated with this idea. I began to entertain the notion that Shangri la might indeed exist and boy! I would like to visit there.

I hunted down a copy of *Lost Horizon* in the Main Library of Toronto on College St. The author was James Hilton and the book was published in 1933. In the book the protagonist was not Bob Conway but called "Hugh Conway." I read the book thoroughly. It matched the movie well. For the remainder of my embodiment I would watch the movie several times.

CHAPTER 18

Race Relations According to the Toronto Comet

One, day in the early summer of 1947, when I was 14 and a half years old me and the equally aged Charles were taken from The Farm to the Glen Echo loop by Hugh Watson. The Sasakis had asked Charles to bring me to their home in Leslieville. I had an overnight bag for a two and one half days stay. We boys were not expected till 8:00 PM so when we arrived at Queen Street we transferred to the Queen Street West line and took a small Peter Witt west to Peale Street. I wanted to show Charles my old neighborhood. We departed the Witt next to the Peale House and walked north toward the Peale Apartment building. We bumped into the Kowalski brothers.

"Where ya going kid?" one of the Kowalskis asked. "And what's with the chink?" One of the Kowalskis grabbed me by the upper arm. The other reared back to take a swing at Charles and quickly was tossed on his ass. While Charles was doing this he said. "I'm not a Chink." The fallen Kowalski could not get up. The other Kowalski ran off. Actually, it was more of a waddle. Charles and I left the scene quickly and boarded the east bound Queen Streetcar and headed to Leslieville.

The next day I saw on the breakfast table at the Sasaki residence an article in the Toronto Daily Comet. It detailed how rising juvenile delinquency in Toronto was becoming a major problem.

Why is it that two hard working teenagers, the Kowalski brothers, were assaulted on the streets of Toronto by a viscous gang of hoodlums? The hoodlums made anti Polish remarks!

The article reported that one of the brothers had his hip broken by the assault! No witnesses ever came forward and many had seen the brief altercation. For a while the Peale Street area became quieter. One Kowalski simply could not terrorize the neighborhood as effectively as two. I read the small article in the Comet. When I got back to the Farm asked Hugh Watson to telephone the Comet to ask them how they got their information. While I sat beside Hugh a phone call to the news room was made.

"I have it on good reliable information that your recent story on teenage hooliganism is inaccurate," Hugh said. "The Kowalski brothers had a run in with two smaller and slightly younger boys. The Kowalskis then tried to assault them. One of the boys was an expert in self defense and countered an attempted blow from one of the Kowalski. There was no teenage gang of hoodlums attacking them."

There was a pause, and then Hugh Watson was heard to say, "I see," over the telephone and then he hung up.

"What did they say to you?" I asked.

"The Toronto Comet reserves the right to interpret the news as it sees fit," Hugh answered. "The Comet prides itself on being the 'paper of the working man.' During its history in Toronto it has had more labor problems than any other daily newspaper in North America," Hugh added.

The Sasakis were an interesting family. The two oldest sons, about 20 and 21 years old were finishing up rehab school. This was preparation to enter the University of Toronto. They were never trained for combat but for intelligence work translating Japanese signals. They spoke very little Japanese. I never did learn the first name of the elder Sasaki or the first name of his wife. The elder Sasaki was 5'10" tall and the wife about 5'4". It seemed to me that they were always bowing. I had a chance to meet the two older brothers. Physically they seemed to be younger versions of their father as was Charles. The conversation was directly completely at Charles and me. It was harmless talk. Their house although built possibly around 1901 was neat and clean. It came to be known during the dinner conversation that Walter Abercromby KC had a major hand in assisting the Sasakis to relocate from the west coast to Ontario. Their clan was an extended family. The Sasakis settled throughout the province with Charles' parents settling in Toronto. Charles and I after dinner went out on a stroll about Leslieville. No mention of the encounter with the Kowalski brothers was forthcoming. I slept in Charles' bed while the Charles used a cot placed in the room by his parents. We talked a bit about life. Then we fell into a deep sleep.

Both Charles and I took the trolley up to the Glen Echo Loop on Sunday afternoon where Hugh Watson was waiting for us with the De Soto. Hugh was standing in the riders' waiting area and escorted us from the loop to where the car was parked a few yards further south on Yonge Street. Hugh and I drove back to The Farm after dropping Charles off at Willington.

When we arrived at The Farm Lem, by himself, was waiting to see me. This was a clear violation of the terms he agreed to when he signed the agreement regarding my custody in Abercromby's office almost a year earlier. He was supposed to make arrangements with Hugh or Margaret Watson before he could visit.

"What's a matter?" Lem asked, "Surprised to see your old man?" I felt trepidations over my body.

"Was the old bugger coming to take custody of me?" I thought. "Maybe they could give him some money and he would vanish." I did not speak to my father. Lem had been waiting for two hours in the library for me. He did not make the required advance call on the telephone but went to The Farm on speculation. Lem's "live in" girlfriend Pat had tossed him from her apartment for destroying the bed two days earlier. He needed a place to stay. All this Lem related to me. He started to speak but Hugh Watson cut him short.

"You can't stay here," Hugh replied. "You will violate the terms of your signed agreement." It appeared that Hugh Watson was well informed about some of the terms of my inheritance and did not want Lem around. For me, Hugh Watson was a God Send. Lem had purchased a new Buick with the front money he had received from the estate. He had much of his front money left and a sizeable income to boot. While he was working at his trade he would be extremely well off. He had no wife or children to tend to. But he was a natural parasite who had to live off the body and emotions of any host he could find. Once finding that host, he would then drain it of all energy, spiritual, mental, emotional and physical. He showed no gratitude for any arrangement he benefitted from. He was a walking tapeworm. He had the archonic infection. He had drained Agnes and was draining me before I left the Peale Apartments. No female was safe in Lem's presence. He couldn't keep it in his pants.

Agnes would often tell me how Lem would transform into a huge snake when he, on very rare occasions, fell asleep. She would lie beside him in the bed when she would be awaked by a loud hissing sound. At first Agnes was frightened by the apparition in the bed beside her but as time passed she grew more curious about it. She noticed it was almost two feet longer than Lem was tall and had enormous girth somewhat akin to the giant female anaconda that plagued the jungle waterways of South and Central America! She declared on numerous occasions that the thing had a forked tongue. But when Lem awoke he almost instantaneously reverted to human form.

"Pudd Goldberg has to have his right leg amputated," Lem said, as he began a conversation directed at me. "The poor bastard has complications from ulcers in his lower limbs. The leg will have to come off." I was only interested in the oldest of the Goldberg brothers because of the sense of Justice I felt over the fate now descending on Pudd. The fat man who loved to assault helpless drunks by kicking them was to lose the leg he loved to kick with. "Bobby also might have to have the left leg off and maybe Mickey," Lem continued. Bobby was the middle boy and Mickey the youngest. Lem was good at faking real concern and compassion for these three loutish brothers. The three brothers now seemed to be paying a Karmic debt to Life for every drunkard they ever kicked. I started to lose interest in Lem's talk.

Lem changed the subject in his usual way. He started to tell a dirty joke. "You know," he said looking around the room to see if Hugh was paying attention. "I've been to the doctor and I told him, there's something wrong with me. Everything I eat turns to shit!"

Hugh Watson was losing patience with Lem. Lem continued: "Hal Summers had a massive heart attack and died last week. Poor man, he died so young. He was so good to you. He was 49 years old. Your Uncle Spike has moved with Lily to a new apartment near Wilson Avenue and Bathurst Street. Agnes wanted them to move into her new apartment. 'Bathurst and Wilson, in North York was really in the country,'" Agnes commented when she heard this news.

"Mr. Noble," Hugh Watson spoke, "You will have to leave now. Bobby has things to do."

Lem became indignant. "What did I ever do to Robert that he should treat me this way?" It had never once occurred to Lem that he neglected his children, cheated on his wife, and he never said a kind word to me or his other children. I tried to give Lem my love. One day I mentally threw my hands and arms up in the air and thought "What is the use." Lem said good many kind words about other people's kids but nothing ever about his own. I would often hear him say things such as: "Oh little Danny Evans is such a wonderful boy but he is so naive. We were taking about girls at his father's house and someone asked: 'What should a girl never move when she's dancing? I answered: 'her bowels.' You know what Danny said? He said, 'don't be silly, everyone know girls don't have balls.'" Such was Lem's "love" for children.

Garth Evans, Danny's father adored his youngest son but there were heavy sparks flying when he dealt with his older son Keith. The older boy possessed a new 1946 Ford Roadster his mother paid for on his 16th birthday. The older boy had an independent streak. Garth Evans hated him for it. He did not want to enter his father's jewelry business. He wanted to become a policeman. This bothered his father.

"What a dumb job," he would often remark. The father seemed to detest the older boy. There is much to be learned about parenting in this World. Hugh Watson had words with Lem as he was escorting him off The Farm. At any rate, I never saw Lem again. His funeral was a closed casket affair so it was literally true: I never saw my father again.

CHAPTER 19

Justice at King George V Academy

I arrived back at The Farm on a Monday about two weeks after visiting Charles' family Hugh Watson had placed a late afternoon edition of the Toronto Comet on the kitchen table. Charles and I were both sitting at the kitchen table. Margaret had laid out some milk and cookies for us. I preferred a Coke. Charles indulged himself with the snack while I began to read the Comet. The head line blared.

Head master of Establishment School hauled into Court over claims that he sexually abused some of his young students.

It seemed that head master Percival Proctor had seduced three 12 or 13 year old boys into having sex with him. What kind of sex I couldn't discern. The article was vague in details. Proctor, the headmaster, had these boys over to his apartment on the grounds of the school not as a group but individually. Once in his apartment he would make the boy strip completely and proceed to have oral sex performing some dirty act on the boy's member. One of the boys had claimed he had told his parents about headmaster Proctor's performance on him but the parents dismissed the boy's story as a fabrication. The boy was, after all "placed," at King George V Academy so that his wild behavior could be brought under control. It was only when the other two boys confessed their relationships with Proctor to their parents that word began to make it around to the other parents. Parents began to call each other on their telephones.

Finally they began to meet each other for social gatherings and began to share information. In a few weeks they had confessions from three boys about Proctor's pederasty! The police were called in. Police interviews were conducted with the three boys who hardly knew each other. Police Staff Sergeant Hammond of the Toronto Police Service was handling the case. While I was attending King George V Academy I avoided Proctor but when I came close to him I felt a tremendous odious vibratory action emanating from him. It made me cringe. Proctor's face was pock-marked. There was a reference to "pock-marked Proctor," in the Comet.

On the following Tuesday I found another edition of the Comet describing some of the day's details on the Proctor trial. The Comet was sarcastic in its reporting.

> *Educator of one of Ontario's Elite Schools cries on the witness stand. He says he is sorry for the harm he has caused his young students. "Can they ever forgive me?" He pleads.*

The comet reported that the courtroom was packed with parents and interested onlookers. I wanted to attend the trial but Hugh Watson would not allow it. As the days progressed Hugh told me that Proctor had probably twice as many victims as had come forth at King George V Academy. These other victims were probably "ashamed." Hugh told me that Proctor had in all likelihood left his previous employment in England because of similar trouble that now plagued him in Canada. A few later issues of the Comet summed up the trial by printing the court's sentence of Proctor to five years in the Ontario Prison system with mandatory counseling. Hugh Watson said Proctor would have a very hard time in jail because fellow inmates would not like his predilection for young boys. Proctor would be considered a "diddler." Nothing whatsoever was heard of Proctor after that issue of the Comet for some time. There was no Mrs. Proctor or any children. It seemed that the Board of Governors of King George V Academy could have had the man checked out before they hired him!

Then about two years after his trial was over and article appeared in all three Toronto dailies. It was short and to the point. It was from the Canadian Press.

> *Pedophile and former headmaster to the elite has eye scooped out by another convict with a rusty spoon in a provincial reformatory. Percival Proctor, a pock marked educator of rich Toronto youth had to be taken Sunnydale Hospital for emergency surgery. Two vicious cons serving life-time sentences for extortion and murder apparently did not approved of 'diddlers' and showed this by maiming Proctor.*

CHAPTER 20

Some Communists are Disillusioned

In 1946, the Iron Curtain descended over Eastern Europe. It seemed odd to me that many of the Jews emigrating from war torn Europe seemed to be ardent communists. While people in the United States and Canada, for that matter, went into a "Red scare," most of the world slept on. In Canada we had the famed Gouzenko case. By late June 1947, I was 14 and one half years old and I seemed to stop growing. At 5'9" in height and 140 pounds I was taller than average but I had been at this stature since my 14th birthday. To me I didn't seem older even though six months had passed quickly since that birthday. I went to visit Agnes in her "new" apartment in Niagara, the former village where she experienced her childhood. I made this visit after numerous requests to drop in. Agnes would not visit The Farm. The visit dragged slowly and I left her apartment at 6:00 PM. I walked east on the south side of Queen Street toward Bathurst Street. At the corner of Pontiac Avenue and Queen a large crowd was assembled. There was a provincial election scheduled for about three weeks in the future. The notorious J.P. Cohen was going to speak to the gathering crowd. J.P. Cohen was a Member of the Provincial Parliament for the Riding of Niagara. He also represented the Labor Progressive Party, a communist political organization. J. P. was the only standing member of any Provincial parliament in Canada or the Federal parliament or for that matter who was an openly declared Red.

Some folding bridge chairs were available and I sat in one. A few minutes later all the chairs were occupied and a large standing crowd had assembled as well. It was a pleasant late June evening and sunset was over two hours off. I wanted to hear his speech. I wondered why any one of sane mind would vote for him.

"My fellow working class Canadians," J. P. began; "it is almost four years since I stood before you last to speak. The working man of Canada has been betrayed by the government of William Lyon Mackenzie King. As our fighting men and women returned from the war they were promised everything but now nearly two years after that war those poor and downtrodden veterans are still in chains. You must rise up you workers of Ontario. We must arise and throw off our chains." And so did J. P. Cohen carry on. He sounded like the clone of Daniel Breck, he of the Young People's Camp, but lacked the thick Slavic accent. But something strange happened during his 30 minute oration. He made eye contact with me. He stared at me while he delivered the rest of his speech. He didn't stammer or lose track during most of his oration but in the last 10 minutes J. P. seemed to lose control of his mind set. The oration now seemed to come out of him like a well-trained parrot. This was evident by the coughing that began to fill the atmosphere. J.P.'s talk reminded me of the speeches of Hitler. Even though I couldn't understand a word I was captivated by the mystical power of the madman's oratory. It was evident to me that Hitler and JP Cohen were under the spell of black magicians. It appeared that J.P was infected with the archonic disease. Was the whole speech a form of hypnosis? It was like the entire gathered group was in a trance. But like all good things it came to an end. The audience picked up some pamphlets distributed by J.P.'s help. The chairs were folded and loaded into a delivery van. Then J.P. approached me.

"Young man," he said, "I could not help but notice you in my audience this evening. What did you think of my speech?" I offered no comment. "Would you like to join me for a treat at the Paddock Grill," asked J.P. as he gestured across Pontiac Avenue towards the Diner. I was familiar with the Paddock. By reputation and by my experience it made the best "all beef" hamburger in the city of Toronto. The older man and I went into the diner and sat in a booth. J.P.'s helpers who were in the diner did acknowledge JP's presence. They left JP and me alone in the booth. I ordered an all-beef burger and Coke now available in the six and one half ounce bottle. J.P. ordered a coffee. Again J.P. asked: "What did you think of my speech?"

"Are they really your words?" I replied. There was a long silence for about one minute. J.P. Cohen began to sob. I was becoming uneasy. The hamburger was however, good. The Coke was from an iced bottle and it was good. J.P. Cohen mumbled some quiet words.

"I have faithfully parroted the words of Moscow for 40 years. I have spent time in prison for my loyalty to the party. I have destroyed my marriage and my children. They are not my words. I haven't had an original idea since the age of 20 years. All I do now is speak as I am told to speak and rant as I am told to rant. I'm sick of it. I became a communist because I thought communism could change the world. It has, it has made it worse!"

J.P. Cohen began to gather himself. He stopped crying. "This evening I looked into my audience and saw a young Light. My shame intensified. I have betrayed myself." J.P. Cohen started sobbing again but very silently. His aides sitting a nearby booth only looked occasionally at him. I excused myself and made a telephone call to The Farm. It cost me nothing to call collect. I told Hugh Watson I would be one hour late arriving at the Glen Echo Loop. I then told J.P. Cohen that I had to go home. My last words to him were: "don't do anything rash."

Two days later the Toronto Comet carried a feature on its front page. *Sole communist member of the Ontario Parliament, J.P. Cohen shoots himself. Cohen was a champion of the working man's rights. Cohen is survived by his wife and two adult children.*

This was the third man that I met who committed suicide but by this time I had some doubts about Major Duncan's death. I had considered Alistair Duncan's death a suicide. By this time I changed my mind. He was too brave to do away with himself. Then there was Louis Lippschitz. I knew and talked with all three. I felt that to commit suicide was a karmic wrong. The thought that I was some sort of pariah crossed my mind or was J.P. Cohen like Major Duncan and Louie Lippschitz and his mother disillusioned or perhaps sick. Certainly Louis Lippschitz was murdered but the papers called it "a double suicide." Like all socialists or communists, ultra conservatives and liberals J.P. Cohen was a harbinger of hard times. They suffer from the delusion that they are "do-gooders." Perhaps he may have changed when I met him. J. P. Cohen brought nothing of value to his constituents or anyone else he encountered. In the end he brought nothing of value to his own personal life so he ended it.

CHAPTER 21

Deep Contemplation

In mid-July, I wandered alone into the secluded area of The Farm so I could be alone with myself. I found my usual seat on the smooth boulder in the center of the clearing. It was the mid-summer of 1947 and I was 14 and one half years old. I was to enter third form at Willington in September. I wanted to know who I really was and what was I to do with my life. I sat on the boulder and became very still. I lost track of time. Suddenly, after several minutes, I was engulfed in an Intense White Light. The feeling of a slow Divine Strength came over me and a calm Peace such as I had never experienced. I was not frightened. For the first time; my ever busy mind completely shut down. My physical body became a remote part of me. I got up and began to walk in the clearing noticing the extreme beauty in everything I saw. I looked toward the boulder where I had sat and discovered a boy about my age sitting there. I thought: "who is that strange boy?" Then an unusual thought occurred to me: "That is me! I am not in my body." I felt as light as a feather. I wanted to examine what this new me looked like and to explore my surroundings further. Suddenly I was back inside "myself" sitting on the boulder.

It was as if everything in the silent spot was stripped of its human creation. Then spontaneously I thought "What am I to do Lord?" Then I sat motionless for what seemed like hours and then the moment faded. I made my way back to The Farm house.

Hugh and Margaret Watson were sitting in the kitchen when I came in. I noticed that both Hugh and Margaret were staring at me as if both were in a trance. There was a supreme silence in the room. Margaret spoke: "Can I get you a glass of orange juice?" I agreed and sat down at the table with them. I could not drink milk or eat dairy products any longer. They simply didn't agree with me. My consumption of animal products was down to one serving a week yet my health and vitality seemed to be increasing. I never discussed this dietary change with either Hugh or Margaret but still they seemed to sense my new requirement.

Margaret spoke again: "We have a guest staying with us from Scotland, our niece Renee. She is almost 15 years old. We want you to meet her." Hugh Watson left the kitchen for a moment and returned with a fair skinned girl with red hair who walked over and stood beside me. "This is my niece Renee Cummin. Her mother is ill and in a sanatorium and her father passed a year ago." Renee, I noticed, had violet eyes. Margaret Watson introduced her to me. The slim red headed girl took a seat at the kitchen table. I noticed how erect her posture was but it was her red hair and violet eyes that dazzled me. She also had unusual hands, with fingers widened at their tips. Experts refer to those of fingers as being "spatulate." The fingers were abnormally long. I was thoroughly taken with her.

Margaret went on: "Renee is a concert level pianist and has won many junior competitions in Great Britain and Europe. She has consented to play for us. Shall we go into the living room. Renee comes from Elgin in Scotland. That is the legendary home of the Cummins."

The party adjourned to the large living room. I knew the piano in the room was of high quality but I never attempted to play on it. But the piano was always in tune and dusted. Renee sat down at the piano. Then she spoke with a soft Scottish burr: "I am going to play 'The Girl with the Flaxen Hair' by Debussy." I had observed that the piano was made by some company called "Chickering." Hugh had told me it was "a parlor room grand. It is very expensive," Hugh remarked. Apparently Alistair Duncan had played on it regularly until his military duties took him away from his music. Renee began to play. She had a feel for the instrument acquired rarely by young ladies of her age. It seemed as though she had a skill acquired over many lifetimes, but she was not yet 15 years old. Renee finished the Debussy opus and Hugh began to speak.

"Renee will play a second piece. It is 'Chopin's Etude, Opus 10, number 3 in E major.'" I noticed that this was a more powerful piece and was played with greater gusto and power than the first piece. I noticed Renee's oversized hands, out of proportion the rest of her petite body. They seemed especially made for her to play the piano. She spanned 11 of the white keys on the piano!

"The Chopin piece is a study and was not meant to be played at a recital!" the young Scot's lady said; "but I love it so much I can't resist." I noticed that while Renee played the two compositions there was never any music on the stand. Even the way Renee spoke seemed to be musical. Each word was like a note of a song.

"Renee will be with us the rest of the summer before she moves to New York to study at The Julian School of Music. She will be staying with my sister Marjory and her family in Manhattan," said Margaret Watson.

I knew how to read music and could play some elementary music to about the grade 3 level, none of it well. This gave me some appreciation of Renee's mastery of the instrument while just short of her 15th birthday. The young lady rose from the piano bench. The Watsons and I were sitting on the leather chairs scattered about the living room. Renee sat beside me on the small settee.

She spoke: "My Aunt tells me you are a very advanced life stream. She says that people like you become angels. She said you were very beautiful. I can see that is true." I stared at this girl with great intensity. She continued: "I would like to know you better. We have that opportunity the remainder of this summer. Can we spend some time together tomorrow?"

I replied: "I have a quiet spot in the woods I like to visit. Would you attend with me after we eat our breakfasts. We can go there after 10:00 AM." I did not see Renee after she left the living room with Margaret Watson.

I adjourned to the front lawn of the house. It was a 70 yards by

200 yards neatly manicured area that fronted on the county road that served as a southern boundary to The Farm acreage. A private drive ran up one side of the lawn to the house and reached back to the country road on the other side. I began using the lawn as a practice area for my golf game. Hugh Watson had a large six foot deck mower that he could attach to the rear of the Massey tractor and in about two hours cut the grass to about two inches in height. I had discovered a set of steel shafted left handed clubs in an old bag along with a shopping bag of almost new balata covered Spalding golf balls. In one of the out buildings I also discovered some old golf books. One was written by the former golf champion "Bobby Jones." I went for this book because of the first name of the author. Since the clubs were left handed I would have to form a mirror image of the photos in the book to make them applicable for use with left handed clubs. So in May of 1947, I began to hit practice shots with the 7-iron.

For the first three weeks nothing seemed right. The ball went everywhere but where I intended. Then one practice session everything went blank in my head while I attempted to hit the ball and I flushed it. I only hit one more like the first flush shot during that session. Both flushed balls sailed out about 130 yards, curved and went from my left to my right, landed in the grass and stopped. That was it! I had to duplicate that effort which I eventually did. Being meticulous I always counted out 100 of the best balls for practice. When I was done with the 200 to 300 I hit at every opportunity I could find I would wash the balls in Javex and laundry soap mixed with hot water and wipe them clean. Hugh noticing me practicing my golf on the front lawn prompted Hugh to cut the lawn every three days. By late June of 1947 I was becoming the master of the 7-iron. I could "blank out" 90% of the time while I was hitting a ball with it. Hugh and I found an old surveyor's tape in the barn and laid our markers on the front lawn. I started practicing with the 5-iron and found he could hit it about 20 yards farther than the 7-iron would go. I seemed to master it much faster than the 7-iron. I then started with the 3- iron. This when struck properly seemed to fly about 174 yards on average. I decided to spend at least two hours daily practicing with one single club until I mastered the 13 clubs in the set I had discovered earlier.

Golf would have to wait one day when Renee Cummin came on the scene. Both Renee and I went to the secret opening in the woods after breakfast. I showed Renee where I liked to contemplate. I didn't tell her about the White Light that surrounded me the first time I visited that location. Both of us sat on the smooth boulder. I was staring at Renee when it happened a second time. There was a powerful White Light engulfing me. I was completely captured by it. Both Renee and I said nothing.

Finally the Light diminished and I turned to Renee. "This is why I have to come here." I said. "I must come here. I want it to go on forever. You know I left my body." Something new was added for me. Even though there was not a flower to be seen anywhere in the clearing the distinct aroma of burning leaves which I came to know as "sandal wood" was prevalent. Renee did not smell it. Or at least when questioned about it said she didn't smell anything.

"I too have flowers about me, I think they are roses," Renee said in response. "One time my aunt in Scotland, on a Sunday, was driving down the high road to get to a church on time in Elgin. I sat beside her. There was a lorry in front our car as and we pulled out to pass it. You know what happened next? The motor stopped working. Then the lorry moved to the right to pass a horse cart in front of it. I thought we were going to die. But nothing serious happened. The whole car was flooded with the scent of roses! There certainly was an angel with us."

I had found someone to discuss strange occurrences with. Renee seemed fascinated with me and me with her. I asked her again about the aroma of burning leaves. "Well I do smell something," she responded. "But it seems to be a special blessing for you, but I suppose if I sense it, it is also for me." I could not take my attention off of her fascinating eyes. "Shall we come here tomorrow?" Renee continued. Then she stopped for a moment.

"Oh Bobby," she said, "Will you ever succeed in finding it?"

"Finding what?" I replied.

"What you are looking for, The Holy Grail," Renee answered.

When I returned with Renee to The Farm house at 3:00 PM there was a strange gentleman in the kitchen dressed in a gray business suit talking with Hugh and Margaret Watson. "Robert," Margaret said, "I would like you to meet Dr. Barnslow, he is a genealogist and would like to talk with you for some time. Renee shall remain here too."

I examined Dr. Barnslow for a few seconds and asked him: "What type of doctor are you sir; are you a physician or surgeon?" To which Dr. Barnslow replied: "I am a real doctor, I have a Ph.D. in ancient history. The word 'doctor' means 'teacher.' I teach at the University of Eastern Ontario." The doctor opened his briefcase and dumped the contents on the kitchen table. "One of my specialties is family trees," Barnslow continued. "Would you like to see yours?" A long scroll was spread out on the table and secured by two heavy glass jars. "This is your mother's family tree. It goes back to Princess Tea Tempi and beyond. In about 585 BC, the Babylonians invaded Judea and seized the 'remainder' of the Royal descendants of King David. They sent the remainder of the tribe of Judah to Babylon. They murdered the male heirs to David's Throne with the exception of Princess Tea. I suppose we can include Jesus as an heir. The Prophet Jeremiah sensing the impending doom of Davidic heirs took her out of Judah. He took her to what is now called "Ulster" where she married into the Irish Royal Line. That journey took several months by sea and land."

"One of her descendants was King Kenneth MacAlpine; who lived about 850 AD. He became the first King of both the Picts and the Scots. Kenneth's father Alpine, who was the king of Scots married the daughter of the King of Picts. Kenneth was their offspring. I believe that the Beloved Jesus, whose children were alive after his Ascension, had descendants in Scotland some time before the Reign of King Alpine. Those descendants married into the Scottish Royal line. Therefore on your mother's side you have the Blood of Jesus."

"Now for your father, be it as it may that his life has amounted to very little; well he is a descendant of the Emperor Charlemagne. We can say that the Emperor Charlemagne is important because he was the offspring of the direct descendants of King David and Phillip II of Macedonia, the father of Alexander the Great. Perhaps Alexander was a Hebrew. It is also interesting that your father Lemuel we believe also has the blood of Jesus. I am checking on this."

I interrupted: "But isn't my brother Bill the older brother the rightful heir to any birthright?"

"Think about this," Barnslow continued, "Your brother Bill has a different mother. He carries only your father's royal blood. What makes you unique and possibly your sister Marion is that both of you received a double injection of very special royal blood. We estimate that there are 8000 descendants of Jesus living at this time. Perhaps in 50 years there might be 8500. Jesus's offspring and their children comprise the Senior Royal Family of this world. This is called 'The Grail Family.' The modern Christian churches are afraid to entertain the thought of Jesus having a wife and family. They don't want The Lord's surviving heirs even coming close to public attention. It would mean the end of their power. Jesus taught his disciples a teaching hidden since the Beginning of the World. In order to bring about 'Norvus Ordo Seclorum,'or the 'New Order of the Ages' it is important that this senior Royal Line come forth. Then perhaps we can return to the Garden of Eden. The Grail Family does not want a world government. Just that people recognize their own personal Divinity. Man must come to know he is his own master. That he is a spark of the Divine that must be fanned into a Flame."

"But why are my parents such losers?" I asked.

"What a man and a woman do in their reincarnations is their choice. Do not think that your parents have not thought as you do many times. This of course took place in their youth but they chose a path less than desirable. To overcome the world was not for them. You - you are a different story. We are working to check our facts with new methods that do not require the use of musty old charts. We can determine your roots right out of the Cosmos! It is hoped that by the year 2017; some of these methods will be known to genealogists in the outer world. By the 1980's many books will be circulated about Jesus and his Royal Family. They will be scorned by established churchmen. They alone want to tell you what to believe. It is their form of control. Now young man, how do you feel learning something about your roots?" I said nothing.

CHAPTER 22

Renee in New York

I wanted to hike with Renee in the backwoods of The Farm on a weekday morning but she was not at the usual 8:00 AM breakfast. Margaret Watson provided knowledge as to her whereabouts.

"She flew to New York and left the house at 5:30 this morning. Hugh took her to Malton Airport. She will be back on Friday this week. She had to finalize her arrangements for the Julian School. Would you like to go with Hugh to pick her up at Malton when she returns?" Margaret Watson asked. I jumped at the opportunity. I passed Wednesday and Thursday contemplating in the "quiet place" in the woods.

On Friday morning at 10:00 AM, Hugh retrieved the De Soto from the outbuilding and he and I drove to Highway 7 and over to the Malton Road in Peel County that led to the airport. It was an hour before we arrived and parked the De Soto. Renee was due in at Noon. The plane arrived on time. It was a twin engines Dakota. Renee met Hugh and me were waiting near customs gate as she passed through. She spotted me immediately. "I am so glad you brought him with you," she said as she hugged Hugh and then turned and kissed me on the cheek. "Everything is arranged for my first year at Julian. I will be leaving on September 3. My aunt will meet with me at La Guardia.

The de Soto arrived at The Farm about 1:00 PM. Hugh carried Renee's overnight bag into the house. "I had a good time the two days I was in New York," Renee said. "Have you visited our quiet spot?" I nodded my head. I felt an enormous attraction to Renee Cummin.

"Let us visit the quiet spot after lunch," Renee said. "I will change my clothes so I can be more comfortable." The two of us had a quiet non meat lunch consisting of salads of three types and some whole wheat rolls Margaret had baked while they were returning from the airport. Margaret told me that her guest was a total vegetarian.

"Yes that is true," Renee began, "I haven't eaten an animal product since I was five years old. Fortunately our family doctor said I shouldn't since I always regurgitated any type of animal product my mother fed me. You have to know what Scots mothers are like? She stopped complaining when our doctor told her to stop feeding me those things."

Renee and I arrived at the quiet spot at early afternoon. "The last time we were here I had a white light flash," I told Renee. "It was longer than a few seconds this time. I sort of welcome these flashes." Renee looked at me with a look of bewilderment.

Both of us went to the outbuilding after the time in the quiet spot. I showed Renee the golf clubs I found in the building. Picking up the bag of balls I asked the young lady to accompany me to the front lawn. By this time the sun was behind us so that I could hit away from the sun. I dumped the 50 or so balls on the ground and took out the 7- iron and began to hit a few shots. Most of them were excellent shots.

"May I have a go?" Renee asked. I handed her the 7- iron. Renee lined up and took a short little swing with the club. The result was about an 80 yard shot that flew properly. She took several more and when she had hit about 10 balls were duplicating my best shots. She stopped for a moment and removed the 5-iron from the bag and began to hit shots with it. These were also excellent and flew about 20 yards further than the 7-iron shots. Finally after a few minutes she put the two clubs back in the bag and removed the driver. She began to hit the ball this club almost the length of the lawn, nearly 200 yards. The balls landed just short of the road and then bounced and ran onto the gravel.

"Holy shit," I said, "where did you learn to do that? And you did it with my lefty clubs."

"I haven't had a club in my hand for over a year," Renee answered. "I started playing at 10 years of age. I had an old Scottish professional as a teacher. He showed me a few things about the game: you know, like the grip, setup, waggle and so on. I began to pick it up. Shortly after I started I began entering junior girls' tournaments at 12 years old and played four times a week for two years. I stopped playing about a year ago and Angus Beaton, my teacher, said it was a shame. I used left-handed clubs. He said I could be one of the best woman players in Scotland if not the whole world."

"I might say," she continued as she studied me," that you are quite good. Do you play much?"

I had to admit that I had never been on an actual golf course. My ball striking was confined to only a 5 and, or 7-iron. I had intended to start learning the 3-iron but my practice had been interrupted by Renee's arrival.

"It is very hard to find enough time in the day to do everything one likes. I am slightly sorry that I stopped practicing golf. You can see from my staying at your Farm that I practice the piano four hours a day. Where can I find time to practice golf four hours?" Renee was shaking her head. "If you want to be really good you should up your practice time to four hours a day. I know enough about golf to help you. We can start tomorrow." Both of us went to dinner.

CHAPTER 23

Vice Admiral Nelson at Trafalgar

After dinner I went up to my room to contemplate. While lying on my bed I closed my eyes and began to contemplate reincarnation. "After all," I thought, "A life time is too short to spend only one time trying to get it right." While lying on the bed I dozed off. Suddenly I was sailing on a wooden ship on some great sea. I had no control over my body. The vessel appeared to be an eighteenth or early nineteenth century sailing ship. I inspected my clothes. I seemed to be dressed as a British sea captain.

Another officer approached me, stopped in front of me, saluted, and spoke: "We are about 10 miles from the French fleet sir," the man said. "We will catch them in a few hours." Then I went blank and another scene started moments later. I was the naval officer again. I looked through my telescope and heard myself giving orders to the officer I had talked to in the previous scene. "Get closer," I heard myself say, "I want to destroy at least 20 of them."

"Aye," the officer said. I went blank again. Then I was at sea again. My ship was in the middle of the enemy fleet. Ships' cannons were firing from everywhere. I felt a sharp jolt in my back and felt myself fall to the deck. Several seamen and officers gathered around me.

I spoke from this different body: "I have been struck in the lower spine," I said. "I will not last." Then everything went blank. I awoke again one hour later. I felt as if he hadn't dreamed at all. It was a vivid dream; in fact it seemed to border on being a real occurrence.

I went downstairs and Renee was playing the piano parts of Greig's Concerto when I walked into the living room. I sat down on an armchair and listened to the music. Renee was rehearsing for some sort of audition. She finished up the concerto and played two Bach two part inventions and got up from the piano. Renee walked over to me.

"I have just had an interesting experience," I said. "I was in some sort of naval battle and got shot in the back. I fell on the deck of the ship. I don't remember anything after that."

"You have just relieved a past life, or a bit of it," Renee replied. "I think you are going to have many more of these occurrences. Do you happen to remember what name you had or the date?"

"Not a thing, I just seemed to be a bit shorter than everybody else. It was as if I were reliving another life. I didn't feel much in the way of emotion. I was a participant and observer at the same time."

"Do you have any British history books in the library downstairs?" Renee asked. Both of us went downstairs to the small library which contained a radio, desk, and several shelves of books. Beside the shelves in one corner was a small filing cabinet. Renee opened the filing cabinet. "I am searching for books on British Naval history," she said to me. "It appears that Alistair has five of those. The library is cataloged by subject" Renee walked over to the shelves and began to look for the books. She had written something on a note pad she always carried with her. "Ah here are all of them in a nice row." Renee pulled all five books off the shelf, they were quite dusty. She cleaned them and began to look through them. "Does this look familiar?" she asked. She opened the first book up at a certain page which showed a painting of three ships of a small naval unit representing part of Admiral Nelson's command at the Battle of Trafalgar. She brought the book over to me. I was now sitting on the couch in the library I looked at the picture and fainted. I had never fainted before except when I first visited head master Proctor's office.

I revived in about 10 minutes. Renee showed me the portrait of Admiral Nelson in the book. I felt a wave of dizziness once again but

I remained conscious. My last reincarnation had been as the British Admiral!

"Reliving part of a past life can be quite traumatic," remarked Renee. "Can you stand up? I want to examine your back." I removed my polo shirt. "You certainly were shot in the back. You have a mark where the musket ball probably broke the spine. Do you have lower back pain sometimes? - By the way you have a beautiful back."

In time, Renee went off to The Julian School. She was not short of financing for this venture. When I brought this up Margaret Watson said she received an inheritance from a distant uncle. Aside from her scholarship to the Julian School she was well funded for other expenses I would not see Renee for any length of time for three years after she left for Julian. We kept in touch by letter.

CHAPTER 24

Final Years at Willington

I started back at Willington to study my third form courses. The Academy used a semester system of five months duration for each term and taught four subjects per term to each student. This was unheard of in Ontario secondary schools but it served to increase the classroom time from 40 to 75 minutes. There was more individual time for each student that might be used by the teachers. By grade 10 (second form) I was studying grade 10 and 11 mathematics and grades 10 and 11 science. I was taking four subjects a semester and acing them. By the time I entered fifth form (grade 13) I already had my three upper school mathematics, and my physics. The exams for these courses were written the previous June at Vaughan Township District High School. I was studying the two English Courses, Literature and Composition, Chemistry, and Spanish. This allowed me to converse with my paternal grandmother Esther Perez de Leon Hombre Noble in her first language. There was no oral test in Spanish.

I sat in the rocker beside Esther Perez de Leon one afternoon and Esther told me an oral history of her family. It seems that they came from the ancient Iberian Kingdom of Leon. In fact, Leon existed before Spain did. She and Maximilian's ancestors originated from that location. Esther was quite emphatic about one point: her family was in no way, connected to the Jews from Eastern Europe. They were not Ashkenazi. They had lived in Leon since the reign of the Emperor Tiberius. Before that Esther stated that the family lived in the Holy Land and a few centuries before that in Ancient Egypt. They had come out of Egypt during the second Exodus.

"We are descendants of the Hyksos Pharaohs," Esther proclaimed. "You have the blood of an ancient line." Esther reclined in her rocker. She remained silent for a minute. "My mother was a gentile. At least that's what those other Jews considered her. My mother was a "Ballard." Those other Jews are not Hebrews! My mother was also of the line of King David. She married my father Pedro Perez de Leon in 1883. I was born in 1885. Marjory Ballard, my mother was doing missionary work in East Europe when she met my father. She could converse with him in Spanish. I was their only child." Esther paused again for a moment.

"My family fled Leon in 1492 because the Catholic Church wanted all Jews to become "conversos." My mother was born in Kansas. She was doing missionary work at that time in the Ukraine for the Episcopalian Church when she met Pedro Perez. She married him. Pedro was killed in a pogrom two years later. I grew up in Mogolov on the Dnieper River. I married your grandfather in 1903 and later Lem was born, then the others. Lem was born in the old country, the rest in Canada. After your grandfather was released from a Japanese prison camp in 1907 we managed through a rich uncle to secure a passage from a Polish port to America. The boat went to Montreal. We became Canadians. We moved to Toronto in 1910. Your father is not Jewish because I am not, but we are Hebrews. Not all of the Hebrews are Jews. Remember, there are 12 tribes. Only one of them has Jews. Do you know that Saint Paul was of the Tribe of Benjamin? It says so in the New Testament. So how can Paul be a Jew? But he was a Hebrew!"

As for your mother's family; they aren't Khazars. I am certain of this. I don't know what they are; pretending to be Hebrews. All those blue eyes and light hair. I think they are maybe Scottish descent. Most Scots consider "scotch" a strong alcoholic beverage. I think they have never been in a synagogue. Your mother knows nothing about the ancient Hebrews. I think they pretended to be Jews so that they could make business with them easier. Years later I found out that my mother's primary Scots ancestor, a man whose surname was "Graham" fled from Scotland to mainland Europe to escape the gallows the English had prepared for the leaders of the Jacobite Rebellion of 1745. There he hid in the ghetto of Warsaw amongst the Ashkenazi Jews. He spoke no Polish. His children later learned that tongue. I tried to correspond with her by letters but the matriarch could not read or write in English! She was only literate in Spanish.

I finished my final five grade 13 examinations writing them at Willington. I completed my algebra, trigonometry and analytical geometry, physics and chemistry, while in fourth form. Each grade 13 examination in a particular subject was written in Ontario at the same time and on the same day throughout the Province. Kenneth MacAlpine, headmaster supreme, using his profound influence with the Department of Education had volunteered to pay the Ministry official's wages rates for an officer to supervise examinations set by them. These were now administered in the study hall at Willington. MacAlpine did not want to sully the reputation of his school by any hint of the scandal that haunted the local secondary school in an earlier year. The Department of Education officials that supervised the exams at Willington were above reproach.

Strangely, I never did earn my Junior Matriculation. I never sat an examination for grade 12 English, either in Composition or in Literature. I jumped from grade 11 in those subjects directly to grade 13. Nobody at Willington picked up on this. So in late August, 1949 I was an Ontario Honors Secondary School Graduate who had a senior matriculation but no junior one! It was unheard of previously and would cause me some minor problems when joining the RCAF. Different universities also complained about this lack of a Junior Matric.

"How can you possible graduate with a Senior Matriculation with such fine results if you haven't a Junior Matriculation?" all three universities queried. "Such a thing is unheard of." However, three universities accepted me to start in September 1950 at their institutions. I for the remainder of my embodiment would never graduate from grade 12.

CHAPTER 25

The Fledgling Professional

In late June of 1950, Hugh Watson contacted the Canadian PGA office in Ontario by telephone and asked how a young man who just finished secondary school could become a professional golfer. They told him they would send an information package to his home. About one week passed and I received a large brown envelope addressed to me. I opened it and removed two forms. One page was an application to join the Canadian PGA and the other a list of jobs available of all types. There were jobs available for beginning professionals they called "assistants," eight of them. There were two positions for head professionals. On the application to join the PGA they asked for age, date of birth, and the usual stuff about religious affiliation which I chose not to answer. I felt this was not anyone's business and invited discrimination based on race and religion. It was strange that this information was asked for in the 1950's but illegal to request by the 1960's. The paper also wanted to know my history as a golfer. The applications asked for any tournaments I won and what type of scores I shot. This I answered by going back to when I started to play in the spring of 1948. I won the Junior Championship of the Upper York Country Club at 16 years of age, during the summer of 1949. I had reduced my handicap to three by this time and had a good chance to take the men's regular championship except the regular men members forbade me of all chances to compete. By 17 years of age my handicap was down to one. I was convinced I could play to scratch or better if I could play full time winter and summer.

In the summer of 1949, I entered the qualification round for the Upper Canada Amateur Championship and gained entry into the tournament. I played three matches and was disposed of in the third round by the player who ultimately won the title. My long game held up well under this type of pressure but I couldn't putt like I normally did during casual games. On the first hole I had a three foot uphill straight putt for a birdie and my ball didn't reach the cup. I was short on straight uphill putt! I squandered almost all of my birdie chances by making easy pars. Eventually my greens game caught up with me in my third match and I was out of it after 16 holes. I lost three up with two to go. To compete at a high level I had to become better on the greens.

One job for an assistant caught my eye. It said: "A young man wanted to learn the game from a professional's viewpoint." It was at the exclusive Clairmont Golf and Country Club located north of Toronto in North York Township. This was a plush facility about 12 years old which the designers started to build in the mid-1930's and it opened for play in April 1938 to accommodate the nouveau riche who could not get a memberships in such swank places as Collingwood Golf Club where the waiting list was 30 years, or the Seaforth Country Club where the membership had to be inherited, or many of the other establishment clubs. Clairmont was not far from The Farm and Hugh could drive me to the club until I earned my driver's license later that summer.

About 10 days later, there was a telephone call to The Farm from Roy Rollins, the Head Professional at Clairmont. He claimed to have heard of me from some of his better playing members. Could I come, that afternoon for an interview. So an arrangement was made to have Hugh Watson drive me the five miles to Clairmont. When we arrived 15 minutes before the interview Hugh told me he would wait until the interview was over. Then he would receive news on how it went. So I went into the pro shop by myself. I climbed the small staircase and entered the shop. A woman about 35 years of age was behind the display counter. I approached her. There was no one else in the shop. I introduced myself. The woman told me to wait and Roy would see me shortly. After sitting for five minutes Roy came out of his office that was behind the club storage room and repair shop located behind the pro shop. Roy introduced himself to me. He was about 40 years old. I then remembered him from the Canadian Open I was watching earlier. I was following Snead. When the Snead trio came up to a tee on the back nine and had to wait for a threesome ahead to tee off. It consisted entirely of Canadian club professionals. The first two got off poorly struck driver shots and then Roy followed suite and hit a thin drive that hooked 30 yards into the left rough. The spectators watching the action applauded each of club pros hits despite the fact that I clearly saw them all miss their shots. Roy's was the shortest shot barely flying 200 yards and far off line. After the threesome hit their second shots I watched Snead drive off and could accurately measure the efforts of the previous three by comparing them to Snead's effort. The Canadians came up far short.

"You have a good amateur playing record," Roy commented holding my resume and clippings from the sports pages in his right hand. "Maybe I can use you here. Can you start tomorrow morning? I want you here presentably dressed at 8:00 AM." I showed up at the shop at 8:00 AM and was put to work retrieving bags of clubs from the storage room below the pro shop. I was stationed at the door to the storage room while member after member came to ask for their clubs.

The usual request was "Boy, get my clubs." They were offended that I asked for their names. "Why don't you know who I am?" replied one indignant member. "I could buy and sell you." I discovered that these people were very bossy and very rude. Never did a request use the word: "please" or upon delivery of the equipment draw the words: "thank you."

The women members were even ruder than the men. "Boy, do this. Boy, get my clubs from my car." Even though it required a walk of over 100 yards to the lady's car and then a harder walk toting her clubs back to her. She didn't offer to park the car next to the pro shop for a moment so her equipment could be removed. She didn't even offer the keys so I could open the trunk. I was expected to jump and run like a slave. One fat, overweight member added to his request for clubs adding the words "chop chop." One would think he was ordering coolies about.

This went on for about two weeks. I was supposed to work eight hours a day but Roy was always late arriving at the pro shop, usually by an hour, and once or twice a week by two hours. This kept Hugh waiting in the parking lot while I carried on doing his duties in the pro shop. When I added up my total hours for two weeks in came to 110 hours. It was so late at night I could not play or practice any golf.

One Monday a particularly mouthy woman called Doris Waterford wanted her clubs. "Get my clubs boy," she demanded. I left her alone in the pro shop while I headed for the storage room. At first I forgot to find out the woman's name. I stepped back into the shop to find out her name and caught Doris Waterford helping herself to a box of a dozen top line golf balls which she swiftly placed in her large tote bag. "Will I charge those balls to your account?" I asked. Mrs. Waterford, who didn't see me return back into the shop.

"What balls?" she asked.

"The ones in your tote bag," I replied.

"Why of all the nerve!" Mrs. Waterford replied. "How dare you call me a 'thief.'" By this time her shrill and loud manner had attracted two other members who stood there and watched the whole scene. Mrs. Waterford started to leave the shop. I stepped over and seized her bag; turned it over at the counter and out fell the box of a dozen balls and two unopened packages holding golf gloves. Mrs. Waterford, the shoplifter, was caught in the act. Usually the pro shop employees removed price stickers from the inventory when a member purchased something. These were still on the merchandise.

Mrs. Waterford became silent; possibly for the first time in her life. I took the merchandise and placed it in the stockroom. "From now on Mrs. Waterford, you are no longer welcome in this shop, unless there is a member of the professional staff in here with you." Mrs. Waterford looked to the two other members as if pleading to them for their support. They walked out of the shop. The next day Mrs. Waterford went to the club secretary to complain about the rude service she received in the pro shop from the young upstart boy. The secretary came over to the shop to talk to me.

"Now young man, the club secretary started, we expect employees of the club to treat our members courteously."

"Bullshit," I replied. "I caught her thieving from our shop. I have the names of two members who witnessed this. I handed the club secretary the two names. I never heard another word about the incident. Every time during a weekday when Mrs. Waterford would come to the shop and asked for her clubs I made her stand outside; I locked up the shop and went into the downstairs storage room and retrieve them. One time she arrived with her husband. It was raining hard outside.

"This is Mr. Waterford, boy," he is vice president of the Union Bank. "Get my clubs."

"Would you please step out of the shop and you too as well Mr. Waterford." Mr. Waterford looked puzzled. I would not resist the chance to make her stand out in the rain.

"Why must I step out of the shop?" he asked.

"Because your wife is not allowed to be in the shop alone," I replied. "Since she is with you I must ask you both to step out. She could also use some instruction in how to treat the employees of this club." Mr. Waterford looked back at his wife and said nothing. They left the shop while I locked up. I retrieved their clubs and they went off to the first tee. The rain got worse. I would observe on later occasions how she treated her spouse. She called him "hubby wubby" and "doggy woggy" on numerous occasions, but only if other people were within earshot. If he had a leash attached to his neck he would have been, in her eyes, the perfect mate.

Roy, in the meantime, would continue to take advantage of me. He would show up later and later to relieve me. Work week hours were running at 55 per week on the average and Roy insisted that I pay full retail price on everything I wanted to purchase from the shop. "Boy have I got a deal for you," he would say. Then he adroitly would slip a windbreaker or some piece of material over me.

I would reply: "I can't afford it." I was usually thrifty with my money and didn't want to waste it. I knew Hugh Watson would outlay the cash I needed for just about any purchase. Hugh himself was suspicious of Roy. I hadn't been paid for over four weeks. I talked with Roy when he came in on a Friday, one hour late, to relieve me in the shop. "Roy I haven't been paid for over four weeks, how come?"

"You have to ask me for your pay if you want it" Roy said, "You didn't ask so I didn't give it."

"Well I am asking now."

"I will have your check tomorrow when I see my accountant." Roy relieved me almost two hours late the next day and presented me with a check. Even at 40 hours a week or 80 hours pay for two weeks at 60 cents per hour I was owed $48.00. The check was for $30.00. "Where's the rest of it?" I asked.

"My accountant has to deduct unemployment insurance and income tax," Roy replied.

"Well where's the deduction statement?" I enquired. "By law you have to issue a statement with any check an employee receives." Roy grew silent. "And another thing," I began: "You are always late when my work time is over. You should be me paying overtime. I took this job so I could play and practice my game. I have had no time to do either."

Roy grew sheepish. "I'll be on time with relief for you from now on," Roy answered. "I am very busy. That guy that picks you up every evening; what's his name? He drives an old De Soto."

"You mean Hugh Watson?" I replied. "Why do you want to know?"

"Well the McConnell kids are here up till six PM every day. Could you get Mr. Watson to take them home?" I was amazed at the request. Roy not only worked at the club running his pro shop and providing service for the members but he somehow figured he had to provide limousine service for the members' children.

"I most certainly cannot," I replied.

"You are very selfish," Roy replied, "I guess I'll have to do it myself!" Roy got up to leave the shop. I put my arm out and stopped him.

"My hours are over for the day, if you leave this shop before I do I will leave right after you and leave the place unlocked."

"But who is going to take the McConnell kids home?"

"Let them walk."

I finally started to get some time off to play and practice my game. I made an arrangement with Roy to work for nothing if Roy would sign and validate my CPGA papers. This Roy did this willingly since this allowed him to hire a teenager, who wasn't interested in golf, to work in the shop. Roy was slow in paying me my back wages so I confiscated several dozen golf balls and gloves, equal at a wholesale price, to what I was owed. "Let us call it even," I told Roy, "now you don't owe me a cent." Roy had already signed the CPGA papers before this latest confrontation.

Then an interesting event happened in the pro shop while I was on duty. I answered the telephone and the caller asked for Roy. The caller was informed that Roy wasn't in. "Well tell him to call Mac Bennett when he comes in from the PGA Triumph Supply Company." I informed Roy about the call to which Roy replied: "Let him make an appointment to talk with me on the telephone the next time he calls. You set it up so he calls when I am on duty."

The next day Mac Bennett called and I told him to call back after 5:00 PM. Bennett said: "What kind of shit is this?" and hung up. The next day Bennett telephoned again. I said Roy wasn't in.

Bennett said, "I expect your cooperation on this matter."

Then I asked Bennett: "How much does he owe you?"

"Never you mind," Bennett answered. "That's not your business."

I told him: "If I don't know where he stands with you; why should I help you?" I was able to determine that Roy owed Bennett's company over $10 000! Later I discovered from Mac Bennett that several professionals in the Toronto area owed Bennett's employer as a group almost $300 000! Such is the legacy of being a golf professional! There was greater folly in being a supplier to one.

Most members at ritzy golf clubs overpay for equipment which is no different from that sold by sporting goods stores and discount golf retailers; all were made by the same manufacturers but sold under slightly different labels. I believed that all the golf balls were essentially the same, just labeled differently. The difference was in the price the end user paid.

CHAPTER 26

Playing with the Members

I went out to play with Roy a few times. I always warmed up for 40 minutes before I teed off. The club had a five acre practice area about 250 yards long and 100 yards wide which was located behind the parking area. It was about 100 yards from the pro shop and located between the first and tenth tees. I was almost finished with my warm up when Roy approached me. The practice area was only used by the better players.

"It's time to tee off," Roy said, denying me any chance to have a few practice putts. A member called "Arnold Banks," who I recalled was the "chop chop," member was waiting on the first tee. Banks was a man who admitted to being 54 years old. He was about 5'9" tall and weighed about 200 pounds. I never saw him warming up. Banks professed to be a 4-handicap.

"What will we play for?" Banks inquired.

"Let's play for a dollar a hole," Roy said. "If two tie all will tie."

"I don't want to play for money," I replied.

"If you're going to be a pro," Roy said, "you've got to be able to play for money." With that settled Mr. Banks teed off first. He hit a passable drive on the short 475 yards par 5 hole that went about 225 yards down the fairway. Then I teed off and hit my drive about 245 yards. Banks muttered some remark about "being out driven by a skinny 17 year old kid." Roy hooked his tee shot about 220 yards into the left rough which was three inches high. The ball sank into the long grass. Roy was away so he hit his approach shot first. It was low screamer with a 4-wood that scurried along the ground and stopped about 50 yards short of the green. Roy had struck the ball and topped it. Banks hit a 4-wood also, semi topping the ball. It finished besides Roy's ball. Then I decided to play it safe and to hit a 4-wood which I reckoned would be short of the green by perhaps 10 yards. It would be an easy par 5. I flushed the shot from the middle of the fairway, it took off with the high launch angle that I usually had on my shots, bounced on the fringe of the green and stopped six feet from the hole. I heard Mr. Banks remark: "that kid has a horseshoe up his ass." Both Mr. Banks and Roy hit their third shots short of the green and only Roy could chip his fourth shot close enough to be certain of paring the hole. "That putt is good," Roy shouted to Banks.

I said: "Just a moment, that putt is not good." Mr. Banks picked up his ball when he reached the green without marking it. It was 4 feet from the cup. Banks had committed a rules violation. No competitive golfer gives away a 4-foot putt. I sank the 6-footer for an eagle.

"Shit lucky punk," Banks was heard to say. Both Roy and Banks were down one hole.

By the fourth hole both Roy and Banks were down $3.00 each to me. As we were approaching the fourth tee two members of the club with caddies sent their caddies to the clubhouse and became spectators watching our threesome. At the sixth hole two more members joined the gallery. By this time Banks and Roy were down $4:00. Roy announced that he had business in the pro shop, quickly left the threesome and headed back to the clubhouse. This was an excuse to avoid being beaten by an 17 year old. This was Roy's favorite ploy when he found himself loosing during a match. Banks on the 7th tee said: "double or nothing?"

I said: "why don't you pay me the $4:00 and we will call it quits." Banks muttered something about a "gutless kid who had no spirit of competitiveness and was afraid to play for $4.00."

"Okay," I said, "double or nothing." I teed off on the 210 yard par three with a 2-iron trying to reach the front edge of the green. Again the ball flew perfectly and landed on the front of the green and stopped four feet from the hole.

Banks hit a 3-iron, the wrong club, to show me and the gallery which had now swollen to six members how much bigger and stronger he was than his opponent. He cold topped the ball and it went 50 yards. He turned to me and said: "are you trying to hustle me?" Again it was double or nothing.

The six members in the gallery snickered. Banks lost that hole. He was down $8.00. And so on it went. Banks struck his shots more and more poorly while I, playing in a trance like state, was near perfect with my shot making. On the 420 yard uphill 18th hole I drove off first hitting the ball to about 190 yards from the pin. There was $32 riding on me if I won the 18th hole. Banks happened to get off a decent drive and was beside me in tee shot length. I had to hit first and was going to use a 4-wood for the long uphill second shot. It was getting darker. Instead Banks violated golf etiquette and hit first, His 2-iron was struck thinly but rolled onto the middle of the green 10 feet from the hole. Banks was lucky. My 4-wood was flown high but overshot the pin by 25 feet. I had a straight slightly downhill putt. I lined it up, made my stroke, and the ball went into the hole.

"Holy shit," Banks remarked, "Don't do this to me." If Banks made his putt he would halve the hole with me and still be down $16. He rolled it 8 feet past the hole. I had won $32. "I will not pay a cheating hustler," he said and walked off the green. There were six witnesses to Bank's antics and none of them liked Mr. Banks.

I would continually see Arnold Banks around the clubhouse and would constantly ask for my winnings. "I am not going to pay up until I am good and ready," he would reply. "You care too much about money, are you a Jew or something like that?" Banks was proud of being a Mason and bragged about his 32nd degree ranking in the Scottish Rite. The Masons were supposed to be about brotherhood. Why did he spew all the bullshit about Jews that constantly flowed from his big mouth? The six gallery members leaked the story of his loss to the 17 year old assistant professional around the club. Banks was not only the subject of derision and ridicule but members began to chide him for being a sore loser and dead beat.

One day Banks walked into pro shop when I was on duty, threw $32 on the floor, spat on the money, and said: "here you goddamn cheat, is your filthy lucre." Three club members caught the act. I put a paper towel over my hand and retrieved the money off the floor; cleaned it in the washroom sink; and placed it in a fresh paper bag behind the display counter to dry it out. Banks was infuriated. He expected me to be more dignified and refuse to accept the money.

Banks had too much whiskey one Friday evening and despite warnings from other members not to drive away from the club by himself got into his pricey Cadillac. He forgot to make a left or right turn, whatever it was from the club driveway unto the side road. Instead he went straight ahead, across the side road and into a wrought iron fence of an expensive house across the road. There was excessive damage to the Cadillac and the fence. Police were called. Banks had his license suspended for three months and had to pay damages for the fence to the owner of the house. He was a good citizen.

Roy owed me $4.00 from the three ball match with Banks but never offered to pay up. I took his money in pro shop merchandise. I even left a receipt for payment of the gambling debts Roy owed. When asked earlier for payment Roy remarked: "Why should I pay up, I never finished the match." It gradually occurred to me that Roy was far from the player he claimed to be. "Do you know how close I came to playing on the US PGA Tour?" he often remarked.

"Not very," I finally answered.

CHAPTER 27

Playing with Good Players

I had the opportunity to play several rounds with Jim Kelly, a former Province of Upper Canada Amateur Champion and winner of many local amateur tournaments. He earned his living as a physical education teacher in the local secondary school in Vaughan Township. In his early 50's he played to a legitimate 1 handicap. "Why didn't you ever become a professional?" I asked him.

"There is no money in professional golf right now," Jim would always answer. "Maybe in a few years there might be." Most of the other low handicappers at the club were never able to play at or better than their handicaps when they played with me. I suspected they posted lower scores then they actually achieved. I felt the same way about Roy. For all the talk about his great rounds he could never produce one while I played with him.

As the months passed the weather turned cooler after mid-September. I began to practice more. I earned my driver's license in August of that summer and picked up a new Dodge Coupe from the local dealer. The insurance rates were high on the new vehicle and would not come down until I turned 25 years old. I allowed Margaret Watson to use my car for shopping and everything else she needed it for. Everything was fine as long as I was picked up and delivered to the golf course. My handicap was down to scratch by the end of November. I had scored in the high 60's on 10 occasions. My best score was a "66." Roy, in the meantime, constantly boasted to the club members: "I taught Bobby how to play!" In actuality, there was nothing I could learn from Roy! Roy would saunter over to the practice field when I was hitting balls; shake his head after watching me hit a few shots and walk away. He never offered any instruction whatsoever. Beside that, if Roy offered advice I would have totally ignored him. I firmly believed that anyone achieving the status of head professional should be an excellent player. Roy didn't seem to measure up either as a player or a teacher.

Ivan Fletcher, who owned a GM dealership in North Toronto, was a member of the club. He was about 5'10" tall and was heavy set. He was a foul mouthed loud man and the consummate bully. He never lowered his voice on any occasion. He never requested anything in his life from anyone but demanded it. When I was going off duty in the pro shop one day Ivan Fletcher entered. "I want to play nine holes with you," he demanded. "Roy says you are off duty in 10 minutes. I'll see you on the first tee." Ivan then sauntered off not waiting for a reply from me. I went off duty and ignored the invitation. I went to the practice area instead. When Ivan saw this he went over to the area and started to scream.

"How dare you refuse to play with me," he hollered at me. He then started to shake his fist. Several members started gathering at the scene. I kept on hitting balls with my pitching wedge. Fletcher in the meantime was losing his cool. "Why you god damned insolent kid," he screamed, "How dare you ignore me?" Fletcher had turned red in the face. He reared back and attempted to slap me. Without a moment's thought, and strictly as a reflex action, I flipped the 200 pound Fletcher on his ass. I learned this move from Charles Sasaki and had mastered it. I did not realize what I had done. This was a similar incident to what happened a few years earlier with the Kowalski brothers on Peale Street. About 20 members witnessed the event. They were laughing at Fletcher and this was an insult to him. "You saw what he did." Fletcher pronounced as he turned to the audience. "He assaulted me."

"You threw the first punch." somebody from the audience yelled. "That's what I'll tell anyone who asks. I'll say the same," another man said. With that everyone left the practice area including Fletcher.

The next day at the shop Fletcher came in when I was on duty. "I hear you need a car," he remarked. "Have I got a deal for you!" With Fletcher it was business as usual. Fletcher's son was also a club member.

He was a young married man with an attractive wife. His son was quiet and mannerly. He certainly didn't learn that behavior from his father. The wife came into the shop a few days later.

"I have to apologize for my father in law," she said after introducing herself to me. "I hope you don't judge all the Fletchers by that blustering oaf."

When I returned to The Farm that evening I had a letter from Renee. Margaret reported that her three years at Julian were ending soon and she wanted to visit me for a week at The Farm. I became very excited. Hugh was growing concerned about me. While he thought my playing golf was a good exercise and got me out into the fresh air he felt that my choice of working as an assistant professional was a poor choice for future employment.

"It is a good avocation," he remarked, "but a poor vocation. If you want to play for prize money that's fine and dandy with me; at least you are your own boss." It was not the game Hugh disliked but the club membership and Roy Rollins. He referred to them as "constipated ass holes." He told me that he had Walter Abercromby check up on Roy and what he discovered would make my skin cringe. The information from Abercromby and was relayed via Hugh Watson. "Roy has some shady friends," Hugh related. One of them, a Paul Pennington had conned Roy into investing in a mining company. Roy took the money he needed to pay pro shop bills and buy merchandise with and tossed $20 000 in the mining stock. The money evaporated. I realized that to be conned you have to have larceny in your heart.

Before his discovery as an "operator" Pennington was a senior assistant professional at an exclusive Toronto golf club. One of the less savory members of the club saw him "operating" in the pro shop and said he was wasting time as a professional and suggested he join his stock brokerage company. Pennington proved to be very good at this. He made $70 000 in his first year. One stock, "Breakridge Mines" was his best seller. One of the Toronto dailies ran a one quarter page article in their business section along with a picture of Pennington. The articles even featured a profile of "young Paul Pennington, the brilliant entrepreneur." Within a year all the investors lost their money. There were rumors of "false assays and seeded mines." This the public never read about in the Toronto print media. Roy Rollins was one of those investors. The lost money forced him to shun paying his bills for pro shop supplies. Eventually suppliers refused to sell to him. He was on his way to bankruptcy. Two years after I ceased working with him he took a job selling fish to fancy restaurants. No golf club wanted him as a professional after his contract with the Clairmont Golf Club was up. Perhaps it was for the best.

I was asked to play with Pennington. Paul Pennington could not break 90. Maybe it was good that he retired from professional golf! In Pennington's personal view, he was better off as an entrepreneur. Whatever, Pennington never paid green fees to play at Roy's club, the Clairmont Club. He was always Roy's guest. Occasionally, he would purchase golf shirt or something relatively cheap as a token of gratitude to Roy. Roy drooled when he talked about Pennington's business acumen. Pennington reminded me of Hal Summers the private investigator.

I opened the letter from Renee. In it she had some interesting things to say:

Dear Bobby;

I will be finished up at the Julian School at the end of July this year. I will be going on a short concert tour my agent has set up for me. It will consist of a two months tour at several medium sized concert halls located in Dallas Texas, Boston, Philadelphia, Atlanta, New Orleans, Los Angeles and Birmingham, Alabama. After that I will be returning to my aunt's home in New York and then on to Toronto. All has been arranged with my Aunt Margaret. I will be coming to The Farm in early October. Oh how I wish to see you again. My aunt Margaret has told me you have been working as a professional golfer since late June this year. This must be quite an experience. I have a recording contract to fulfill after my tour. I am making good money. Some of the newspaper reviews have said that I am a gifted pianist. Love, Renee

CHAPTER 28

Renee's Triumphant Return

It was mid- autumn when Hugh and I retrieved Renee from Malton Airport. She had three large valises with her and Hugh hired a porter to help with the luggage. We departed the airport at 2:00 PM. I noticed that Renee still had her school girl figure.

"What happened on your tour of the States?' I asked.

"Oh nothing much," Renee replied. "I didn't see much of any city I visited, just hotel rooms and trains. My Aunt, from New York, traveled with me as well as my agent. I don't think I can take more than two trips a year like that. My recording sessions were easier. At least I could return to my aunt's house after a session. It takes a strong person to do all that traveling."

"What did you record?" I asked.

"I recorded all 14 standard Chopin Waltzes, the Preludes, the classic three Beethoven Sonatas, and some Mendelsohn. My agent says they can sell 100 000 copies of my recordings. He says this will set me up financially for a long time. But for the next two weeks I am not going to touch the piano, just loaf."

Renee was not true to her word. She resisted the piano for two days. She carried all her music with her from her aunt's residence in New York City. She opened her music bag, unloaded it, and laid it out on the parlor grand in the living room. I noticed a collection of ragtime music bounded in a paperback format on top of the stack. "What do you think of this," Renee asked, as she ran through Scott Joplin's "Entertainer." "It's called a 'rag.'" I was impressed. This was the first time Renee ever played anything but a classical piece while I was present.

There was still enough daylight present for me to practice on the front lawn of The Farm. "When you are done with practicing can you come and watch me hit a few?" I asked.

About 4:00 PM I dragged out my set of lefty clubs from the trunk of the Dodge coupe and set up on the front lawn with my back to the sun. This made my target line go south. I pulled out my 5-iron and began to loosen up. The balls, after a few shots, began to carry about 160 yards. I was heading for my 18th birthday in December. Thoughts about working three more years as an assistant professional, especially in a shop like Roy Rollins operated, were repugnant to me. I loved playing golf and working on my swing. I detested the majority of club members at the Clairmont Club and ceased to work in that pro shop at the end of September. At this time the greens keeper, Leigh Smith closed the greens and tees at the course. The members could play the course if they used temporary greens outlined on the fairways and temporary tees. The pro shop only opened after 9:00 AM and closed at sunset. Yet there were still members who could not respect what the head greens keeper requested and when Leigh Smith was out of sight they would play the course as if it weren't partially closed. Members were requested to remove their clubs from storage at the club after October 31. It was now almost a half year since I completed my senior matriculation at Willington Academy. I did not have a definite idea of what I wanted to do with the rest of my working life. While deep in my thought I did not notice Renee standing behind me.

"You are hitting that ball well," she commented. "Let's see what you can do with the 3- iron?" I replaced the 5-iron in the golf bag and withdrew the 3-iron. The 3-iron shots were carrying over 185 yards. They had a 10 yard hook to them. "Your rhythm is much better than the last time I saw you. What are your scores like?"

"I am playing to scratch," I replied. I wish I could play and practice over the winter."

"You will have to get out of this area for a few months," Renee answered. "You might need a set of clubs with stiffer shafts. That hook you have; it disturbs me. In competition it will betray you."

I was staring at Renee's intense beauty without let up. "I love you," I said, When I realized what I had said I began to apologize. "I am sorry; I don't know where that came from!" Renee did not seem surprised. "I feel the same way about you," she replied. "I didn't really come back here just to see my Aunt Margaret you know."

I continued: "I want to spend this winter in Central Florida. Some friends I made among the other assistant pros told me there are mini tours available there that are open to any type of pro from anywhere. I figure it will cost me about $2500 to play and accommodate myself from early January next year until April. Then if I am playing well I will play in some local pro tournaments up here. If not I'll do something else." I looked at Renee. "I have all sorts of money," I said. "Would you like to come along, all expenses paid?"

"I have recording contracts to fulfill and two minor concert tours booked. I can't commit to anything until May next year." I was disappointed. I did not realize the heavy schedule Renee had before her.

"Let's not plan anything for six months after your tour is over," I said. "We need time for ourselves. We will meet here in early May. Don't worry about expenses."

"Silly boy," she replied, "I can manage my financial affairs. I don't need your millions."

"I will not attend university this fall although I have been selected by three so far," I blurted out. "I am going to try my hand at playing professional golf on something called a 'mini tour' which starts in Florida in early January. It will cost me $1500 in US money to play in 15 tournaments. I will have another thousand in other costs. The tour finishes in early April. Of course my accommodation and meals will be funded by me, also my transport from tournament to tournament. I am taking my Dodge to Florida. I have also had Walter Abercromby help me obtain a Canadian Passport. I will take $3500 in traveler's checks. I have six dozen new balls I received from various suppliers to play with."

Renee stayed on at The Farm for two additional weeks. Then she left for New York to start on another three month tour she had been contracted for another recording session with RBC Records. Hugh and I packed her baggage in the aging De Soto and left for Malton on a late November day. I felt very alone at The Farm. Renee had promised to keep in touch with me by letter. I continued to break in a new set of clubs with stiffer shafts especially selected for me by Jim Kelly who spent an afternoon with me and introduced me to Ken Gray, the head professional at Mount Vernon Golf and Country Club. Ken Gray, now in his early 50's was considered one of Canada's greatest playing professionals. But he had a position at Mount Vernon that afforded him a decent living. His playing abilities were displayed only at local Canadian PGA events. Had Ken Gray attained the support he required in his younger days possibly he might have become one of the greatest players in golf.

My new left-handed clubs initially felt heavy and rigid to me but Ken Gray had advised me not to alter my swing, just hit balls until I got used to the new clubs. So until I left for Florida in mid- December just after my 18th birthday I worked on my ball striking. I tended to flight every shot with the new clubs to my left, but one day while snow was still off the ground I stopped the flight my shots took to the left and started hitting them straight along the target line. They would hook slightly and then land with little roll. I had the "feel" of the new clubs.

I packed mostly casual clothes in my car and my golf equipment. I did however take along a light gray suit, two white shirts, two decent ties and a pair of dress black shoes. I had stopped growing at 16 years of age. At 5'10" tall and 145 pounds I felt comfortable in my body. But my hair was still curly and defied combing. I shaved every other day with Gillette Blue blades which the Gillette Company bragged: "gave the slickest shaves ever." They were always dull. I carried a clipping from the Toronto Comet that defined several routes to Daytona, Florida. I ventured out alone on a lengthy journey to a strange country. When I reached Highway 7, I headed west towards Detroit. From there I would make my way to Florida. The trip took two full days to reach the southern part of Georgia.

I started out on the third day and after a few hours driving found the road that would take me directly to Daytona. When I arrived in Daytona I stopped at a local golf course to ask for directions to decent accommodation. There was a young woman about 18 years old at the counter in the pro shop. The golf course was called "Southern Pines."

"Excuse me," I began, "I just drove down here from Toronto to play in some pro golf events. They are supposed to originate in Daytona Beach, Florida. Can you help me?" I opened a paper with all the tournament dates and the location of the courses where they were to be played. No course holding a tournament was greater than 60 miles from the center of Daytona. "Where would I stay to play this first event?" I asked the young lady.

"Do you know," the young lady remarked, "that this club is the first stop on the tour you signed up for. Did you ever stop at the right place! By the way our name is the 'Southern Pines Golf Club.'" I had begun to refer to myself as "Bob" over the last several months. I felt "Bobby" was a childish name. I had major difficulty trying to understand her manner of speaking. She had a tremendous southern drawl. She frequented her speech with the expression "you all." It sounded to me like "yoll."

"Are you really from Toronto?" she asked. "My name is Debbie Wall," She informed me that she minded the pro shop for her father who owned the course. It was a semi private course her father had developed in the late 1930's on scrub land outside Daytona. She got around to telling me her mother's family had emigrated from Toronto to Alabama in 1906 and settled in Birmingham. "My father's real name was 'Walburg.' He shortened it to 'Wall' when he came to Toronto from Germany in 1932. Shortly later he moved to Alabama. He met my mother in 1934 down here. We have been called 'Wall' ever since."

"What are you telling me all this for?" I asked. "I am really a total stranger." I thought about her remark that her father emigrated out of Canada in 1906, while my mother's family had done the reverse in the late 1890's.

"I sound like a real 'cracker,'" Debbie went on. "I guess it's something I'll live with the rest of my life. Oh if you were only Jewish. I could bring you home to meet my dad."

I never discussed my family origins with strangers. "Does being a

Sephardim count?" I asked Debbie. "My ancestors came from Spain and Scotland. People say I don't look Jewish. When I went to a Jewish summer camp the kids called me a 'goy.' I didn't seem to fit in with those Russian Jews. There is even information from my paternal grandmother. She said 'her mother wasn't Jewish.' I guess that makes her a goy."

"Where are you going to stay while you are playing down here?" she asked.

"I don't know," I replied. "Recommend something."

"Come home with me after I lock up the shop; Dad would love to meet you."

Debbie drove further away from Daytona Beach as her and I left the pro shop locked and secured for the long dark night. It got dark at Daytona at about 5:30 PM during the early winter as opposed to the 4:45 time of Toronto. After a short drive of 10 minutes we arrived at Debbie's home. It was an old southern house that reminded me of "Tara" the home of Scarlet O'Hara from *Gone with the Wind* fame. At least that's how it appeared to me after I had viewed the movie at the local theater some years earlier. The pickup truck that Debbie drove was fairly new and could carry three people in the front seat. There was a huge circular driveway leading up to the main entrance to the old plantation house. The house seemed to be located on a very large lot. Debbie drove to the front door and she and I left the pickup. An elderly black man came out of the house and drove the pickup away. Debbie led me through the front door. "Welcome to 'Canaan,'" she said turning to me. "This is the home of the Walls."

I stepped into a large anti room. "Come with me and you can meet my father Michael;" Debbie said as she motioned me through the exceptionally large living room into a library that situated off of it. We both entered the library which was at least 24 feet by 24 feet in area. It must have contained thousands of books. There was a gentleman, I reckoned, he was about 45 years of age sitting at a huge desk located at the window side of the room. He apparently did not hear his daughter enter. "Dad, I want you to meet a visitor from Toronto," she said, to the man at the desk as he looked up. The man rose from his seat and walked over to me. He looked over me for a few seconds as if evaluating my Spiritual Energy and offered his hand.

"My name is Michael Wall," the old man said. "What is yours?" Michael Wall seemed to have a similar southern drawl to his daughter. After all, he came from Germany in 1933! After 17 years in the Deep South most all of his German accent had been totally eradicated. He never told people he was a Jew. The established Christian community wondered why his family was never seen at any local church services.

"My name is Robert MacAlpine Noble," I answered. "I am a professional golfer and came down here to play in 10 tournaments on the mini tour. I still haven't found a place to stay and my car and things are over at your club."

"Not to worry about that," Michael replied, "I'll send Adam over to the club with Debbie and we will get your car. Do you have the keys?" I wondered who these people were that would want to deliver my car to their house. They didn't seem to care one bit about the fact that this was my first evening in their locality and they seemed to completely trust me on first glance.

I handed the keys to Debbie and she left with the Black gentleman in the pickup. I was alone with Michael Wall. "So young man, how did you happen to stop at my golf club?"

"I wanted directions to some place where I could get accommodation for the night. Then tomorrow morning I was going to look over the location of our first tournament. I didn't know it was Southern Pines." I looked at Michael Wall intently.

"You will stay with us tonight," the older man told me. "There is only my daughter, myself and three servants." He motioned me to take one of the seats in the library. "I am a widower. I lost my wife eight years ago to a heart condition. She had just celebrated her 40th birthday. She was from Toronto, originally. Great people come from Toronto. I was visiting some friends up there who wanted me to purchase some land down here for them so they could build retirement homes. This happened in 1939 right before the War began. Their representative's name was Walter Abercromby. Is he still practicing law up in Toronto? What a great guy he is! He is something called a 'King's Councillor.'"

Michael paused for several moments. Then he asked me the typical question that all Americans ask a Canadian. Never mind that Canada was larger in area than the USA. "Do you know Walter Abercromby, he is a Canadian?" He went over to a small refrigerator near his desk in the library and removed a pitcher of orange juice. He poured two large glasses of the drink and gave one to me. My attention on the man was 100%. "I don't reckon you know him?" Michael asked as he sipped the juice. "After all doesn't the Toronto area have about 1 000 000 people?"

This last statement from Michael absolutely stunned me. The older man wanted to know my background. "My father was a Sephardic Jew," I related to Michael. "I don't think he ever cared about anything spiritual. My mother's family originally came from the States. A family tree I recently saw shows her ancestors arrived in America early in the first half of the 19th century. To be precise it was in 1847. They settled in Charleston, South Carolina. The original man who came to America fought in the Civil War on the Confederate side. Then they began to spread out over the whole country. I have 26 first cousins and many more 2nd cousins. I have seven first cousins I have never even met. I don't know any of the 2nd ones. I have to study this more closely. The genealogist says I might have the Blood of Jesus. For a Jew I seem to be too much interested in Jesus! Besides everyone seems to say I don't look Jewish. I have even been called 'a goy.' Why do the Jews seem to hate Jesus so much?" I noticed that Michael Wall did not wish to answer that question.

"Have you ever considered what the Great Avatar might have looked like?" Michael asked. He then answered his own question. "He was about six feet tall and weighed about 175 pounds. He had reddish blond hair and blue eyes. He had a fair complexion. Does this describe your typical Ashkenazi Jew? He was described as the most beautiful man in the world! He is also my heavenly mentor." Michael stirred from his chair and brought a bound volume from a shelf in his library. The title on the book was: "The Walbergs." He opened the large tome to a page titled: "An abbreviated family tree of the Walbergs." On this page was a diagram of the history of Michael's father's family. The book was passed to me. "Look at this page," Michael remarked. "It shows my descent from King David through the Emperor Charlemagne down to my father Laban. Interesting isn't it? "What intrigued me was the insertion of a separate line from Jesus connecting into the father's line and into that of Charlemagne that seemed to occur after 900 AD. "Now turn to page 54," Michael instructed.

I flipped the pages until I came to page 54. This page showed a family tree from Michael's mother's ancestors. Michael's maternal ancestor appeared to originate in Wales and there seemed to be an ancestor who was some sort of Welsh King who married a descendent of Jesus. Michael retrieved the large tomb from me. "You can study this at your leisure another day." At that moment Debbie entered the library.

"Bob's car is outside in the driveway," she reported. I continued to speak with Michael while Debbie sat in one of the easy chairs in the library.

Michael continued: "Dinner will be served shortly," he announced, you will join us. We will be pleased to have you."

The group in the library entered the large living room from the library via a door leading directly into it. There was a buffet arranged on the large table. "We are not flesh eaters in this family," Michael replied. "You may select whatever you like from the table. Our cook and housekeeper Bella, and her husband Adam have been with us for 17 years. Bella's husband is the man Debbie went with to retrieve your car. His full name is "Adam Barclay."

In short order Debbie, Michael and I were seated at the large oak table and sat on cushioned chairs. Michael noticed my interest in the dining room table and chairs. "This dining room set, the 12 chairs and the table date back to about 1824. They were fashioned by John Rugby, the famous cabinet maker, for this particular house. The original family that owned it was Clayton Barclay and his wife Dora. He built the original house and occupied it in 1823. This was almost a complete wilderness back then. It was Clayton Barclay who started to cultivate oranges commercially. There were other crops, some cotton and some wheat. He also began a lumber mill that no longer exists. It is now a shopping area. Soon he began to prosper. The Barclays, who help us run the house, have ancestors that were slaves on this property. That is how Adam got his family name. Clayton Barclay was an interesting life stream. He didn't believe in slavery. When he was rich enough he purchased slaves to keep them out of the hands of cruel owners. He actually allowed them to escape from this plantation. I believe the escaped slaves traveled north on the 'Underground Railway' until they reached safe haven in what is now south western Ontario. Some town called 'Sandwich' was the terminal up north. There they were granted asylum by the people up there." The town of Sandwich, Ontario has become the city of Windsor. It has about 400, 000 people. It is directly across the river from Detroit.

During the Civil War Barclay sent his sons, now young men west to California to start on agricultural ventures out there. This was to keep them out of the Civil War. By the Grace of God, Barclay was spared a great many of the abuses wreaked on southern properties during the Reconstruction era. I consider it a pity that Lincoln had to die in 1865. He was the South's greatest friend. This area was too far south to be of any interest to the Yankees. When we bought the remnant of the plantation and this house we only modernized the heating system. We installed a cooling system recently that they call 'air conditioning.' We restored the property to its pre-Civil War state. I bought the property from Clara Barclay, a great grand-daughter, who at that time was a widow with no heirs that lived near her and no children. The woman was very advanced in age. I made a fair offer according to her attorneys, and it received approval. Bella and Adam were working here maintaining the estate I made it clear they would be welcome to stay on with us. In a short time we trained Bella to be a vegetarian chef. She and Adam are almost vegetarians now. Their children two boys both stayed in the Army after the War and are still serving today. I must begin the Grace."

"O 'Mighty I Am', when Moses questioned you for your name, you said: 'I am that I am.' 'I Am' is my name and my legacy forever!'" Michael stopped a few seconds and then continued. "For your ever abundant supply 'I Am' eternally grateful. Amen." The meaning of the Grace went over my head. Still, it intrigued me.

The food was excellent. Bella had an assortment of every salad imaginable to mankind. There were pickled eggs, a large bowl of garden salad, some sort of breaded things that I thought reminded me of breaded chicken legs, rolls baked from flours made of several grains. Different fruit salads were on the table. I thought: "nobody in this room could possibly eat all of this."

"Bella and Adam will take this around to people in need," Michael responded as if he were reading my thoughts. I, who on occasions could be overwhelmed by a prodigious appetite was satisfied with small samples from several dishes. The cooking and preparation equaled that of Margaret Watson. I thought momentarily of Agnes and her overcooked meat dishes, burnt coffee, and wilted salads.

"She was doing the best she could," I thought. I had lost a great deal of my anger since I was no longer in her company. I went to practice on Southern Pines the following morning finding my way to the club and arriving at 8:30 A.M. I unloaded my clubs at the parking lock and hauled my golf bag up to the pro shop. Debbie was there and talking quietly with the pro shop help. One was an older man about 50 years of age and the other a woman slightly younger. "This is Arthur Cole and his wife Mary," Arthur is our assistant greens superintendent. Debbie said, as she acknowledged my presence. "I have told them all about you. We have a small driving range where you can warm up if you want." Mary Cole produced a large bucket of range balls and handed them to me. Debbie asked: "May I walk around with you?"

Debbie and I went over to the practice range and I began to warm up by hitting a few sand wedge shots and then working up to clubs used to hit balls longer distances. I then gathered up my clubs together and went to the practice putting green Debbie said nothing during the warm up. When we arrived at the first tee a youth about 18 years of age joined us.

"This is my Sam White," said Debbie in introducing the youth who was the same age as me. "He is the nephew of the Coles. He stays on our property and helps out with grass cutting, general maintenance, and so on. Adam is a trained carpenter and Sammy is apprenticing with him sort of part time. He will caddy for you."

The opening hole was a long par 4 and I went after my first shot with a driver. It was a good effort winding up 245 yards from the tee.

I played quite well on the first nine holes scoring a one under par 34. There seemed to be no other players on the outward nine but coming back on the inward nine we passed through several foursomes. "The course gets real busy at 10:00 AM," Debbie remarked. I had carded a 34 coming in for a 68. "That's two under," Debbie said. "Keep that up for three rounds and you will do quite well." The course was 6500 yards long.

The tournament would run on Wednesday, Thursday and Friday with Tuesday being a practice day for the players. I played an additional practice round. Sammy White caddied for me for the two practice rounds and would accept no fee for his services or did the pro shop charge any fee for the range balls. "It is my pleasure Sammy always responded, I don't charge for having a good time" I would also caddy during the tournament."

When the tournament began on Wednesday, 102 players teed up. I warmed up for an hour then arrived on the first tee at 10:15 AM. My two playing partners were Americans, one from Milwaukee and the other from Cleveland. Both had caddies and I had Sammy White. The two American pros were about six feet tall and were much heavy set than me. They both could hit their drivers about 20 yards past the 240 yards I drove the ball. In addition they seem to use a 5-iron where I would hit a 4-iron or a 3-iron to the greens and on longer holes where I used a 4-wood, and so on. However, they lacked the accuracy in shot making I displayed. All three of us scored 69's that first round. There was a cut off line in the tournament after the first two rounds. The top 45 and ties would play the final round on Friday. If you made the cut you were guaranteed a payoff. I was paired with two older professionals for the second 18 holes. Both were "Class A" club professionals about 40 years of age. They seemed to be much less skilled in the tee to green game then my previous playing partners. They both scored in the high 70's. I scored a 71 the second round and survived the cut. In my third round I scored 78 and finished 3rd last. I took 36 putts that day. The average pro considered 30 putts adequate. I got $75:00 in prize money. For the self-supporting player this would have covered weekly expenses. I thought, "What a way to make a living!" This made me wonder what

I was doing trying to compete, even at this low level. It was equivalent to a Class A professional baseball league.

Weeks passed by. I was playing well in tournaments making the cut in all but two events. My putting seemed to be a big factor in my scoring. Under competitive pressure a six foot putt for a birdie seemed a gut wrenching affair. One older gentleman watching the minor league tournament players approached me in the dining room of the clubhouse and introduced himself. He started a conversation with me. I recognized him as Nelson Burns, a prominent player from the mid- 1930's until the mid- 1940's. Nelson was the winner of five major championships and over 50 US PGA events.

"I can help you gain the three strokes you need to improve and become a top notch player but it will take two years of dedicated work. There are some areas of your swing that need refining. These areas cost you power. Your putting stroke is crap. But with work in two years you will be there."

This commentary made me think: "I have worked hard and long on my game. I play slightly better than scratch and yet I still needed to improve." When the tournament schedule finished in mid- March I ventured up to Nelson Burns club located inland from the Walls' residence near Daytona. Burns told me he would always be available any weekday. The drive took about one hour. I found out from discrete enquiries that Nelson quit playing in the top line professional tournaments when he was about 38 years old. This was in late 1946. He had played for 13 years near or at the top of his game but he began to go downhill in January, 1946. While most of his serious competition was away in military service Nelson was unable to enlist because of a series of lingering maladies. He had asthma and this nixed him at medical exams. Another serious defect was cramps in the legs and type 1, diabetes which he had to take insulin for after the age of 20 years. Otherwise, Nelson still looked robust. He stood 6'2" tall and weighed perhaps 190 pounds. He originally came out of southern Mississippi from a fairly well to do family who inherited even more wealth from a rich uncle. Nelson inherited his fair share. He played golf using the income of his inheritance to support him until he got established. It didn't take long. He was married since the age of 22 years to Louise Turner but had no children. In one short final season all the maladies started to take a large toll on Nelson. He quit competitive golf at the end of that year. He retired to his estate near Orlando in November, 1946. He played casual golf from then on and taught a small group of promising pros. I felt privileged to be asked to work with him.

I drove through the gate of the club and parked my car. I enquired about Nelson Burns at the pro shop. "I am sorry, Mr. Burns is not at the club today," the young lady at the pro shop said. "Are you expected?"

"I was supposed to drop in to see him whenever I was in the area," I replied to the young lady's question. "My name is Robert Noble" The young lady picked up a telephone and dialed a number. She talked to some unknown person on the telephone and mentioned my name then hung up. "Mr. Burns wants to see you," the young woman replied. "Can you drive about five miles down the road to his home?" I replied affirmatively. She picked up the telephone again. "Mr. Noble will be over shortly," she said and put down the receiver. She looked at me and said, Mr. Burns lives down the Pines Road about five miles. When you reach the road outside the club turn left and drive for about five miles until you reach the Eagle Ranch. The entrance is on the right hand side of the road. Go up to the main house."

The short drive up to Nelson's ranch allowed me to think about the venture I just completed in Florida. I had finished in the money in 12 of 15 events. I made $550 which was exactly equal to the expanses I ran up for food and gasoline traveling about from tournament to tournament. If it hadn't been for the generosity of the Michael Wall and his daughter Debbie I figured I might be out close to $3300. It was a great deal of funds in 1950, to pay for three months food and tournament fees. That money could have purchased a new Ford convertible; a stripped down model but a new one nevertheless. I didn't have a sponsor for balls and clubs. I was able to practice at the tournament sites because it was included with my entry fees to play on this "Class A" minor league tour. I had offered money to Michael Wall on many occasions but the gentleman refused to accept it. I secretly donated $500 to the Salvation Army on behalf of Michael Wall. I had told the Walls I would be back after the final tournament to say goodbye and head back to Canada. The weather in central Florida had warmed up considerably.

I spotted the entrance to Nelson Burns' Ranch and wheeled my car right and drove up to the main house. It was a medium sized house which looked as if it were built in the last five years. The bricks were an almost white color. The sign which hung over the main door was a smaller version of the sign at the main entrance to the driveway. It said: "The Eagle Ranch." I parked my car in what appeared to be an enlarged part of the driveway and walked to the main door. "I am Bob Noble; "I said as a woman about 45 years old answered the door.

Presently, Nelson Burns arrived at the front door. I noticed he seemed stooped over a bit and had lost the catlike walk he possessed when I saw him in newsreels from the 1940's that were studied earlier by me. "Ah the teenaged professional golfer; I am so happy to see you." The older gentleman oozed dignity. He grasped my right hand and shook it vigorously. "We will go out back. Do you have your clubs with you?"

"They're in my car, I can get them," I replied.

"Then do so," Nelson replied. Nelson went to his telephone in the hallway and dialed one number. "Bring the cart to the front of the house," he requested. While I was retrieving the golf bag from the trunk of my car a four wheeled buggy came puttering up from the outbuilding behind the house. It was the forerunner of what was to become the modern gasoline driven golf cart. I looked at it with amusement. The old man who was driving the cart placed my golf bag on the rack at the rear of the cart. Nelson and I got into the cart and drove over to the rear of the outbuilding. What was behind the outbuilding was a large well-manicured practice field about 150 yards wide by 260 yards long. It was so situated that the sun never shone directly at the player if he stood at either end. The field was surrounded by tall mature palm trees.

"I spend four hours working on the cutter each day that I mow. I do it myself," Nelson commented. "Cutting grass is very therapeutic. I have a special deck mower that cuts an eight foot swath. It has three rotating blades and can be set as low as one and one half inches above the ground. It is something we rigged up in our workshop. A large mower manufacturer bought the plans from us last year. Our people are going to get royalties from them when they start producing them for the commercial market."

I thought of the clumsier rotary type machine that Hugh Watson used back at The Farm to mow the front lawn. It was towed at the rear of an old Massey tractor. Unless the grass was less than three inches tall the machine always produced a poor cut. In wet weather two cuts were needed: one high and the second lower.

"Do you play anymore?" I asked.

Nelson pondered the question for a few seconds. "Not the way I used to," he answered. "I lost half my swing arc in a little over two years. Nothing I tried will bring it back. My tee shot length has dropped from 265 yards down to 235 yards and still continues to drop. I have severe arthritis in my lower spine."

"Is there any cure for it?" I asked.

"It's a karmic thing," Nelson replied. "Until I learn to reduce that karma I am stuck with it. I met a lady once about five years ago. She said that stuff about karma. I asked her how to get rid of karma? She told me: 'to raise my Spiritual Energy.' I guess my Spiritual Energy is still low because my condition has worsened. I live a clean life. I don't smoke, I don't drink, I don't do narcotics. I attend church once a week. I do the usual things a good person is supposed to do. I keep asking the Good Lord what to do."

Nelson went to the back of the cart and opened the lid on something that appeared to be a soda pop cooler. It was filled with golf balls. They were contained in sack like containers with each container holding about 30 balls. The balls were all Titleists! "Get your five-iron and hit me a few," Nelson commanded.

I emptied the sack on the ground and set up with the five-iron. I selected a large palm tree about 80 yards down the field as a target. "I got cold since I left the golf course," I announced. "I will only try to hit these shots to the tree." I took a half swing with the five-iron and the ball sailed on a solid line toward the palm tree, hit the tree halfway up the trunk and bounced back toward us. With each subsequent shot the ball went about 15 yards further until after five shots I reached my maximum distance of 165 yards. "Now I am warmed up," I said as I turned back to look at Nelson. As I struck more and more shots with my five-iron my left handed hook got larger. The ball spun wildly to the right as it landed.

"That hook won't do!" Nelson observed. "You will have to alter your grip with the right hand, your top hand" He came over to me and drew out a fountain pen from his shirt. "I am going to mark your hands with key lines. When I am done you will place your hands on the club handle so that the lines fit together precisely. If you do it correctly you will have the ultimate grip or pretty close to it."

When he finished talking and marking my hands I placed my hands on the club handle matching up with the lines on my right and left palms. I showed it to Nelson. "That's it," Nelson exclaimed. "You supinate the right hand too much." I began to practice the changes Nelson recommended at Nelson's private range. I had made arrangements to leave Florida originally in early April but decided to stay on till late April. I telephoned Hugh Watson at The Farm and informed him about my change of plans. Nelson would drop by the range once a day to check on my progress. After three weeks I had mastered the change in grip to the extent that I could assume it without any conscious thought but my shots, while no longer hooking, had lost any semblance of a curve and were flying almost dead straight. I began to hit the ball well again but would have to compensate for the 10 yard error with my driver. I arranged to stay an additional week to be certain the mastery of the new technique would stay with me.

One day I came to my final hours in Florida. I packed my car with my luggage with the help of Adam Barclay and his wife. I gave Adam $100 as a love gift for their kindness to me. My car had been serviced by a garage that Michael Wall used and everything was set. Debbie Wall was not there to see me off. While I loved Debbie but it was not the feeling I had for her that I experienced while around Renee. I told Michael Wall I donated $500 in American funds to the local branch of the Salvation Army in Michael's name.

"But how can you afford it?" Michael asked. I related to Michael that I had inherited a vast fortune and valuable property from a certain man I befriended right after the War. I told Michael I would never be short of money. Michael had a present for me. It was packed into a small 18" by 18" carton and sealed up with tape. "Don't open this till you get home." Later I discovered a comprehensive record created by Mr. Wall detailing the history of all the Jewish Families that came to America after 1800. How he ever compiled all this information I never did find out. Agnes Posnaski's family was listed in the tome! These relatives of Agnes never settled in the United States permanently. They moved into Canada in the late 1800's.

I drove over to Nelson Burn's Estate to have one final practice session. It was to make certain that I would keep what I had learned and not revert to my previous technique. I went to the practice range. After hitting about 50 balls I had moved up to the clubs meant to hit the ball further until I was hitting shots with my driver. Then I felt a sharp pain in my lower back. I could not hit another shot after that incident. I did not want to say anything to Nelson Burns. I needed to sit down and rest. My pain was exhausting me. There was no further golf shots struck in Florida. I promised to correspond with Nelson Burns after I reached my home in Ontario. This I did once a month regularly until I abandoned golf for a different vocation. Nelson had sent me seven reels of 8 mm Kodak movies of various professionals that I could study.

"Certainly progress with your golf is important to me," Nelson commented, "but I would really like to know if you find what you are ultimately looking for. I am also trying to find it. My wife is trying to find it."

The first leg of the trip took me to middle of Georgia. The pain from the lower back was excruciating forcing me to abort two hours of daylight driving and find a motel to accommodate me. This I succeeded in doing. The next morning I awoke at 9:00 AM. Most of the discomfort I experienced was gone and I felt more comfort in driving. I drove for eight hours with only a short stop at a diner for food. I stopped in Northern Kentucky for sleep and continued North the next day. I was ready to motor on by 8:00 AM. Late that night I reached the Rainbow Bridge at Niagara Falls N.Y that would take me into Canada. I had a large hassle with the customs officer on the Canadian side.

"How long have you been away?" he asked. When I answered four months and that I was playing golf as a professional. There was some lecture from the customs officer about filling out a Canadian income tax form. The officer decided to search the car. The contents of the trunk were tossed onto the pavement. "What are all these balls for?" the officer asked. "Are they for resale?"

"These are my practice balls," I replied. By now the balls, numbering over 300, were loose and rolling around on the floor of the trunk.

"How do you get them out of the car," the officer inquired.

"I drive the car onto a steep hill, open the trunk and they fall out," I answered.

"And how do you get them back in?" he asked.

"I chip them in," I answered.

"How much did you win?" the officer asked.

"Not enough to write home about," I answered. The customs officer was laughing when he waved me through. He helped me to pack the trunk.

"Teenagers," I heard him say as I drove off.

I reached The Farm five hours after I crossed the Rainbow Bridge that spanned from Niagara Falls, N.Y. to Niagara Falls, Ontario. I was tired when I pulled into the driveway of The Farm. There was a strange car parked in front of the house. Hugh and Margaret Watson came out of the house to greet me. "We were so worried about you," Margaret blurted out," you should write more! We have a visitor." Renee had come to The Farm the day before. She never stayed in my farm house but with the Watsons in the small house. Renee never freeloaded. I declined an evening snack and went up to my room and prepared for bed. I wanted to visit Renee but instead fell into a coma like sleep. I had never inspected the small house after I took up residency in the main house. I felt strange at first, sharing the big house with Bill my half-brother and Marion my sister. There was Agnes of course but she was always carping about living in the sticks. She stayed on for nearly one year and abandoned The Farm for an apartment in Niagara. Agnes was not a rural person. The smaller house was about 1200 square feet in living area. Hugh Williams had asked for funds from the Duncan Estate and worked on finishing the basement. Hugh completed about 800 square feet of recreation area with an office. It was a fine residence for a retired couple who entertained the occasional visitor. The large house was strictly reserved for me and my siblings.

CHAPTER 29

A Promising Career Ends

In the morning, I rose from the bed and showered. I lacked a heavy beard so no shave as of yet was necessary. The soreness in the back had disappeared. I was in time for the large breakfast Margaret usually put out so I dressed according to the weather forecast in comfortable but heavy pants, a flannel shirt and a sweater with complete arms. It was to be 65 degrees Fahrenheit with no wind and sunny, not bad for a latter April day. I wanted to have a talk with Renee, eat at a slow pace and then practice for four hours. This was the usual regime since I started altering my golf stroke with the changes Nelson Burns recommended. I would then have a small vegetarian sandwich and a Coke and go back to practice for three hours in the afternoon. This usually resulted in the hitting of 500 balls. I knew the Coke was not exactly good for me but it was the one of the final vices I vowed to rid myself of if only the strength would come to do so. Besides the Coke tasted especially good if it was directly from the small six and one-half ounce bottle. The fountain drink was always flat.

I entered the large kitchen. Renee was sitting at the table. When I had entered the room she turned her head and glanced at me. I felt she had grown more beautiful with the five months that had passed since I last saw her. She smiled at me which I felt made her seem more enchanting. Hugh was sitting at the table. Margaret had laid out a buffet type breakfast similar in fashion to that Michael Wall had served at every meal in Florida while I stayed at their estate. I wondered why

Margaret went through such trouble. On the table were home fried potatoes, scrambled eggs, these made properly by scrambling in the bowl first not in the actual pan, fruit salad, fresh squeezed orange and grapefruit juice, whole wheat rolls, and numerous other goodies. There was enough to feed a platoon of professional football players.

I loaded my plate with some fruit salad and poured a glass of orange juice. When I finished that I took a plate of scrambled eggs, one roll, and some home fried potatoes. Margaret always prepared the breakfast using only high quality foods. She always fried the eggs in fresh butter. In deference to my growing vegetarianism the Watson couple had slowly converted their personal menus to suit that style as well. Hugh Watson quietly left the table. "I have necessary work to do," he said as he rose from his chair. Margaret was sitting in the pantry listening to the soap opera, "Our Gal Sunday."

"I am giving up playing the piano in public," Renee said. "The constant travel, the hotels and the large cities are becoming difficult to take. Besides, I hate audiences."

"But why do that?" I replied. "You are at the beginning of your career."

"I have made some money doing this but enough is enough. Royal Broadcasting Corporation has offered me a contract and royalties to record a great deal of music. We're starting with Chopin's Nocturnes and moving on from there. Of course, I need time to learn some of the other Composers' work. I know very little Bach. Things like that will keep me busy. I would like to live here at The Farm but I need your permission according to my Aunt Margaret. You are the landlord! I will pay you for food and accommodation. I insist on it."

I fought off the urge to invite Renee to stay at The Farm free of charge. I instead asked, "What do you think is a fair price." I had heard a sum of "$150.00 per month" as an answer. Can you afford it?" Renee nodded in agreement. I rose from the dinner table. "I want to practice my golf swing. I had some instructions from Nelson Burns this winter. He says I need two years of work to master them. Will you excuse me.?" I was wondering why Renee would pay for the privilege of staying at The Farm when I would be willing to have her as a guest. When I arrived at the practice area the answer hit me; Renee wanted to pay her own way. The same thing happened to me in Florida when Michael Wall refused to accept my offer to pay. Advanced life streams pay their own way and with more than money.

There was no pain in the lower back as I slowly dispatched 10 shots with my pitching wedge. The ball flew for 100 yards and they were all well struck. As I moved on to hit balls with the 9-iron there was no pain. I had struck 20 balls. I struck 10 balls with the 5-iron and no pain, then 10 with a 3-iron. I pulled the 4-wood from my bag and began to hit shots. I felt a small twinge in the lower back on the second shot. The pain worsened on the third shot, and increased sharply with next three. I had hit 51 shots with various clubs and had excellent results but after that I became progressively more crippled and in greater pain. I abandoned the balls in the field then put my 4-wood back in the bag and slowly struggled back to the house. I went to my room and lay on the bed. I fell into a deep but short sleep and awoke at noon. I entered the dining room. Renee had already entered the room, Hugh was there and Margaret was laying out another buffet. Margaret turned and after watching me she asked, "Are you alright dear?"

"I am in agony," I answered. "I can hardly walk. Maybe I'll visit a doctor tomorrow if I can drive." I ate very little at that lunch. Their concern for me showed up in their faces. Renee also showed concern. Renee said nothing during lunch.

"I think Bob should lay down for the rest of today," Renee commanded when everybody had finished eating. She was a very formidable young lady. When they rose from the dining room table Renee led me to my room and I lay down on my bed. I was awake again at 5 AM and changed into my pajamas, and went back into the bed. I hated wearing anything to bed and usually slept nude. Since my pain in the lower back and left leg was more frequently occurring I was afraid there would come a day when I couldn't get out of bed. Hence I wore pajamas. I awoke at 8:00 A.M fully pain free. So it was off to the practice field. On my way I did not want to disturb Renee at her piano practice. I fed at the breakfast buffet and 30 minutes later was on the practice range. The first 30 balls with the 9-iron, 7-iron, and 5-irons were pain free but as I started to strike balls with the 3-iron the pain in the lower back returned This pain led me to quit hitting shots as I was unable to walk properly let alone strike a golf ball. I retreated back to the house leaving the balls on the practice field. I went up to my room and lay down. Despite the pain and discomfort I dozed off until it was time for the buffet lunch. I was still in moderate discomfort as I went downstairs for the buffet. Renee and Hugh and Margaret were sitting at the dining table. They gave me a look of concern. "What is the matter dear?" Margaret asked.

"I guess maybe I should have laid off on my practice," I replied. "I was in no pain when I got up." I will take it easy for the rest of today, Maybe I will take tomorrow off and go ahead with it the next day after that." Two days later I was ready to resume working on my golf swing. I was in no pain but it started again after 25 shots and I was forced to quit hitting balls. I rested for two more days, but during this interval I noticed an excruciating and frequently recurring pain in my left calf. Sometimes it was so severe in would cause me to double up. Finally after two more days I decided I had enough. I went down stairs for breakfast and saw Margaret, Hugh and Renee at the table. "I want you to make Bob an appointment to see my doctor he told Margaret." At 2:00 PM Hugh drove me to see Hugh's family physician in Richmond Hill, a Doctor Phillip Maclean, MD.

"Your leg is turning blue," Maclean commented as he told me the obvious. "How could an 18 year old boy have such a condition?" Dr. Maclean kept pawing the left my leg. "I want you to see an orthopedic surgeon friend of mine in Toronto," he said as he wrote some information on a paper. He handed the paper to Hugh Watson. "Wait in the reception room for a few minutes and my receptionist will get you an appointment." He turned to Hugh Watson and said, "We will take good care of your son." While waiting. Hugh and I sat for about 15 minutes on separate chairs. The receptionist came out of her office and approached Hugh Watson. Here is your appointment. It was for three weeks later. The office was in North Toronto.

"Hmm," Dr. Fallov, the orthopedic surgeon commenced, "this leg is bad. Why didn't you come here at an earlier time. We might have to operate. This leg requires immediate attention."

I thought: "why not wait another week and the leg will 'Fallov'"

I endeavored to explain to the surgeon that my pain was growing steadily worse each day and the leg bluer. I explained that I had tried three times to reschedule the appointment earlier but Fallov's receptionist cackled: "I am sorry but Dr. Fallov has a very busy schedule. He just can't change his schedule to please the patients!" The surgeon, with the strange name of "Dr. Fallov" seemed uninterested in what I had to say. Instead, he continued on, in a pompous manner, because he believed that God had ordained him with infallible judgment. The surgeon went on with his talk. "You have some sort of nerve disease in the lower leg. If it gets any worse we may have to amputate. I am scheduling you at the Brantwood Hospital for the date marked on the card I am giving you today. We want to observe this condition."

I thought, "Well you can observe it long enough until it's too late to do anything but amputate?" I managed to slip on my pants in the examining room. "May I have my file?" I asked Dr. Fallov.

"Off course not," Fallov answered, "We don't give patients their files. That's unheard of. Imagine, a patient wanting to see his records. I decide what's best for you." So we all have free will according to the Divine Law unless the doctors decide otherwise.

I, in discomfort, got into the De Soto with Hugh Watson and started to drive down Yonge Street towards the Brantwood Hospital. In a very short distance I said a silent prayer. "Beloved Jesus, heal what ails me." I glanced out the window and saw a sign: "Dr. Theo van Damm, DC., Specialist in Pain Management." I asked Hugh Watson to park the De Soto in front of the office entrance. I entered the office and asked the receptionist: "what type of Doctor's office is this?"

"A clean one," she answered. "Doctor van Damm can see you right now, he just had a cancellation. Go into the examining room." There was no one in the office. I paced around the room for a moment. A plump gentleman entered the office from different door than I entered the room.

"Young man," he said, "You have a serious back problem. I want to X-ray your lower back." Dr. Van Damm was observing me through a one way window from another room. I was escorted to an X-ray machine in an adjacent office. Dr. van Damm asked him to lie on a table near the X-ray machine and took two pictures of my back. "Wait a few minutes while I develop these pictures," the rotund man said. "Wait in my office."

After about five minutes of waiting the Doctor returned with two large celluloid positives of the X-rays. He placed them on a viewing screen and beckoned me to come over and see the screen. "You have twisted your spine and it has been moved about one half of an inch towards the left. It is pinching your sciatic nerve. You must have terrible pain in your left leg. I can fix this fairly rapidly. Do you have 20 minutes right now? I agreed to let van Damm work on me. He showed me how the spine was pinching the nerve. Van Damm did some sort of manipulations on my back then took one more X-ray. Dr. van Damm returned to the examination room in five minutes. Van Damm attached an electrical device to my left leg at the top of the leg and at the ankle. A current was passed through the leg. After a few minutes I was detached from the electrical machine. "How often does the pain shoot through the left leg?"

"About once every half hour," I answered.

"The pain will recede and occur about once an hour, then in a day or two, about once in two hours, then in another day about twice in a day, and then in about 10 days completely disappear. I need to see you tomorrow and for the next 10 days to continue to regenerate the sciatic nerve. Would you write down a description of how you came about this back pain, when the leg pain started, and what your medical doctors wanted to do about it."

I followed through for 10 days of treatment. Each day Dr. Van Damm checked my back then used the electrical device. There was no treatment on Sunday so the Doctor could attend Church. I presented him with an account of my adventures with Drs. Maclean and Fallov after the end of the tenth visit. Dr. Van Damm read it slowly. He turned to me and started to tell a story.

"An American soldier serving in Japan during the occupation in

1948 had developed a severe problem with his penis. He went to the army doctors but they wanted to amputate his member. Finally in desperation he went to a Japanese doctor. The doctor examined the soldier's penis and shook his head. 'What do your 'Amelican' doctors want to do?' he asked. 'They want to amputate,' the soldier replied. 'Amelican doctors, Amelican doctors' the Japanese doctor exclaimed, 'always want to operate, you wait three weeks and it fall off.'"

And so I didn't need an extensive amputation to save my blue leg. I often wondered how an amputation could save the leg. All these things do is create medical waste. It game me great pleasure to cancer future appointments in the hospital. But I began to look into alternative medicine carefully. After Dr. Van Damm's treatment was over I did not trust M.D.s any longer. I began to grow suspicious of inoculations when various people told me those shots ruined their health. Margaret Watson, for example, three weeks after Dr. Maclean insisted she have a shot to prevent flu developed some sort of illness. Her hands trembled. This occurred during the previous Autumn. There was a lot of hassling from Dr. Fallov's office about why I was not having surgery. "The disease in the leg could spread to the entire body, he screamed over the telephone. "The leg might have to be amputated." I felt I should not reveal the name of Van Damm lest I create a problem for the chiropractor. I began to suspect that if Louis Pasteur were to return to Earth and healed the sick the Medical Association would attempt to have him arrested for practicing medicine without a license. So did I feel that they would also condemn Jesus Christ for healing without a medical licence.

I kept in contact with Dr. Van Damm over the next few years. Van Damm had many high level patients: high ranking military officers, politicians and other noted medical practitioners. Yet he was continually hassled by the Medical Association. An article appeared in the Toronto Comet concerning a former patient that accused him of harming her with his brutal treatments. This was verified by certain medical doctors, among them Dr. Fallov, who upon examination of that lady, several weeks after her treatment from Van Damm proclaimed that the chiropractor had done her serious harm. "Such quacks should be put out of business," he pronounced. Actually the lady was in good health and wanted to sue Dr.Van Damm to make money via a law suit. A shady lawyer was hired to pursue the case but two M.D.s who were patients of Van Damm vouched for him because they needed Van Damm for personal problems they suffered from. Such is medical ethics.

Dr. Van Damm commented that I had a marking on his lower spine that looked similar to a healed up entry wound from a bullet. He told me never to hit more than 50 balls before I played. There was a chance I could re injure the back. Of course, I had no way of practicing for any long period of time. I noticed I was sore after hitting slightly more than 30 balls. I could still hit putts, chips and pitches but no more than 50 of those in any one interval. As I played that summer my handicap rose from 0 to 2 and my length off the tee with a driver did not increase but dropped to an average length of 235 yards. Not good enough to ever make it as a professional tournament golfer. I needed a new profession. I would never be satisfied as a "run of the mill player." Earning money was not a major consideration in choosing a vocation. It had to be something that interested me, made me happy, and was worthwhile doing. It had to be something of benefit to everyone I had to be excellent at my work. But what was it to be? What type of vocation would a "control freak" turn towards.

So one day in July, 1950 Hugh Watson drove me to the Glen Echo Loop. I was attired in my blue suit, had on a lighter blue shirt, and decent dark socks, and black shoes. I was dressed like the epitome of a young business man. I rode the Yonge trolley down to St. Clair Avenue to the RCAF recruiting office on St. Clair Avenue near Yonge Street. I was 18 and one half years old, didn't wear spectacles and other than my recent back injury which was now giving me no trouble, was intent on joining up. I carried with me a transcript from the Department of Education showing my Grade 13 Provincial Examination results from the examinations written in the months of June of 1948 and 1949. It showed nine firsts had been earned. I had sat the examinations in English Literature and Composition, Chemistry, Physics, Trigonometry, Algebra, Analytical Geometry, and Spanish Composition and Literature. There was no indication on what my actual numerical rank was in any subject, just an indication that I had firsts. I had left Willington Academy a bit over a year ago. I also carried a birth certificate with me. I also had a passport I acquired with the assistance of Walter Abercromby K.C.

The Flight Sergeant at the counter gave me a basic application to fill in. Then I went to a quiet small room behind the recruiting counter and wrote some type of intelligence test that I was allowed one hour to complete and then taken out to the front of the RCAF office again. I sat there for 15 minutes when the Flight Sergeant, a man named Fraser, walked over to me.

"Mr. Noble," the Flight Sergeant began, "you show on your tests a high ability to learn. Would you be willing to undergo a medical examination this afternoon?" I was pleased to be called "Mister." So I was sent up Avenue Road to a medical building at 2:00 PM for a medical. I had about one hour to wait so I stopped in at a book shop about a block from the building and perused the occult section of the store. I picked up a copy of something written by Emmanuel Swedenborg, originally written in Swedish, but translated into English. The book looked interesting so I purchased it after I had read several pages. I then left the book shop and headed back to the medical office for my 2:00 PM appointment.

"Dr. Conner will see you now," the medical receptionist stated. It was exactly 2:00 PM. It was the most prompt and well-kept appointment ever kept by any medical doctor or dentist I ever had. Oddly enough, there were no other patients in the office. But even with no other patients in an office waiting to see the medical professional these appointments were usually one half to one hour late in being fulfilled! "The doctor is busy," was often the excuse. I thought, "Busy with what?" Dr. Conner was still in his 20's.

"You are Robert MacAlpine Noble?" he asked.

"I am," I replied.

"I have to give you a comprehensive medical. Flight Sergeant Fraser informs me that you are a good candidate to train as an Observer. So let's get started." So with that the comprehensive examination began. The doctor performed the usual checks of blood pressure, heart, eyesight with extensive tests of color vision and everything else. I had never undergone these tests earlier with any other physician. The examination took over an hour. After I dressed myself, Doctor Conner entered the examination room. "You'll do," he pronounced. He signed some documents, sealed them in a large envelop and gave them to me. Take these back to Flight Sergeant Fraser as soon as you can.

"Are you a regular doctor for the RCAF?" I asked.

"I am a reserve medical officer, I entered as a Flight Lieutenant," Dr. Connor said. "I needed funding after completing pre-med school and the first year medicine at the University of Toronto. The RCAF paid my way, gave me a living allowance and bought my books. For this I return the favor by serving in the Reserve. Performing these examinations is a small task for the help they gave me. They even paid me at university. Besides, I am early in my medical practice. These examinations are helping set me up in private practice."

One part of the eye test was to test for visual clarity conducted by having me read eye charts. This gave me no difficulty. But to me the world was always flat. Each eye when used together did not reach a central point of fixation. One eye looked slightly in a certain direction when sighting over a long distance and the other eye in a different direction. I was slightly cross eyed. I judged distance by switching from one eye to the other, many times per second, when viewing. This gave me a semi feeling for depth I could not gain any other way. In 1956, I would discover this problem when visiting a highly skilled ophthalmologist. Had the RCAF been more astute they would have rejected me as a flight cadet. I made the half mile walk back to the recruiting depot. My birth certificate and grade 13 exam results were still at the recruiting office. Only the receptionist was in the office. I turned the envelope from Dr. Conner over to her. I was ordered to remain in the office. So I sat down and began to read a current copy of *Air Force Monthly.*

CHAPTER 30

The Flight Cadet

When Flight Sergeant Fraser returned to the recruiting office he received the medical reports from the Receptionist who was standing behind the counter. The woman was a civilian. The Receptionist had photo-stated my papers. They were returned to me.

"Mr. Noble," the Flight Sergeant began, "Are you available in early September to report to our Station at Aylmer, Ontario to begin your initial training. The details are in this envelop." I received an open brown manila envelope. "If you haven't the means of transport to Aylmer, we will provide it. Are you married sir?" This last question caught me off guard. "We can't accept a recruit for flight cadet training for observer or pilot unless there are exceptional conditions, if he is married. I am going to send you home now and want you to go over the material in this envelop. Call me on the private telephone listed on the 'orientation page' if there are any questions."

I left the recruiting office, walked over to Yonge Street and hopped on a Yonge Street car that was heading north to the Glen Echo loop. The construction of the new Union Station to Eglinton subway was causing some havoc with the downtown street car traffic. Peter Witt trolley cars and trailers had been diverted through residential areas while the main part of Yonge Street downtown was being torn up and then covered over with heavy wooden planking. The trolleys still ran and were not replaced with motor buses such was the respect the TTC had for its originally purchased new street cars: the large Peter Witts.

They had carried riders up and down Yonge Street for nearly 30 years! I had purchased a Toronto Comet to read while the trolley journeyed north towards Glen Echo. There was an interesting item in the paper describing how horse bones over 10 000 years old were discovered under the old paving on Yonge Street in the downtown area during recent excavations for the subway. It certainly disproved claims that wild horses originated in North America from the early Spanish explorers who brought them from Europe. I had called Margaret and left a message for Hugh to retrieve me at the Glen Echo Loop. It was only a little after 3:00 PM. No real rush hour traffic would begin until after 4:30 PM. Hugh was waiting at the Loop. We walked south on Yonge Street one block to where the car was parked and got inside. Hugh drove.

"I've joined the RCAF!" I declared. Hugh said nothing. We motored in the now aging De Soto north to The Farm. The body of the car was still rust-free. The car's interior body parts were sprayed with oil by Hugh every year to prevent corrosion. The car still looked immaculate. Hugh handed me a letter from a realty company, I. J. Baird Developments, Inc. This Corporation wanted to purchase The Farm from me. Walter Abercromby was the final authority over any sale of property that I inherited until I reached the age of 21. The realty development company was offering slightly over $1 000 000 for the property!

"I don't want to sell. It's the only place I have ever lived in where I felt happy. Wild horses are not going to make me sell. Where else would I live? I didn't consider the fact that I might be residing off The Farm while in RCAF service. Where would you and Margaret live? Where would my brother and sister live?"

We arrived at The Farm. I had remained a silent passenger in the De Soto for the last three quarters of the time it took to complete the journey to The Farm. I was depressed over the thought of selling something I treasured. I naively believed the developer could buy my property out from under me because I was a minor. I called Walter Abercromby KC after I reached The Farm. Walter Abercromby answered the call immediately.

"Do I have to sell my Farm?" I asked.

"Not if you don't want to. You know sir," Abercromby continued,

"Your Farm and the buildings and the house were all purchased and constructed for Major Duncan before the War. The whole shebang cost him $55 000. It cost another $25 000 to furnish it. The current lease fees earned on it pay the taxes. Income from your estate support Hugh and Margaret as well as you and your siblings. The Watsons have looked after it for many years. An appliance manufacturing concern had leased 10 acres of land at the rear of the property. They erected a storage facility and operate a warehouse there. They paid $50 000 in rent per annum. This was for the grounds alone. The warehouse is not your property. With the income from your money you never need to worry about maintaining the place."

I, while only half listening to Abercromby; replied, "I do not care, it is not for sale."

"Terrific," replied Abercromby and he hung up.

I spread out the contents of the package I received from Flight Sergeant Fraser on the library desk. Hugh and Margaret had joined me I examined one document that informed me that I had been selected as a flight cadet and would be sent to Winnipeg, Manitoba if I was successful in the first three months of training at Aylmer, Ontario. An "Observer" was the title given to an RCAF officer who had his wings and successfully completed training as an officer and was a skilled navigator and administrator. In the US Air Force they called them "navigators." It would take one year for me to be commissioned a Pilot Officer and a second additional year for me to win my wings. There was a document explaining that my initial commission called a "Short Service Commission" and was to be approximately four and one half years long from the time I fully entered the service. After that I would stay in the service with a promotion to Flying Officer if I was deemed suitable as an officer.

Other documents informed me what to wear when I reported for initial duty just after Labor Day. I asked Hugh if he would be willing to chauffeur me to Aylmer, a possible journey requiring about four hours from The Farm. Hugh decided we would leave Monday afternoon. There were other papers to sign and certain things to relay back to Flight Sergeant Fraser. These were hand delivered to the Recruiting

Station later that week. Final arrangements had been competed in about 10 days. Hugh located a small hotel in St. Thomas, Ontario a few miles west of Aylmer that could accommodate Renee, me, Hugh and Margaret overnight if we arrived on Labor Day. We could drive to Aylmer the next morning in less than 20 minutes.

There were several days left before I was to report to Aylmer. I had some additional contact with Flight Sergeant Fraser. Fraser had been a gunner on a Lancaster Bomber during the final two years of the War. He had only attended school to the age of 16 years when he left to work on the family farm. He was an above average student but the excitement of the War fascinated him. He was from Jarvis, Ontario. In June 1943, he joined the RCAF when both parents passed on suddenly. Their passing occurred after he turned over the management of the farm to his older brother Jeff and Jeff's wife Elaine. They had two small children, both boys. Jeff had been refused by all three branches of the Canadian military because he suffered from a heart murmur. "No sweat," Jeff thought, "Now if ever it comes down to it I can't be drafted."

After completing the Gunnery course situated in his home town of Jarvis. Ontario, John Fraser was promoted to Sergeant and sent to England. This was in December 1943. He was 18 years old. He was assigned to an RCAF Lancaster squadron and served a full tour of duty from late January 1944 to December1944. He was awarded a DFM for assisting to fly his badly damaged Lancaster back to its base in England when the pilot and co-pilot were seriously injured by flak. His plane crashed upon attempting a landing but every crew member survived without further serious injury. There was no fire in the aircraft; that was the danger that all allied aircrews were prone to experience because of the high flammable nature of aviation fuel. This occurred in a raid over Europe in late 1944. He spent the remainder of the War helping to train gunners. When the War ended he was a WO1. He stayed on in the RCAF with a reduced rank of sergeant after the war, but first went to Rehab School in Toronto to complete his Junior Matric. He did this in 10 months and entered the RCAF a second time in June, 1946. He regained his former rank as flight sergeant in 1950. Fraser intended to serve for another 14 years and then retire and pursue some other line of work. By that time he would have 20 years of service. He didn't run around much and lived a frugal life saving his pay. He often thought about owning a sporting goods store. He even entertained thoughts of settling down on a permanent basis in Jarvis, Ontario.

On a clear and sunny day, a Tuesday, right after Labor Day in September, 1951, in the morning at 8:30 AM, I was a slim 5'10", 150 pound young man who in my own evaluation of himself had failed as a professional golfer was off on another venture. I, Robert MacAlpine Noble, still undecided about who I was, what I was doing on the Earth and what purpose my Life served to that very point in Time. I hugged Hugh, kissed Margaret on the cheek and began my formal entry into the RCAF. An RCAF corporal explained to Hugh and Margaret Watson that it was best to leave me to my own devices. I talked for a few moments to Renee.

"I am at a loss to explain why I am doing this," I began, as I looked at Renee. "Maybe this is right for me? I will contact you as soon as I am settled in and give you my address." I turned away from Renee after she kissed me on the lips. Every other cadet was watching from the side of the large room where formal indoctrination was to go on. There were also rude remarks cast my way by the new recruits.

"Over there," the corporal pointed. "Take your bag and wait over there." A large WO2, over six feet tall and over 200 pounds was standing in front of the group of 30 flight cadets, all not uniformed, while they waited. I was the last to join the line. When I had joined the group the WO2 raised the clipboard he was holding and began to call the roll. "Answer Warrant Officer," if you are here," he ordered. After roll call the group was taken to a special stores unit where they were outfitted with training uniforms. There were four duty shirts, a winter uniform, similar to that worn by the other ranks, a field hat, a pair of black boots, many pairs of Air Force blue hose, two ties, and two gym outfits. "You gentlemen are going to sweat a lot over the next three months," the WO2 said as the 30 candidates were lined up neatly in two rows of 15 outside the stores building. "If you survive the three months you will have a uniform allowance. This will provide you funds to visit a good tailor we will inform you about. You will be provided with funds for uniforms suitable for potential officers of the Royal Canadian Air Force, in other words they will fit. The successful candidates among you will be sent to navigation school in Winnipeg."

I was surprised when all 30 candidates were bunked two to a room. I figured out that our quarters were possibly used by officers in the service during World War II. Each room had a separate water closet, sink, and shower. I had expected the type of barracks room I had seen in so many of the World War II depictions in the movies. Revelry was at 6:30 AM rather than 5:00 AM so lovingly illustrated as the sleeping situation of the US Marine Corps "boots." I was shown where to store my bag. I knew how to properly make my bunk from my time at Camp Young People. At least those commies had shown me how to make a bunk.

"Flight Cadet Noble has his bunk made up properly," the WO2 screamed to the Sergeant accompanying him as he began his inspection of the flight cadets' quarters. The first room he stopped at was mine. I seemed to be the only cadet in the room when another Flight Cadet, a young man of about 20 years entered the room. The WO2 looked at the arriving cadet and turned to me. "This is Flight Cadet 'Albert S. Barker.' He is a graduate of Prince of Wales College in P.E.I. He was late arriving because his parents' car had a flat tire near St. Thomas, Ontario. You will instruct him on where to put his gear and how to make his bunk." The WO2 saluted me and turned smartly and faced the Barkert as the NCO started to leave the room. I returned the salute, and so did Flight Cadet Barker. The WO2 caught a glimpse of the salutes. He turned around. "Never return a salute out of uniform and without your cap on, you fucking sons of a bitch, - sirs!" There was a pause of a few seconds before the WO2 said "sirs." As I was soon to learn all training personnel such as the sergeant and WO2, no matter how senior their rank had to address all flight cadets with the title "sir." This "sir" was always included along with some vile profanity.

"Jeez," Flight Cadet Barker commented, "I was an Air Cadet for three years during high school. I should have remembered how to and when to salute. I can make the bunk but check it anyway to see if it's done right." Barker was typically from the Maritimes. His accent gave him away. There are three major Canadian accents: that of the United Empire Loyalist, this was the way I spoke; the Western Canadian: and the Maritime. It was plain to me that Albert S. Barker was from the Maritimes. The "S" in his name stood for "Something," a name given by his parents because they could come not up with anything else. It was meaningless like the "S" in Harry S. Truman the current USA President. Albert's parents had a wry sense of humor. Albert's father started out running a chain of three precursors to what would become typical supermarkets. The three stores were all successful and serviced P.E.I. and the small city of Charlottetown well. They were planning a large market in Somerset an even smaller city in P.E.I. Barker's enterprise would produce a fortune for the family, which would by the year 2015, number in the billions of dollars. Albert wanted no part of the family business. After graduating from Prince of Wales College at 18 years he worked for his dad for one year. He signed up for training as a flight cadet at almost the same time as me. He flew in on a Trans- Canada flight from Charlottetown which stopped in Montreal first and then proceeded to Toronto. The plane was a DC3.

"That damned thing flapped its wings to get here," Albert S. Barker commented, "but I made it." Albert's aunt and uncle who lived in Toronto had made arrangements to bring him to Aylmer. Albert had apparently done well at Prince of Wales College earning first class honors in all of his subjects. P.E.I. had no grade 13. Completing grade 12 there was similar to grade 13 at Willington.

There is no end to bullshit. Cadets were to rise at 06:30 and shower and shave. Then they did almost one hour of rigorous Physical Training including a 25 minute run outside their quarters if the weather permitted. This entire physical education training ran from 06:40 to 07:30 hours. Of course the showers they had partaken of at about 06:30 hours were rendered useless by the end of the morning PT session. Albert approached the WO2 in charge of the quarters. Albert suggested it might be more advantageous to shower and shave after the morning physical training session. The flight cadets would then be fresh and clean for the remainder of the day.

"Get the fuck out my office, sir," the WO2 screamed at Albert. "The

RCAF has thought long and seriously about these training programs." Oddly, two days after Albert visited the WO2's office, a bulletin was posted on the common room of the flight cadet's quarters explaining that all cadets had the right to shower after morning physical training. They were allowed 30 minutes to do this. The very early morning showers were to be eliminated. Score one for Flight Cadet A. S. Barker.

The afternoon classes were filled with instruction. This included some interesting history of the RCAF: its contributions to the Allied War Effort in World War II, some detailed sketches of Canadian RCAF war heroes; and how to behave as an officer. It also included one hour of drill instruction marching around the indoor gym located in the center of the flight cadets' quarters. During favorable weather parades were held outside. Very little was mentioned about actual flying. The food was served in a cafeteria so I could select dishes which fitted my decision to become over the remainder of the year more a vegetarian. There were also several films dating from WW II about venereal diseases and how to be cautious and avoid them. On film the lectures were always delivered by some unctuous officer with an RAF moustache who held usually held the rank of squadron leader or wing commander. Usually that officer wore no wings. I assumed he was a medical officer. Cadets from Quebec who were not sufficiently capable in English were billeted with Cadets from predominately English speaking parts of Canada.

Time went fast. Three months had nearly passed but no flight cadet had been granted a leave from their quarters. They had not even visited the nearby town of Aylmer. I had come to notice that the total number of flight cadets had dwindled somewhat. It was down to 22 by the time two months passed. This I deduced from the four unoccupied rooms in the 15 unit building. When someone left the program roommates were juggled around so that there were always two per room unless there were an odd number of cadets. After two months there were no dropouts. Then the last day of training at Aylmer came. Albert S. Barker was still around and so was I. On the last day of basic training after washing and showering up the cadets lined up in parade formation in the gym.

"Today is the final day of training for all flight cadets attached to this group," the WO2 commented. For once he didn't shout. "Your gear must be packed at the end of instruction at 14:00 hours. You will remain in your uniforms. There will be some final instruction. There is to be a formal affair and dinner tonight in the officers' mess at 17:30 hours. When that is done you will rise tomorrow at 06:00 hours, clean up and prepare for transport to Winnipeg, Manitoba to begin your training as air navigators. I have enjoyed training what's left of you. Transport will be by Dakota, two such air craft will be provided."

Most of the instruction consisted of orientation of what to expect once the cadets settled down in Winnipeg. This was given by a Squadron Leader Chester, who was second in Command of the basic flying school. Chester was a Bomber pilot during World War II. He had eight medals from his war service including a DFC and ED. Chester, after a full tour of duty piloting a Lancaster, was funneled back to Canada in mid-1944 to head up a training command under the British Commonwealth Air Training Plan. He was relieved to be out of the dangers of night bombing raids. A buffet banquet was served along with copious quantities of hard liquor. Most of the flight cadets were under the legal drinking age of 21. Such is rigorous discipline! I spoke with Squadron Leader Chester for several minutes after Chester had sat down beside me at the dinner table. Chester invited Albert Barker and me to each sit on the one side of him. Chester began to speak

"A lot of people think that pilots are the glamour people of this air force. Well that is bull shit. Let me tell you what I think. One night, when we were bombing Calais, we ran into some heavy resistance from night fighters. The squadron split up and ran for England. As a pilot I would have been all over the sky. Our navigator got us home. On my own I probably would have landed in the Channel!" Squadron Leader Chester leaned back in his chair, took a sip of Scotch from a small glass and continued with his talk. "This navigator was 22 years old. He dropped out of the second year of mathematics, physics and chemistry at the University of Toronto to enroll in the British Commonwealth Air Training Plan. He asked for assignment to become a navigator. He saved my bloody life that evening."

"What became of him?" Albert asked.

"He died in a plane crash in February, 1945. His plane exploded on landing. God, what a tragic waste of a good young man! He was navigating a plane for someone else by then. After the War I called on his parents. They were from Toronto. The dad was an Orangeman. That boy could have gone places." Chester stood up. "I would like to offer a toast," he said. "Gentlemen, I salute this class of Flight Cadets, may they ever find their way." Squadron Leader Chester sat down. The entire dinner party applauded.

Navigation school was fairly academic. After one year as flight cadets Albert and I were to be commissioned pilot officers. I had invited Agnes, Hugh and Margaret Watson to the Commissioning Ceremony. I was to pay the expenses for the three days hiatus. If Renee was available she was to come as well. Only the Watsons showed up. Agnes did not want to be dragged into "igloo country." Renee was engaged with the RBC with recording sessions. In early September 1951, I was almost 20 years old and my friend Albert S. Barker and 20 other flight cadets were commissioned Pilot Officers. We had become the "lowest of the low."

While I was sitting on the makeshift stage in a makeshift auditorium that doubled as a gym I spotted a senior NCO seated in the second row of spectators. It was Flight Sergeant John Fraser. After the ceremonies I invited Flight Sergeant Fraser to join me and the Watsons at our dinner table. Fraser accepted.

"I dropped by to see some of the Flight Cadets I recruited. There are five of them. It makes me feel good when someone I recruited makes it as far as you have. Your CO tells me you are at the head of your class," the Flight Sergeant remarked. "I hope to be there when you earn your wings. I am going to stay in the Service. I am up for promotion in another two years."

Time passed quickly. Of course there were endless administrative duties to be performed by the "lowest of the low." Another year in the RCAF was coming to a close. One navigation problem, a trick problem, was asked by the instructors of the observer candidates. It went like this: "A pilot wants to fly on a course of 330. His airspeed in still air is 300 knots. He has a head wind of 60 knots coming on a course of 110. What is his final speed on his desired course of 330 and what course must he fly to achieve it?" I knew how to solve it and so did Albert Barker.

It was a splendid moment of Triumph for both potential observers. See Appendix 1. In all, 14 observers graduated. Those who did not get their wings were reassigned to train in air traffic control. The successful candidates were posted all over Canada. Some candidates were posted to Europe. Albert Barker and I were assigned to instructor duties.

One of the great thrills for graduating flight cadets is the "Wings Parade." A high ranking RCAF officer presents these wings. The ceremony was held in the large hangar of the station. A temporary stage was constructed with a public address system. Pilot Officer Barker's parents were there accompanied by a young lady who was Barker's fiancé. A small band of seven musicians played "God Save the King," then the "Royal Air Force March Past." There were 14 candidates who received wings. Thirty candidates had begun the program at Aylmer almost two years earlier. I had no kin attending the wings parade. Hugh and Margaret Watson were present but Agnes did not attend. "It's too cold up there," she remarked. Renee was busy recording Beethoven for RBC. All the newly winged observers received a set of five wings. Two for use with two winter uniforms, one for the summer uniform, one for the dress uniform and one for their flying suits. I would keep all my uniforms after I left the service.

CHAPTER 31

My Final Military Flight

I n mid- December, 1954 a training flight for four flight cadets in basic air navigation started out from Cold Lake, Manitoba and steered on course 350. On board was the pilot of the North Star, Flight Lieutenant Beery. He was the commander of the aircraft, Flying Officer North, an experienced aviator but a trainee learning to handle the North Star, four flight cadets, all training to be observers, Pilot Officer Albert S. Barker, and me. Barker and I now had early two and one half years of service on active duty since we received our wings. We were teaching flight cadets making their first flight. We were navigation instructors. It wasn't our first flight. We didn't mind doing the in air training our service provided but the endless and boring administrative duties were dulling my interests in the RCAF.

After about 30 minutes out from RCAF Station Cold Lake the first hint of trouble became apparent as the power dropped rapidly from one engine, the outermost starboard engine of the North Star, a four engines DC4 conversion. This conversion had Rolls Royce inline engines installed replacing the radial engines the Douglas DC4 usually had. The four Merlins produced 1700 HP each about 300 HP more than each radial. This re-engined craft could out range and out speed the original design by a considerable margin. The top speed rose by nearly 60 miles per hour. This aircraft was unique to Canadian Flying. The machine could manage to stay up under three engines provided the power on those engines was at a maximum. The three Merlins had a total power nearly equal to that of the four radials. It was decided by Flight Lieutenant Beery to return to Cold Lake.

The North Star did an 180⁰ turn onto course 170 which would carry it back to Cold Lake. If we were off radar Beery would steer us on a correct course until we came in range of the station's radar system. But the North Star, at an altitude of 5 000 feet and being airborne for 60 minutes was out of radar's range. It had flown nearly 200 miles from Cold Lake. To get in radar range it would have to climb several thousand feet or fly closer to the station. Climbing was out of the question. Flight Lieutenant Beery, an experienced pilot with over 10 years of multiple engine time, decided a return to Cold Lake was the best strategy.

I took over the radio and gave the approximate position when the 180° turn was completed. The damaged engine ultimately lost all power and Beery feathered the propeller to reduce drag on the North Star. The North Star was going to make it back to base so we all thought. Then the ultimate catastrophe happened. The original engine failure was on the starboard side of the North Star. Then the second engine on the starboard wing started to lose power. Slowly the Rolls Royce Merlin dropped in RPM. If we lost this this engine the craft would no longer be able to maintain attitude. It would ultimately come down. It was still 25 minutes out of Cold Lake. The North Star had descended to 2000 feet.

"There is no fucking way this shit box can get back to Cold Lake," Flight Lieutenant Beery announced over the North Star's PA system. "I'll try to get as close to the base as possible. Pilot Officer Noble is in charge in the back. He will prepare you to crash land." A crash landing was something I never experienced. True, there was training for that eventuality but this was the real thing coming up.

The North Star was down to 1500 feet when the crew knew it could not possibly reach Cold Lake. There was some bush where they figured the aircraft would come down. We knew area was frequented by fur trappers. We had now reached radar contact with the base. A second engine was feathered. It had malfunctioned. The craft was difficult to maneuver. All the thrust came from the port side making the craft yaw. The crew in the rear of the plane had strapped themselves into their seats. These were no regular passenger type chairs. These had been removed and replaced with radar sets and other navigational equipment. I made certain the four flight cadets were as secure as they could be in case a crash landing occurred but the seats were facing the sides of the North Star. Only the pilots would face along the direction of the Craft's path as it crashed. I wondered if the cadets would remain in their seats at impact or be tossed about during the upcoming rough landing. I would soon find out. A final estimate of our position was determined by me in the last five minutes of flight. I informed Flight Lieutenant Beery and took my position at one of the navigation instructors' posts. I figured we were less than 10 minutes from Cold Lake when the North Star went down.

The craft fortunately landed in a clear area free of trees, skidded for several seconds and came to a sudden stop as fresh fallen snow piled up in front of wings and fuselage. Beery had switched off the two engines that were running just before impact. I had radioed Cold Lake and given my estimated position at the last possible moment. When the North Star stopped everything around was white. I was the first to get out of my seat. One wing of the North Star had severed off from the fuselage of the craft. There was an odor of aviation fuel hanging in the air. Fortunately there was no wind or the conditions would have been impossible to survive in. The outside thermometer, still intact indicated at temperature of -5° Fahrenheit. I went to the cockpit to check on the pilots. They both had extensive injuries. It appeared that Beery had a broken leg as his lower right leg had a zigzag appearance. The copilot, Flying Officer North had serious injuries to his face when loose debris flew about during the crash had injured him. I seemed to be unharmed. The four flight cadets were unharmed but very close to a state of panic. Everybody seemed to be alive until I checked on Albert. He wasn't moving. A loose piece of metal piping lying on the fuselage deck had been hurled from behind Albert during the crash and penetrated his upper neck. The pipe severed part of the upper spine and carotid artery. Albert had died instantly. I examined him for a few seconds.

"For shit's sake," I mumbled under my breath. I kept repeating it for several seconds, "for shit's sake." Albert's upcoming marriage was to take place at a local Anglican Church in Winnipeg in just four weeks.

Both the families of Anne Anders and Albert S. Barker were to attend. I was also invited. I had become Bert Barker's closest friend.

"We have got to get out of the airplane," I said. "It is full of fumes. Get the pilot and co-pilot out first and at least 200 feet from the craft. Put a splint on that broken leg. There is a stretcher on the wall and a first aid kit. Use it." The flight cadets put a splint on Beery's leg in short order. By great chance one cadet had taken extensive St. John's Ambulance Training. The orders from me prevented the cadets from panic. I saw to it that the other two cadets assisted even if they only looked on. The riders of the North Star had winter flying outfits on which ensured that they could last a few hours outside and possibly survive. They also wore lined thermal flight boots that were designed to keep the feet warm. Beery was removed to about 200 feet from the plane and then North joined him. Last to be removed was the corpse of Pilot Officer Barker. When all the members of the crew were at a safe distance I scouted the surrounding area. There was some bush about 50 feet further away. I discovered a trapper's cabin inside the bush not more than 250 feet from the crash. It was sensational luck. The door was padlocked. I returned to the wrecked North Star. More luck was with me. I found a crowbar in the airplane about two feet long. I retrieved it. The survivors of the crash struggled and carried the injured Flying Officer North and Flight Lieutenant Beery to the front of the fur trapper's cabin. I snapped the padlock off the door. The crowbar also deftly removed the apparatus the padlock was attached to. Everything had rusted to the point where the metal was almost too weak to resist any force. The padlock broke off easily. Three flight cadets moved the pilot and co-pilot into the cabin. Luck again prevailed. There was a stack of dry firewood and a wood burning stove inside the cabin.

"Get a fire started in that stove," I commanded. "We might as well be warm. Listen up everybody. We can't walk back to Cold Lake in this weather and I don't exactly know how far that is. We are going to wait it out in this cabin. We are lucky we got far from the plane. It could explode at any minute." As I was saying this there was a loud "poof like" sound. The North Star had burst into flames right near the end of my speech. The fireball could be seen from some distance. This utter destruction of the North Star was an Act of Providence. A search party was within a half mile of the reported position that I had relayed to Flight Lieutenant Beery. The rescue crew saw the glare from the fire and within a few minutes had located the burning wreckage. It took a little more time to locate the cabin which by that time had a fire going. The rescuers could see the glow coming from the fire in the cabin. The rescue crew had a track propelled rescue vehicle sufficiently large enough to carry all seven of the survivors. They were transported by the crew of the rescue vehicle to the halftrack and placed inside. There were two paramedical personnel and a trained driver. A total of 11 RCAF people including Albert's body, were taken back to Cold Lake. All the survivors of the North Star crash had made it to RCAF base Cold Lake, Manitoba. We waited only three hours to be rescued! The only fatality was Pilot Officer Albert S. Barker, aged 23 years, two months of Charlottetown, Prince Edward Island. I had left a printed message for the fur trapper in the cabin. It gave the contact number at Cold Lake. The trapper returned to use the cabin in mid-summer and was compensated for any damage to his property shortly after that.

My time in the RCAF would be up at the end of December, 1954, just after my 23rd birthday. I faced two choices. Resign my Short Service Commission or stay on in the Service. If I stayed on I would I be elevated in rank to Flying Officer and would possibly be assigned training duties for the entire term of four plus more years. After that I could remain in the service indefinitely reaching the rank of Flight Lieutenant with very little chance of another promotion. That was almost exclusively reserved for officers with university degrees preferably in engineering and science. The fastest promotions were reserved for graduates of one of three Canadian Military Colleges: the Royal Military College, College Militaire Royal de Saint Jean, or Royal Roads Military College. I considered instead, going to a civilian university. I had been out of a formal school atmosphere for over five years. I had applied to a new engineering school just starting out in south central Ontario: the University of Waterville. I asked for a four days leave in mid-December, 1954 to write some tests and present some credentials to the admissions committee of this new university. A course was to begin for pre year engineering students with no engineering specialization. It was to be run on the cooperative form of education where the year was divided into four almost equal time intervals. Two of these intervals, not in consecutive order, were devoted to studies and courses while the other two were dedicated to practical work in science and engineering.

I booked a hotel room in the local small city of Waterville, Ontario and arranged a berth on a DC 3 flying to RCAF Station Downsview the evening before. From there I arranged for Hugh Watson to meet me at the Station and drive me to Waterville. Hugh would have to wait until Friday at about 3:00 PM for me to have time to make arrangements to return to Cold Lake. I did not have to report for duty till 08:00 hours on Monday. I carried a formal letter of recommendation, that I had not even opened from the Station Commander, a transcript of my grade 13 exam results, my service record to date with the RCAF, and a description of my duties as an officer for the almost three and one half years I had been commissioned.

On Thursday morning in early December, I, 1954 finally arrived at the campus of the newly established University of Waterville. There were no permanent buildings erected, only portables. Hugh and I reported to a desk in a large, well maintained old factory building where many chairs and desks were set up. This was the only building I saw. I presented my letter from the university to the clerk sitting at the desk. I took a seat at the desk numbered "15." It had already been assigned to me some time earlier. There were about 40 other candidates already sitting at desks. There was room for about 20 more. Soon the room was completely filled. There were now about 10 men supervising the proceedings. One man approached a microphone at the front of the room.

"The tests you are about to write are to help us determine how successful you will be with engineering training. Personal interviews will be conducted with each of you by some of our staff as well. Everyone in this room has already been selected to start the course in mid- January, 1955."

Copies of the first test were delivered to all the applicants. They started working on them on a cue from the man at the microphone. Each test took about 30 minutes. There were six different tests given. With washroom breaks of 15 minutes, after each test the whole affair lasted over four hours. After the last test the candidates were allowed to attend a buffet lunch set up near one side of the test room. After that personal interviews were started in private cubicles surrounding the main room where the tests were conducted. Each interview took about 30 minutes and 10 university people were conducting them.

I sat on a bench waiting to be called for the interview. All types of technical material were lying on the bench. I didn't want to read any of it. When I was finally called for my interview it was conducted by a man in a tweed suit, neatly worn. The man smoked a pipe. "Do you mind if I smoke Mr. Noble?" I said I did. The man smiled and stowed his pipe on the large ash tray on his desk.

"I see that you are coming to the end of your initial term of service in the RCAF. According to the letter of recommendation it says you were a highly capable officer and already selected for promotion should you stay on. Are you going to?"

"Not if I am accepted here," I replied. "I have had enough of flying for a while. Cold Lake is very cold."

"How did you win the Air Force Cross?"

"I would rather not talk about it," I replied. I didn't have to. It was already explained in a letter from the Base Commander to the University brass. The interviewers had read this letter. Full details of my actions during and after the crash were documented and were read by the brass right up to the president of the new university. I was to become a civilian again.

The candidates were diverse in their backgrounds. One candidate was a certified Ontario Land Surveyor, another was a Great Lakes shipboard officer, another had been a tool and die maker. I would get to know all of them well. These future engineering students were all out in the work force for at least three years since they left secondary school. They would complete the five year program in about four and one half years and some would pursue graduate degrees. Some would achieve Ph. D's., all of them earned at reputable graduate schools. Little did any candidate realize that their school was to become famous worldwide for its quality and for the competence of its graduates.

Later, shortly after I returned to Cold Lake, the RCAF base

commander, Group Captain Jack Dutton DSO, DFC informed me that the RCAF could and would finance my five year program at the University of Waterville if I so desired. When I graduated I would be a Flying officer again in the RCAF but with two years credit in that rank and promoted to Flight Lieutenant in half the time it would take me without the university degree. I could arrange to have's my cooperative work experiences with the RCAF. That might count as another 18 months of military service and push me up the promotion ladder faster.

There was the visit I promised to make before I started at the University of Waterville in January 1955 to call on Anne Anders, who was the fiancé of Albert S. Barker in Prince Edward Island. I did not entirely anticipate this venture with joy.

I packed my uniforms and gear on my last day in the RCAF. The base commander covered for me and I packed my instruction manuals and navigation tools carefully. I had signed no agreement to be sponsored through the new University of Waterville. That would have committed me to three years compulsory service after graduation. I had arranged for a moving agent with a van to take my goods into Winnipeg. There they would be shipped by rail to The Farm. Being the type I was, former Flying Officer Noble, AFC, had discovered I was upped one rank the day before I resigned my commission. I quietly left the base at Cold Lake and made my way to Winnipeg in the GM van I had engaged. I smiled as I contemplated my almost unknown promotion. I was no longer the "lowest of the low." I had distinguished myself as a junior officer. I had been decorated by my Service, and I was completely lost as to what I wanted to do with the remainder of my life. I especially recalled the comment made to me by Flight Lieutenant Beery, who from his temporary wheel chair made an interesting remark to me just after I received my AFC. Berry said: "I'll fly with you anytime."

Two flights were necessary to fly me to P.E.I. I arrived at the Charlottetown Airport one hour late. I had sent advanced notice ahead to both the Barker and Anders Families stating my ETA. I figured that they would probably have gone home from the airport since I was an hour late. I was tired from all the travel and wished to lie down and go to sleep.

CHAPTER 32

The Barkers and the Anders

It was later December, in 1954, when I, a tired young man, deplaned from the Bristol Britannia that had transported me from Toronto, Ontario to Charlottetown P.E.I. My luggage had been removed from the turbo prop and wheeled into the building that constituted a passengers' receiving area and also doubled as an administrative area. There were five people waiting for me in the terminal: three women and two men. They were two older couples, each in what appeared to be their late 40's or early 50's. They approached me.

"Excuse me, young man, are you Pilot Officer Noble?" one of the men asked.

"Just Robert MacAlpine Noble, sir, no longer of the RCAF," I answered "I am sorry to be so late. It was, for a short time, Flying Officer Noble." It was typical of me to apologize was someone else's wrong doing; in this case Trans Canada Air Lines.

"Well, let me introduce myself. "I am Andrew Barker, Albert's father," the man answered. This is Albert's mother Helen Barker, his fiancé, Anne Anders, and her parents Peter and Jane Anders." I studied the five people present. They had waited for over one hour for the late arrival of the Britannia. They seemed poised and calm. Andrew Barker grabbed my luggage and our party left the small terminal. Mr. Barker owned a small Cadillac if there is such a thing. After loading my luggage into the trunk our group drove off. I shared the back seat with the Anders and his wife while the Cadillac made its way towards Charlottetown. It arrived at an approximate 3000 square foot two story dwelling in the downtown area of the small city.

"This is our humble abode," Mr. Barker commented. "You will stay with us tonight. We won't have it any other way!" They parked the Caddy in front of the main door and a servant came out to unload the trunk of the car. In the living room of the house a conversation developed about the crash of the North Star. Mr. Barker was especially anxious to discover if Albert had behaved well during the crash.

"He behaved as a good officer should," I responded, "With a calm and courageous manner worthy of all officers of the RCAF. His end was the result of an unlucky accident. He relayed messages to the station right up until the end. I want you to understand that I spent over four years with him through our initial training and through navigation school. We were both assigned as instructors after we won our wings. I did not happen to meet you at the wings parade. I noticed Mrs. Barker crying. I always felt strange when a woman started to weep. Agnes used to do this often when I lived with her. I still resented Agnes who had not accepted an all-expenses paid trip to Winnipeg where I was to receive my observer's wings. According to Agnes, "Winnipeg is a place not in Canada!" Nobody of my family was there, only Hugh and Margaret Watson. I considered the Watsons now my family.

"When do you have to report back to your station?" Mr. Anders asked finally breaking the silence he maintained since I was introduced to him. Albert's fiancé was silent throughout the conversation. She also appeared a bit lost by the conversation. I studied the fiancé for as few seconds. She was a petite woman in her early 20's, slim and attractive in her appearance with dark hair and the most beautiful blue eyes I had ever seen. Anne Anders had a different beauty than Renee. There was an air of peacefulness about both pairs of parents. After several moments I answered Mr. Anders question. "I am leaving the RCAF, or rather, I have already left it. In January I am starting my pre engineering course at the University of Waterville. It will take me four and one half years to complete it. I have had enough of flying for now."

"Albert had written me that you are a total vegetarian," Mrs. Barker said, as she engaged with me for the first time. "We have a buffet laid out in the dining room. Shall we go in there?" I thought it odd that where ever I was invited to dine my host always seem to prepare a special menu for me. It made me feel privileged. So we six people went into the dining room of the "modest" abode to eat. In talking with Andrew Barker it was revealed that it was only in the last 15 years of his life that he had any large success as a food retailer. He had been born originally in Toronto and he was the son of a professional baker but he moved with his family to P.E.I. to get a new start in life. They had only one child, who was Albert. Andrew Barker had been a hard worker all his life but he grew restless in Toronto and wanted to move to a quieter local. In a new development in Charlottetown he opened a little bakery. He poured his love into the venture. Within two years his debts in establishing his business were paid off. As is the secret in all successful ventures he looked to duplicate his venture but slowly and without expanding by going into debt. In two more years he had a second bakery but expanded this one into a small gourmet store specializing in gourmet food. He would make shopping trips to the surrounding farms to purchase special products. By the time he was 10 years in P.E.I. he had outgrown the two original bakeries and built a small plaza with 15 stores and some room for business offices that wished to locate there. Andrew Barker began to make it big in his early 30's. Now at 45 years he was one of the wealthiest men on the Island. But Albert was their only child. Mr. Anders, who I discovered, was a Family Physician located in Charlottetown, had been a friend of the Andrew Barker's since he settled on the island 24 years earlier with a young wife and child. It was Dr. Anders, he of Norwegian extraction, who assisted in the delivery of Andrew's first and only child: a male heir. Dr. Anders had told me that she could bear no further children. Albert was to be the first and the last.

Even if Andrew Barker wanted to stop accumulating wealth it was now being thrust upon him and he sensed a deeper understanding of how he must use it to make Canada and the world a more perfect place for people to live. He was not a philanthropist in the outer world sense.

He was no such being like the original John Davison Rockefeller who use to give away dimes. He had learned that true philanthropy was hidden from the outer world. When Andrew Barker gave; he gave in the Silence; "not letting the left hand know what the right hand was doing. Then the Heavenly Father who sees in secret shall reward thee."

I looked at Mr. Barker and said: "I will be leaving this area tomorrow afternoon at 2:00 PM and flying to Toronto. From there I want to set my affairs in order at The Farm. I will be starting pre engineering course at the University of Waterville. There are two elderly people who care for my place. If I give you my address and telephone so can we keep in touch."

Mr. Barker nodded his approval. "Why are you not staying in the Air Force?"

"I haven't made up my mind as to what I want to make of my life. I just turned 23 years old last December 1. I should know my life's work but I haven't a clue. At least I don't have to work for a living if I don't choose to." All five strangers to me looked at me strangely when I mentioned working. They didn't know why I didn't have to work for a living. Mr. Barker excused himself from the room and reappeared two minutes later. He had a small volume of English poetry in his hand which he passed over to me. There was a book mark in the volume.

"Young man, would you please read this piece I have located for you in this volume before you retire tonight. It might be helpful to you in finding your way." With that Mr. Barker handed the book to me. "Leave it on the bed when you are ready to go." The meeting went on for another two hours. I asked Dr. Anders why he had not introduced himself as a "doctor" when they were first introduced.

"'Doctor' is what I do for a living but it is not who I Am," he answered. "One time while I was playing golf with Andrew about five years ago we hooked up into a foursome with two young professionals. We all introduced ourselves. Well, I have forgotten their names but I remember the comment one of them made when I told them who I was. Of course I said I was 'Doctor Anders.' Never mind my first name. I was a 'doctor.' The young man said, 'my what an unusual first name! For what reason did your parents name you 'doctor?'" I got the message right then and there.

The word 'doctor' does not describe a title confirmed upon its holder like an earldom or knighthood. It merely means I work as a physician. It is time the medical professionals stopped thinking about themselves as people of royal stature and infallible judgment. Why if Jesus Christ would return to Earth this day and heal the sick he would quickly incur the wrath of the medical associations because he was unqualified, at least according to them. There is even a movement under way to have a law in PEI passed to not allow anyone other than a qualified MD to call himself a 'doctor.' The word 'doctor' means 'teacher.'" With that calm but intense dissertation the physician then put on his hat and coat and left the "modest" Barker residence with his spouse.

Andrew Barker then added a few words of his own. "Do know what type of specialty Anders had when I first met him?" Andrew queried. "He was an obstetrician. He stopped doing it and became a GP because he got angry when the medical profession started referring to having a baby as a 'miracle of medicine.'" Anders said to me, "I thought it was a natural occurrence'"

So as I lay on the bed in the humble abode I opened the volume of English verse at the place the book marker indicated and began to read. It was a sonnet by the 17th century poet John Milton:

How Soon Hath Time
How soon hath Time, the subtle thief of youth,
Stoln on his wing my three and twentieth year!
My hasting days fly on with full career,
But my late spring no bud or blossom show'th.
Perhaps my semblance might deceive the truth,
That I to manhood am arrived so near,
And inward ripeness doth much less appear,
That some more timely-happy spirits endu'th.
Yet be it less or more, or soon or slow,
It shall be still in strictest measure even
To that great lot however mean or high,
Toward which Time leads me, and the will of Heaven,
All is, if I ever have grace to use it so,

As ever in my great Taskmaster's eye.

I read the piece several times over. I was never one for poetry but this sonnet somehow got to me. I felt to be in a situation similar to that of the poet. I recalled that Albert Barker was going to remain in RCAF service for at least 20 years. He was going to marry, get his service pension than perhaps take some sort of management position in the ever expanding enterprises of Andrew Barker. Now this was not to happen. I undressed and retired for the night. Oddly enough I fell into a deep sleep without my usual tendency to ponder the Universe trying to reason out why bad things happened to good people. It was the first time since early childhood that the sleep of innocence occurred.

I awoke without the aid of an alarm clock. The room where the Barker's had accommodated me had an attached washroom containing a crapper, sink, and an enclosed glass shower. Mrs. Barker, I recalled, had decided to bed me in Albert's room. There were no books in the room. Some framed pictures of his parents and Ann Anders sat on the dresser. Oddly enough, much of Albert's clothing was neatly stored away in the two enormous closets and the large dresser still contained his hose and under garments. It became apparent that Albert had abundant affection from his mother. Perhaps he had too much, I judged. I began to understand why "Bert," which was Albert's preferred nickname, wanted to strike out on his own. For certain, young Albert Barker was going to make it in the world by himself. Mrs. Barker and Albert's fiancé were waiting in the dining room for me when I came down. Mrs. Barker apologized for her husband's absence. He had left the house at 6:30 AM to tend to his business.

"My dear," Mrs. Barker spoke, addressing me. "I have packed you a lunch, vegetarian style, for your trip pack to Toronto. Are there people there to meet you?"

"Mr. Hugh Watson will pick me up at Malton Airport. He had done this many times." I started to dig into the scrambled eggs and natural hash browns Mrs. Barker had carefully prepared. She poured a glass of fresh squeezed orange juice. Studying Anne Anders made me miss the Presence of Renee. She was staying at The Farm, practicing her music six hours per day and making numerous recordings for the broadcasting company RBC that held her contract. She had written me that she had made a lot of money from record sales, enough to set her up for life. She was thinking of purchasing an abandoned farm in Norfolk County, which had rundown buildings but excellent soil and was about 160 acres in size and had above all, an enormous water supply. I wanted to throw in with her but in a special way. Renee was going to be at Malton Airport when my plane landed. I would speak with her then. With developers after The Farm I wanted to find a new place to set up living accommodations. My main problem was what was to become of the Watsons, my older Brother Bill and Marion, my younger sister? Norfolk County intrigued me. I wanted to know more about it. I knew that Norfolk was tobacco country and was somewhat in the vicinity of Aylmer where I received my initial training in the RCAF.

CHAPTER 33

A Married Couple

The Bristol Britannia flew from Charlottetown to Montreal, took on and discarded some passengers, refueled and flew the short distance to Malton Airport located in the nearby suburb of Mississauga. I admired the efficiency and power of the four engines turbo prop. It was far quieter than the North Star. What's more, the Britannia was a proven aircraft. I hoped that Trans Canada would not ditch these planes in a ridiculous attempt to modernize their fleet. The craft set down at 5 PM, EST and taxied to the terminal where the passengers disembarked. I discovered Margaret and Hugh Watson and Renee waiting for me. After picking up the small suitcase I had with me I got into the old De Soto. The care lavished upon the car by Hugh was a great factor in its continuing performance even though it was almost 16 years old. The vehicle was becoming a collectors' item. We headed back to The Farm. I was alarmed when I looked at Margaret. She was pale and stooped over. When I hugged her that great energy she always held seemed dissipated. Renee sat in the rear seat beside me and the Watsons sat up in the front. Renee wanted to know what the Barkers were like.

"They are a quiet compassionate couple," I answered. "Albert was their only child. Mrs. Barker can't have any more children. You know, there is a tremendous power about Albert's dad and his mom too. Time was short there. It was almost as if they wanted me to fill in for their son. Mrs. Barker must have almost smothered Albert with her doting on him. I promised to write them once a month to let them know how I was doing at university. I also met Anne Anders, Albert's fiancé and her parents. Mr. Anders is a rebel MD. Albert's fiancé was very quiet when I was with the Barkers. Mr. Anders is descended from Norwegian stock."

In time, the De Soto pulled up to The Farm house. I went into the library with Renee. "I have something to ask you about the property you are purchasing in Norfolk County. I located Norfolk Country in one of Mr. Barker's many atlases of Canada. You know it's not too far from the new University of Waterville, possibly about an hour's drive. If you live there I could call on you maybe twice per week."

"And just how are you going to get on with your studies?" the red headed young woman asked. I read some of the information the university sent you. It said the pre engineering and engineering courses are quite difficult and part time jobs and excessive commitment to other activities should be avoided. You men are all the same. You need constant mothering!"

"I know that," I answered, "would you be my constant mother?" I grew edgy when I asked this question. I wanted to marry Renee. I did not want my fiancé to be stranded without a husband, like Anne Anders was. "If we were a married couple we could live together. You would be Mrs. Noble. Does that sound good?"

"I have been waiting for you to ask me for ages," Renee replied. "When you start university we will get a suitable apartment in Waterville. I can't have you traipsing back and forth between my farm and Waterville. When spring comes I am having a new two floors house built on my property that we will move into permanently. When do you want to get married?"

"It's now December 22, I have been thinking of sometime soon, like tomorrow or the day after." So Renee and I made what was to be a lifelong commitment to each other. Agnes was contacted at the Niagara Apartment and invited to come up to the Wedding scheduled for December 29. Hugh Watson would fetch her from the city and bring her to The Farm. Agnes had never met Renee. Agnes would not refuse the invitation.

Hugh delivered Agnes to The Farm at 1:00 PM. It was December 28. In a few short days the Watsons had seen to everything. Agnes was decently attired but frumpy. Not a tall woman Agnes, now in her early 50's bore a startling resemblance to the movie actress Claudette Colbert. Lem often referred to Agnes as "Claudette Goldberg." During the pre-wedding luncheon break Agnes was introduced to Renee. The two women stood apart by four feet while they conversed for a few minutes. Renee came over to me. "I don't think your mother approves of me," she said. "She called me a 'schiksa.' She also said my son should have her approval before he married. I was flabbergasted."

"Well don't give it a shit." I replied. "That's her in all her goodness." All told there was a professional caterer brought in from Richmond Hill to lay out a buffet, strictly vegetarian, for 12 guests. Agnes wandered over to the table and inspected it. I heard her remark: "is this kosher?" I chuckled at Agnes's comment about the food. A woman who knew as much about Hebrew culture as Genghis Khan, maybe less, did pretend to spout off the ancient Hebrew lore like a rabbi. Like a rabbi who had spent 20 years in deep study. Agnes had never been inside a synagogue except for her father's funeral. She married Lem at the Toronto City Hall. I was suspicious that she might not be Jewish at all just as Esther Perez de Leon Hombre Noble suggested. None of her siblings or parents had been inside a Jewish place of worship. For her mother, funeral services were conducted at the facilities of the local Jewish undertaker. Benjamin's Memorial Temple handled most of the Jewish funerals in and around the Toronto area.

No guest was allowed to take any more food after snacking briefly until after the wedding was performed. The Watson's were there, so was Renee's surviving aunt from New York, so was Walter Abercromby, and a few friends of mine who I Invited on short notice to come. Charles Sasaki, B.A.Sc. and now a P.Eng. and University of Toronto graduate was there. Bill Noble and his wife Dorothy were there as was Marion my younger sister. Since he was kin of Renee by marriage Hugh Watson would act as the father. I had contacted Kenneth MacAlpine, the head master of Willington to attend which he did along with his wife. I had never thought of Kenneth MacAlpine as having a wife. He was almost six years older than when I last saw him. Kenneth MacAlpine's appearance had not appeared to change. There also to conduct the service was Reverend George Latticomb, an Anglican Priest who Hugh Watson had contacted to conduct the service. At 3:00 PM, Reverend Latticomb asked the guests to assemble in the large 30 feet by 24 feet living room of the Alistaire Duncan Estate, which I had owned for over 10 years. I accompanied the Anglican priest to the front of the room where a makeshift dais was assembled. The dais was covered in a light violet rug that had gold trim. The scene was absolutely ethereal. A professional musician began to play Brahm's Wedding March. I looked to the back of the room and saw Hugh Watson escorting Renee. I almost fainted such was the spiritual energy present in that room in late December, 1954. I felt a tremendous heat in my body.

I suspected Renee did not hear much of the ceremony that lasted a few minutes but certain words and phrases spoken by the Reverend Latticomb would stick with him me the rest of my embodiment. The reverend referred to Renee as: "A Queen of the Blue Race" and me has "A Scion of the House of Jesus and also a Scion of the Blue Race." Later when everybody made a beeline for the table of food the Priest walked over to Renee, kissed her on the cheek, and said: "I am pleased for you today Princess. A union of your two lines can only serve to raise everyone. When the guests are gone I want a private audience with you both."

Renee and I went about greeting the guests. Kenneth MacAlpine introduced his wife to Renee and me. MacAlpine's wife was named Jean. She was tall, nearly 5'10" and dwarfed Renee and me in her high heels. I found out that the MacAlpines had two married children, both boys who were still in Scotland. They were professors and working at St. Andrew's University teaching physics. The MacAlpines were waiting for grandchildren.

Kenneth MacAlpine approached Renee and me with his wife alongside. The tall man spoke; "Reverend Latticomb is a personal friend of mine. He has been searching for enlightenment from a young age. He will be giving up his ministry soon so that he can live by himself. He is a widower. He wants to explore what he is evolving into more thoroughly. I told him about you and Renee's background. In a few years there will be many controversial books written about Jesus and his wife Mary Magdalene. The World is rapidly approaching The New Permanent Golden Age and you two are to be an important part of it. May I salute the bride?"

Eventually the guests left. There was an auxiliary table full of wedding gifts. Renee and I began to explore them. One guest had left me six dozen Titleist balata golf balls. While these were the balls of choice for a tournament professional they were far too fragile for use after playing real golf with them to be tossed into the practice bag. They bruised easily. There were two of the usual toasters and a set of cooking utensils. On and on the gifts went. There was a book wrapped up in plain brown paper that looked interesting and it was addressed to both Renee and me. It was called: *Magnificent Obsession*. There was no autographed gift card, just a handwritten note that said: "To a seeker of the Light."

Things were carefully stowed away in the trunk of Renee's new vehicle, a large Ford station wagon. It was an ideal rig to move luggage, kitchen utensils and those heavier wedding gifts about and of course to stow toasters. Hugh Watson chauffeured Agnes back to her Niagara Apartment. She did not want to spend the night at The Farm. This would entail a long afternoon for Hugh. Margaret went along for the ride.

Renee commented to me about Margaret: "she looks very sick," as the middle aged woman walked slowly out the door. Two days later on a late afternoon Margaret Watson, the wife of Hugh, entered the Brantwood Hospital in North York. She would never leave it on a permanent basis while she remained in embodiment.

A five minute meeting between Reverend Latticomb and Renee and I took place in the Duncan Estate library when all others had left.

"You two will go all the way," the reverend said, "All the way."

"What do you mean 'all the way?'" Renee asked.

"You will both make the Ascension," Latticomb answered. Latticomb ended the meeting there and then.

On that late afternoon Renee and I made the drive to Waterville. I was to begin my classes the first Tuesday of January, 1955. A small apartment was subleased by Renee for us to occupy during the week, and on weekends if the weather became inclement. Things went well for us. We settled into the one bedroom unit. It was untidy at first occupancy. Classes and topics seemed to be crammed together to the highest possible density. The philosophy of education, initiated by the University of Waterville, was to cram as much material as possible into the brains of its students in the shortest time possible. The pre engineering class consisted of 135 members when it started. After the final examinations were graded three and one half months later there were 67 candidates left. I, Robert MacAlpine Noble had ranked 4th from the top.

While Renee was in Waterville, The Music Department of the small institution down the street, called Waterville Lutheran College approached her to be a guest key board instructor on a three month contract. Renee, being a "retired" concert artist, had attracted attention. So both Renee and I were busy. One unfortunate discovery both Renee and I made was that there was nothing in the manner of decent eating places in Waterville except the "Charcoal Steak House." Renee and I were now total vegetarians. The cafeteria cooks at Waterville Lutheran College must have trained at the "Agnes Posnanski School of gourmet cooking." Both of Renee and I lost 15 pounds during that first semester. Near the end of my first term I was called into the Coordinator's office. This was a position designated to one "Octave G. LaVigne," a bilingual Québécois, who harmonized the role of various industries with Waterville University. Since Renee and I were from the Toronto area La Vigne placed me on assignment to Webster J. McPhee Co. LaVigne never talked about this placement with me. He sprang it on me. Renee and I returned to The Farm in Vaughan. I prepared to start my first work assignment on Monday, early April 1955.

CHAPTER 34

At Work in the Field
of the Engineers

Webster J. McPhee was located on the Queen's Quay. This ran along the shore line of Lake Ontario and was situated between York and Bay Streets. Time was wasted driving my Dodge coupe down Yonge Street to the new Eglinton Avenue terminal of the recently completed Yonge Subway. It had opened for passengers in April, 1954 and was rapidly reaching its maximum passenger capacity. Still, it was Toronto's first rapid transit line and was long overdue. I got out of the Dodge at Eglinton Avenue at 7:00 AM and told Renee: "I'll take the subway to Union Station and walk the rest of the way." And I proceeded to do so.

Carl Wilson, the general manager of the large engineering office employing 60 draftsmen and designers, and 25 professional engineers was assisted by Louis Hayes the chief draftsman and the chief engineer was Charles Findlayson, a dour Scot who was formerly the chief engineer for Vincent Aircraft Manufacturing, a now defunct venture that produced the "Hurricane" fighter for the RCAF during the war. To my shock Webster J. McPhee was an American company whose head office was located in Akron, Ohio. They were engaged in drawing up the plans for a large steel mill to be located in south central Ontario. I was introduced to Carl Wilson. Wilson began to talk.

"I graduated as a civil engineer from Ohio Tech in 1942. Of course the United States was getting ready to go to war. This was just after Pearl Harbor. You foreigners up here wouldn't know anything about arming to fight a war." Carl Wilson was as parochial as they come. Beside that I resented being called a "foreigner" in my own country. While he spoke Wilson dangled a cigarette from his lips. The ash accumulating on the coffin nail was three times longer than the unburned portion of his smoke. He seemed totally preoccupied with his narrative. Charles Findlayson, the dour Scot, nodded his head with every word. "We haven't discussed your pay. You will commence as a 'draftsman trainee' at $1:00 per hour. That title draftsman trainee" gave me an idea almost immediately I wasn't to be considered a student engineer but a flunky. We have many plans that need redrawing immediately. If you are good at this and come back for a second tour with us you will get a big raise." With that final comment the long column of ashes broke free of the cigarette and fell upon Wilson's silk tie and blue shirt. As he brushed off the ash he went into a one minute coughing spasm. Obviously he thought smoking was good for him. There would be many times during my stay with his company that he would burst into a coughing spasm accompanied by taunts from the office staff such as "atta boy Carl I hear you coming." He was still outside the office.

I was assigned a drawing table. I found out I had to purchase my own pencils, set squares, and measuring scales. It was going to cost me $10 up front to work for McPhee! The McPhee Company loved Canada! The dunderheads, all Canadian big shots, that would come to own the mill would not consider finding a Canadian company to design what they were engaging Webster J. McPhee to do.

The trek each morning from The Farm to the Queen's Quay was wearing out both Renee and me. Ultimately Renee and I engaged a room in a clean hotel on a weekly basis from Monday to Friday to avoid the four hours of driving and subway riding. "Oh well," I thought, "It comes with the job." A great deal came with the job. Drawings were coming off the drafting board at a phenomenal rate. I had aced the introductory courses in engineering drawing at Waterville. While working at my drawing board I found I was bordered on each side by two young men in their mid- 20's. They were talking while talking a coffee break about wages.

"Geez," one said to the other, "$2:50 an hour is shit pay for what I do." I focused on this item. I was earning $1:00 an hour and seemed to produce two drawings for each one the other two made. It dawned on me that I was being taken advantage of. The McPhee Company also liked to send me on errands about 15 minutes before quitting time. "Will you run these drawings over to Norman Cade and Company so we can get an auto positive and two blue prints of each," Findlayson would order. "Then go home after that." The trip uptown to the blueprint company could be walked in 30 minutes but Finlayson would insist that I take a streetcar. This cost money but the McPhee Company didn't seem to offer any form of reimbursement. I did 10 of these errands for the McPhee Company in my last four weeks with them. By the time I returned to the downtown hotel room it was well past 6:00 PM. Renee was upset. I should have been there by 5:20 PM. By the conclusion of the work term I had paid 12 weeks of hotel bills at $1200.00, had put out $5:00 in TTC fares for errands. I had worked 60 hours overtime with no pay. I later found out under Ontario Labor Law I had not been paid for my services at the level of legislated minimum wage.

When approached about this, Wilson, after a short spell of coughing, replied, "we don't have to pay minimum wage to you, you are a student." Ontario Labor Law's designation of "student" was meant to apply to teens working at summer jobs or part time after school hours. It did not define adults, people over 21 years of age as students. I began to document every incidence of perceived violations of labor law. I asked to see Mr. Wilson for a few minutes about a week before I was to return for my first full semester as a regular engineering student. "What do you want to see me about?" Wilson asked? He motioned with his right hand for me to sit at the table. I noticed a tall well-built man of about 30 years of age who was sitting in the corner of the office not visible to anyone entering the office.

"I am Leonard Bond," the tall man said as he introduced himself. "I am an assistant coordinator from the Cooperative Department of Waterville University. Mr. Wilson and I were discussing your performance with McPhee Company to date. Mr. Wilson is of the opinion that your effort here is not up to par. He feels you are not giving it the old college try."

I was taken aback. These two were discussing me behind my back. What Wilson didn't know was that he had been overheard bragging about how the company was making unwarranted profits on the speedy and accurate productivity of my work. I appeared to produce as much completed product as the combined effort of the two older regular employees whose drawing boards were on both sides of me. Then their need for a good draftsman seemed to dry up. He was bragging to Findlayson who for the most part nodded his head in agreement. My work station was less than 20 feet from Wilson's office. Mr. Wilson left the door of his office open. I felt pleased that these two members of the senior management of Webster J. McPhee thought I was highly valuable. What I heard from Leonard Bond was an exact opposite. How could they in several instants be very pleased with me and on this day tell a university coordinator I was unsatisfactory?

"Mr. Wilson doesn't think he should assign you a satisfactory grade as of now for your work session. However he has suggested you might show him that you are willing to change your attitude by helping out with extra work from 5:30 to 8:30 PM from Monday to Friday afternoons until you leave. Are you in agreement with that?" Bond asked.

"Will I be compensated for the extra hours?" I asked. "This place is costing me more money to work here than I gross."

"Do you own a car?" Wilson asked.

"I own a vehicle," I answered.

"Well sell the car and you won't need a raise!" Wilson answered.

"But the two guys on each side of me do the work and get two and one half times what I get. What kind of outfit do you run here?" I was catching on. The McPhee Company wanted me to work as an indentured slave. They didn't think I was up to the job but offered extra hours with no pay. All the time this banter was going on Leonard Bond sat observing.

"Those two other guys are married. You are a bachelor. You don't have a wife to support. You don't need a raise." This was Wilson's reply. "Obviously," I thought, "Wilson never read the short biography," I had earlier written and presented to the Admissions department of the university. They sent it to Webster J. McPhee Co.

"I suppose if I had a lot of money you would demand that I pay the Webster J. McPhee to make profits for you. By the way I am married!"

"Get out of my office you insignificant twerp!" Wilson screamed. "Get your paycheck and scram. And you are getting a failure on your work assignment." When I received my check it was short 40 hours. The McPhee Company had gone as far as "stiffing" me for my wages. This I placed in my journal. I made photo stats of all the documents. Renee and I checked out of our hotel, rode the subway to Eglinton, took the trolley bus to the Glen Echo Loop and called Hugh Watson to retrieve us at the Loop and take us to The Farm. But the consequences of the work term did not end there. It was to play on for another three months. Margaret Watson was not at The Farm when Renee and I reached it. "Margaret is in the hospital," Hugh answered to a silent question I was thinking. "They are going to do a biopsy on her chest tomorrow." The doctors don't want us to visit her till after it's done. This should be by 2:00 PM tomorrow. We will find out then."

"Well Renee and I sure have time tomorrow!"

CHAPTER 35

Unjust Dismissal

While I was working at Webster J. McPhee I had a few conversations with Stuart MacCall, a recent arrival to Canada and a graduate engineer from a highly respected Scottish university. These occurred during coffee breaks. MacCall had been working for Webster J. McPhee for two years suffering all types of abuse. He had been sponsored into Canada by relatives living in Toronto. During his work time at McPhee he did his work well but Wilson and Findlayson pressured him by threatening to not sign the documents he needed to qualify as a full P. Eng. in Ontario. From this unsavory practice the McPhee Company was able to "indenture" Stuart MacCall to a work week of about 55 hours for well over a year. I had several days to wait until I could start my first full term of engineering at Waterville. It was 7:00 PM on a Monday evening when I received a telephone call.

"This is Stuart MacCall," the voice said. "I worked at Webster J. McPhee while you were there. You once told me you had a very capable lawyer that you used to solve legal problems that came up over your lifetime. Can I visit you this evening? I would like to talk over a problem I am having."

I told him I lived outside Toronto in Vaughan Township. When Stuart said he could borrow a car to drive up there if he received competent directions. MacCall found The Farm at 8:30 PM. Hugh Watson showed him into the library-office where I was waiting. Stuart looked distraught.

"I have been fired from Webster J. McPhee with no notice. They asked me to pack up my things and leave the office immediately. I asked for my final paycheck and they said they would mail it to me at the end of next week when paychecks were normally issued. They told me I was a poor employee and they were not able to recommend that I be admitted to the Association of Professional Engineers of Upper Canada. What am I going to do?" Stuart stopped to catch his breath. He then continued. "I have worked my heart out for those bastards. I have taken six courses to fully qualify as a professional engineer while I worked for McPhee and studied like a dog to pass those exams; which I have done." They have been dangled their endorsement in front of me every day. I think I have been productive."

I had read the regulations of the Association of Professional Engineers of Upper Canada during several lunch breaks while I worked at McPhee. It seemed to me that passing the exams required to become a successful professional engineer had been completed by Stuart MacCall. Stuart had his engineering degree from a famed Scottish University. He found employment at Webster J. McPhee by reading the bulletin boards of his Scottish university. He wrote to what he thought was a Canadian owned business a letter and enclosed as transcript of his academic record. McPhee responded almost immediately. Within two months Stuart was approved for work in Canada and issued the relevant immigration papers. In time, he packed his books, and had them shipped to his remote female unmarried cousins who lived in Toronto. The cousins were Lena, now a 70 year old spinster and Dorothy Watt a slightly younger spinster. Both were successful career women. After a few days he purchased a plane ticket that would allow him to fly across the Atlantic and eventually land him in Toronto. After slaving away for over two years and studying hours after work every evening he had passed six additional courses beyond his university training in Scotland. McPhee seemed indifferent to his achievement.

"Are you going to run out on us?" Carl Wilson, asked Stuart as he first read the application to join the APEUC (Association of Professional Engineers of Upper Canada). The reply from MaCall was immediate.

"I am going to an evening interview from another engineering firm." Wilsons's bluff was called and he refused to sign the papers. "You are not one of the team. We need you to help us complete part of this project on time. You were asked some time ago to work late to help us. You made up some phony excuse that you had to attend your cousin's birthday party." Thus Carl Wilson, general manager of the Toronto branch of the McPhee Company, loved to berate his employees. But he went overboard with Stuart. He called him a liar, incompetent and a disloyal employee. Stuart did not want to work three to four hours extra time every evening Monday through Friday. Besides if Stuart was incompetent why would McPhee and company want him for extra work? Nobody in the senior management of that company even said "thank you" for your effort. The worst thing was there was no pay for the extra hours! Stuart told me that there were at least a dozen employees of McPhee that had been coerced into extra hours of unpaid work by the senior management of McPhee.

"You are salaried employees of a well-established company. A part of our permanent staff and hired as professionals. Professionals work the times needed to complete a project. Professionals are rewarded with the satisfaction they get from doing a job well. There is more to working as a professional that making money." This was a typical rant used often by Carl Wilson.

Wilson often sounded like a used car salesman on the Danforth. The salesman would have a young couple in sitting in front of his desk. "What do you mean you want to see another dealer," the salesman would shout as he banged his fist on the desk. This was used as a rebuttal when the customer wanted to shop around at other dealers to compare prices. "Show me such a dealer and I'll buy those cars off of his lot and sell them off my lot!" These things aren't pep talks but bullying. It was also true that many employees worked overtime but the client employing McPhee's services didn't really require them. This entire overtime hour thing was nothing more than a "boondoggle." Additional hours were billed to the client for overtime at a time and one half hourly rate of pay. The workers never saw a dime of the money McPhee received for their "service."

I took notes on what Stuart was saying but asked Stuart to write down in detail all the incidents that occurred in his slightly over two years of work at McPhee. He was also to include that it took him over a month to receive his final check and it was short one week's pay. Webster J. McPhee had all employees except Wilson, Findlayson and two assistants to Findlayson punch a time clock. "Punching a time clock," I thought, "would make them hourly paid employees rather than salaried staff." The extra hours worked after 5:00 PM were recorded on a time clock. I began to think that the overtime required by senior management might not even be necessary. There was a feeling in my mind that senior management was only interested in bringing McPhee's work on the project in ahead of schedule. The Webster J. McPhee Company would then be entitled to a huge bonus amounting to nearly a million dollars. A substantial amount of these profits earned by the Toronto office would be returned to Wilson and Findlayson and their assistants as bonuses for their industrious efforts on behalf of Webster J. McPhee. They treated the client like a milk cow. The draftsmen and engineers could count on receiving nothing. Later on I wrote these thoughts into a letter I was sending to Walter Abercromby.

"I want you to see my lawyer Walter Abercromby," I told Stuart. He is a highly successful lawyer. I have known him since I turned 13 years old." It occurred to me that Stuart might not have the funds to pay Walter Abercromby. I opened the wall safe in the library. I found nearly $500.00 on hand. I counted out $450.00 and handed it over to Stuart. "This will cover your retainer. I will phone Mr. Abercromby tomorrow morning and tell him about you. Take all these notes to him as soon as possible."

"I will pay you back." Stuart looked sheepish as he accepted the money. "Right now I am short. I barely made my rent."

"Be available by the telephone from 9:00 AM on. Where are you staying in Toronto?" I enquired. "What is your phone number? By the way you don't have to pay me back. Do you see this house and the land; it all belongs to me. That $450 is a drop in the ocean to me. I didn't give you the money as charity but as an investment. For me that $450 is all used up."

By the next morning Walter Abercromby was briefed by me about

Stuart MacCall and the Law office of Walter Abercromby QC; contacted MacCall and an appointment was set up that day in the afternoon. Stuart MacCall carried within a sealed large manila envelope papers documenting all the abuses Stuart and me had suffered while "employed" with Webster J. McPhee. Stuart and Walter Abercromby got down to serious business at 1:45 PM. During the hour that passed Abercromby accepted a $300 retainer for which he gave a receipt. Abercromby didn't expect to lose the case with McPhee Company but even he was amazed at the ignorance and arrogance that would soon surface when he had dealings with the senior management of the Toronto office. It would further be of interest to discover the greater arrogance of the American parent company located in Akron, Ohio.

When Wilson telephoned his superiors and relayed the news that they would be hauled into court they said, "This is a garbage law suit with only two complainants. Ignore it." So Wilson ignored it. Letters from Abercromby went unanswered. Finally, they were summoned to appear in court and had to find legal counsel on very short notice. A lawyer came over from Akron to advise Wilson, Findlayson, and Findlayson's two assistants. McPhee Company didn't even have the smarts to hire a Canadian lawyer familiar with Ontario Labor Law. The American lawyer was not a member of any law association in Canada. I was back at the University of Waterville for about four weeks when all this began. I thought I had heard the end of this case when the Court ruled dismissal had occurred unjustly in the case of Stuart MacCall. McPhee Company had to pay MacCall one year's wages as part of the settlement, plus legal fees to Walter Abercromby and as well settle with unpaid wages owing to me

After all of these court shenanigans Carl Wilson had to get even with Stuart. Every time Stuart MacCall went for a job interview on his applications he listed his more than two years Canadian experience with McPhee. Some of the prospective employers called Webster J. McPhee checking references on MacCall. Wilson could not bear to give an honest reference. This resulted in Stuart losing several opportunities to gain good employment. Walter Abercromby was consulted again. He requested some of his friends who were engineers ask for references from the McPhee Company. Webster G. McPhee Company was hauled back into court a second time and the ruling went against them again. Stuart MacCall now had enough cash to establish his own consulting company. He also was registered as a member of the Association of Professional Engineers of Upper Canada as a result of turning up the thumb screws on the McPhee Company. He would start that business a few months later with two other young civil engineers. After a year in partnership he dropped the two partners and went it alone. He became very successful. He eventually employed 10 people. The name of their venture was "Aim Engineering." There were three engineers and seven technologists. The bulk of his work was fixing projects larger consulting companies screwed up. His fees were half of what the larger companies charged their clients yet Stuart's clients got better quality work. This work that the larger arrogant companies usually did for naive clients was always overpriced and inferior. Stuart McCall was becoming wealthy. He became a life time friend of Renee and me.

McPhee went downhill as a large consulting engineering company. Two years after the law suits were settled it did what all large incompetent companies generally do when they don't have any smarts. They merged with another declining incompetent company called Hector Wilson and Associates. Together they increased their ineptitude. Such a thing is now referred to as "synergy." The two incompetent companies' negative synergy grew in a greater negative proportion to their individual negative energies. After two more years the merged companies folded their operations.

At this time Aim Engineering started landing some large projects. They had to find senior engineers to help. Advertisements were placed in various journals for qualified staff. One evening Stuart MacCall opened an 8" by 11" manila envelope. The applicant's name was Charles Findlayson. This gave Stuart some sinister satisfaction but he responded with a letter back to Findlayson. The letter's content could be summed up in its final sentence: "We regret to inform you that Aim Engineering does not require a professional with your unique talents." Stuart MacCall when first receiving Findlayson's application wanted to call Findlayson to his office for an interview so he could gloat over him but he was now too far advanced spiritually for such shenanigans.

I was to return to Waterville for my first full term of engineering. I was to report to the office of Octave Jean La Vigne the head coordinator for the University. It was his job to facilitate the procurement of work assignments for the students. He was a gaunt man of about 50 years. He was rapidly becoming the laughing stock among the students of the University. When he posted an engineering student to a work assignment he always signed the notice, "good luck, O. J. LaVigne." In a short time, "good luck, O.J. LaVigne" was appearing on everything attached to the walls and bulletin boards. It was signed under a calendar picture of a man waving goodbye from the deck of a steamer. The picture was part of a calendar page for July. The signature appeared on everything: magazines in the library, posters, and so on. It was insane persecution. The man was trying to do his job, he simply didn't measure up.

I had to visit the office of Octave J. La Vigne. It was a few weeks before the final exams were to start. I arrived at LaVigne's office at 1:00 PM after the Calculus lecture, given by John Evenson. The class was just starting integration of functions. A bit of that topic would be examined on the final tests. The subject was easy for me. I had been taught well by MacKay at the Willington Academy. I figured an easy "A" would help raise my average.

"You have no work assignment set up for this coming term!" LaVigne commented. "How do you feel about returning to Webster J. McPhee?" I was shocked.

"Why would they want me to return there? Do they really want to see more of me? Did you not see the information my lawyer sent to your office. Didn't Leonard Bond inform you of what went on there?"

La Vigne replied: "Why are you asking me this? Certainly everything is okay with Webster J. McPhee. They are such a fine engineering company! And they are located in your own backyard." Octave leaned back in his chair. He resumed his talk after looking at the folder on his desk. It was my "work report." The folder contained a four pages type written report detailing my "work experience" gained via Webster J. McPhee. To me the time I spent there was a splendid lesson in labor relations and employment law. LaVigne had never read it. He was too busy. I told him in no uncertain terms I would not go back to Webster McPhee if they dragged me there.

I said, "This was an office run by thieves." With this remark Octave blew his top.

"You are hereby suspended from this university. Get out of my office." After this incredible interview with LaVigne, I called on the Dean of Engineering who was familiar with the case of unjust dismissal that occurred with the McPhee Company. From this interview I learned that LaVigne had no power to expel anyone from the university. I was advised to ignore LaVigne. I did this and went ahead with my preparations for mid-year examinations. The next day I was called to the Dean's office. LaVigne was there. He apologized. That apology was in front of the dean of engineering and the university president. During the apology I noticed LaVigne hands were trembling. I felt sorry for the man. One month later LaVigne was on a long sick leave. He eventually had a nervous breakdown. Two years later, recovered from his illness, he took an assistant professorship at the university and lectured in electronics. The students who gave him the hard time had forgotten all about him. They were too busy trying to survive their course work. My original class of over 130 students had dwindled down to 35.

CHAPTER 36

Other Work Assignments

The year passed as I attended the University of Waterville and Renee was the guest instructor every other three months term in the music program at Waterville Lutheran College. Our expenses were not a problem but the constant moving back and forward from The Farm in Vaughan Township and Waterville was. It was wearing us out. I tried to visit Renee's farm during the construction of the new house in Norfolk County. Construction had slowed down during the winter months but as autumn approached the builders tried to finish the exterior which they did in late August. They also had the heating system installed. Finishing the interior was less a problem because it kept the inside warm. Renee's farm was leased out to tobacco farmers and they had a "quota" to grow so much Virginia tobacco. The property had ample water. Two large green houses were used to cultivate small tobacco plants. The growing area was almost weed-free. It sat on a huge water table that was between 20 and 24 feet below the surface. The depth of the water table never seemed to get lower. I was looking forward to living there. Unlike The Farm situated north of Toronto this place was well outside the large populations of urban areas. The entire affair, including equipment cost Renee $150 000, including the tobacco quota. This did not include the cost of the new house. This I funded.

There was still the problem of a second work assignment. This I took with North Ridge Gas, a natural gas supplier to South Western Ontario. I had a small portion of my $2.00 per hour wage deducted for union dues. When I asked the shop steward for a union member's book which showed the wages of various jobs the steward screamed at me with vulgar profanity. He said, "For what fucking reasons do you need a Union Book?" I did floor sweeping and garbage maintenance during my three months at the gas company. There was no engineering work delegated to me. This dismal treatment of students was to cease in a few years once Waterville attained a superb reputation. When I finally was leaving the assignment I was presented with a Union Book by the shop steward. Looking for a third work assignment when I competed my first year in the regular engineering course after completing my third term of studies I had a call from Stuart MacCall. Stuart was setting up a practice as a consulting structural engineer in Simcoe, Ontario. Stuart had two partners and each of them put $10 000 into the new company. I got this call in August, 1955 near the end of my second term in the designated engineering course. I volunteered to complete my third work term in Stuart's company. It was situated very close to where Renee was building our new home. Stuart's company was to be called AIM Engineering.

"I don't want any money," I told him on the telephone. I will give you two and one half days a week of free time. Cover for me with the university." I informed Leonard Bond, the new head of coordination at the university that he had found my own employment with a new consulting engineering firm, "AIM Engineers." Bond approved of this venture after checking out the company. As the academic year ended I started working for Stuart MacCall and his partners. I worked Mondays, Wednesdays a full day and Fridays mornings only. On Friday afternoons Renee and I headed back to Vaughan Township and The Farm. The pace was less hectic. No occupancy certificate would be issued for the new property Renee acquired for several months into the future. We stayed in the apartment in Waterville when not inspecting the new property in Norfolk. McCall's Company was hired to supervise the building of Renee's new home. Then after inspecting the Norfolk property we took the new 1956 Chevrolet Nomad station wagon I purchased and drove via Highway 24 and rural roads to Highway 7 and came to Toronto. The new Chevy had a V-8 engine with a two speed "power glide" transmission, power steering and electric windows. It took both Renee and I some time to get used to driving it. It had green upholstery and a two tone green and white exterior paint job. We called ahead to Hugh Watson and said we were coming to The Farm and would arrive between six and seven PM.

I had the growing feeling that something was not right with the Watsons. I was growing more trusting of these feelings because they always seemed to be correct.

CHAPTER 37

Making the Change

Renee and I had to admit ourselves into The Farm house. Inside we found Hugh Watson sitting in the semi dark in the library-study. Margaret had been in and out of the hospital four times since her first visit. The cancer had not yielded to chemotherapy. It was not surgically treatable. Hugh had written Renee about Margaret, during this ordeal, which had worsened over the last month of my academic semester. Hugh did not write to me unless it was "serious." He did not want to bother me!

Hugh turned toward Renee and me. "Margaret is not going to make it. The disease has spread all over her body. Visiting hours are till 9:00 PM. Can we go there now?" Hugh suggested the old de Soto but Renee said to use the new Chevy. We arrived at the Brantwood Hospital at 8:00 PM and went to Margaret's room. Margaret, normally a stout lady, seemed to be all skin and bones. She seemed much older than in her late 60's which I knew she was. She refused to take pain killers and any other medicines.

"I have had my good years," she mumbled. "Now let God do his will. My karma will soon be repaid." For some people cancer is a cleansing of all their karma! Margaret asked to speak with her niece Renee. "Your marriage to Robert was foreordained. You and he are a great couple. I knew you were destined to be with him to accomplish 'The Great Work.' I had a dream one early morning, not too long ago, in which I seemed to be in a more real world than I have ever known. In that dream I was shown my Ultimate Destiny. It is very beautiful over there. Where I go Hugh cannot go for a while but he will join me in a short time. Watch out for him, for a while, after I go."

Then she lay back on her pillow, shut her eyes, and made the change. While I looked at her physical form I saw a White Light that engulfed her frame. That Light retreated gradually until it concentrated only around her neck, shoulders and head. Then it seemed to withdraw from her completely leaving through the top of her head. Renee and I looked at Margaret's body during this five minute interval. Then we looked at each other. Hugh was out of the room when this transformation occurred. Renee and I had witnessed the "Life Essence" pass from the body of Margaret Williams.

I pressed the button beside the hospital bed paging the duty nurse. "Mrs. Watson is gone," I said to the nurse when she entered the room. The nurse went over to examine Margaret's body, now an empty shell. Renee and I knew that Margaret Watson was not that body lying on the bed but had become something eternally unseen by most mortal men.

No autopsy was allowed on the body. No cajoling from the MD's could persuade Hugh Watson from agreeing to one. The "used up" body was taken to an undertaker situated in North York once the proper documents were signed by the medical authorities. The body was then kept refrigerated for 72 hours from the time of her passing. It was to be cremated after a short memorial service.

Three days later about 100 visitors attended a Memorial Session to be held at The Farm. The Reverend Latticomb was conducting the service. This was the man who had previously conducted Renee and my wedding ceremony. Four different parties begged the Reverend to conduct the ceremony. Latticomb could not tolerate the outer world any longer. The 100 or so visitors overcrowded "The Farm" house. Some old, some young and many in between aged visitors sat on the upholstered chairs and the many collapsible bridge chairs that had been on hand stored in an outbuilding for use in just such a contingency. While waiting for the service to begin. Renee played a Robert Schumann piece "Trameri" on the makeshift chapel's piano. Reverend Latticomb began his short talk. Margaret from the midlands of England had the Scottish blood of the MacAlpines! Her single name before her marriage to Hugh was unknown to me. Upon reading my mother's family tree I discovered that Margaret Watson and my mother Agnes shared a common great, great grandfather. This made Margaret a 3rd cousin of Agnes! I began to wonder if my wife Renee was now a remote cousin of mine. She was after all, Margaret's niece. I would find out. I had married my 4th cousin and did not know it at the time.

CHAPTER 38

Hugh Watson Leaves
"The Farm"

Renee and I went back to The Farm after the Memorial Service. We were exhausted from the goings on of the last 24 hours. During the service I had not noticed that Agnes had been brought to the service. Renee and I had not talked to her since the wedding some time before. I spotted Agnes heading towards the limousine we hired for her and headed her off. I began a conversation with her while Renee stood by.

"You could call me," Agnes said, "I'm your mother. How is your wife?" Agnes ignored talking to Renee who was standing right next to me. "You should tell your wife she is very attractive. How long has she been playing the piano?" Finally she turned and talked to Renee directly. "A good marriage is based on good sexual relationships. Both husband and wife should have good sexual relations!" After this idiotic conversation my conviction that the world was insane grew stronger. In fact, I believed it grew more insane every passing day. I felt it was a collection of human beings consisting most of babbling lunatics. What's more I felt the world's leadership was made up of lunatics.

"How did you come to be brought up here?" I enquired of Agnes.

"Mr. Abercromby arranged everything. I want to go home now." With that comment Agnes got into the Cadillac limousine and went back to her flat in the former Village of Niagara.

I laid on the king sized bed with Renee. I had observed the vitality slowly seeping out of Hugh Watson since the illness of Margaret became known. I was concerned about Hugh. Hugh was going to need attention. I knew Hugh had four adult daughters, all married and living in Toronto. I had met two of them at a birthday party for Margaret some years before, but the other two, while they visited The Farm, never met up with me. The four daughters were all present at Margaret's funeral service. Three of them had children of their own. I had seen them all talking with Hugh. I didn't know what the talk was about.

Renee answered the telephone at about 9:00 PM. The woman on the other end was Mary Watson. She was Hugh's oldest daughter. "I want to discuss my father with you and your husband. Can you meet me tomorrow? Dad tells me you both are vegetarians, let us meet at the Chungking Gardens on Yonge Street, it has an extensive vegetarian menu. My sister doesn't want our dad to come with you. What we have to discuss concerns his future." So Renee and I made the short journey from The Farm to the Chinese Restaurant. I wondered why Hugh Watson's future without him being present was even conducted. He was not suffering from any form of dementia. Renee and I had discovered Chungking Gardens it at an earlier time. There was a hospital sponsored by the Seventh Day Adventists near their location. The Chunking Gardens had a special menu catering to nonmeat eaters which included staff of the Brantwood Hospital. The Hospital staff patronized the eatery and the management began to serve them non meat dishes. Even the frying oil was vegetable based.

On the first occasional that I dated Renee we stopped at the Chungking. We were both 18 years old. I had the old de Soto and had earned my license a few weeks earlier. Renee had a recording session with the Royal Broadcasting Corporation for 10:00 AM the next morning. Renee and I partook of a full order of sweet and sour "nippet balls," a vegetarian concoction deep fried in vegetable oil. On top of that we had a full order of vegetable fried rice and a full order of vegetable chow mein. It was delicious but our eyes were bigger than our stomachs.

We packed over half the dinner in takeout cartons and brought it home. When we arrived at The Farm it was discovered that we had left some of Renee's music lying on the dinner table back at the restaurant.

A quick telephone call was made to the Chungking Gardens. The restaurant would hold the music until Renee retrieved it later that evening. So a return trip was made. It wasn't a long affair. The owners of the restaurant, all members of an extended family were happy to provide this service. While Renee was talking with one of the waitresses the main owner spoke to me. "That young lady," he said, "possesses formidable life energy."

Renee and I were seated for about 15 minutes when three people approached us. We had taken a booth seating six. The restaurant wasn't busy. A stout lady of average height and about 40 years of age introduced herself as Mary Watson. Her husband Keith was with her and he had the same type of build as her mother. The other lady, possessing the same figure as Mary, was introduced as the second oldest sister. Hugh Watson had four adult daughters. He had served in World War I in the Canadian Army as a volunteer but he never saw action. He was responsible for training fresh recruits. He was discharged as a sergeant. During his time in England he had met Margaret who maiden name was "Cumming." They returned to Canada as newlyweds. I did not know Hugh's actual age but I guessed it to be about 68 years.

"Dad loved to live in the country," Mary began, "he and mom have been on your farm since the mid 1930's. They brought us up there. Some of us spent the war years there. Since mom died, and even while she was ill, Hugh got very down. He perked up when we visited but me and my three sisters became worried. We would like Dad to come live with us. Our children are all at university. There is enough room for him at our home. Would you object to Dad moving in a few days?"

Renee and I felt it strange that Hugh's oldest daughter would need permission from us to move their father. The three people sitting at the table with Renee and me were all at least 20 years older than us. "I want what is the best situation for Hugh," I said. "To tell you the truth I have been worried about him for a time."

"Then it's all set," Mary said.

"If it is okay with Hugh" I said. "He is always welcome at The Farm."

"Dad didn't want to leave the farm. He was always concerned about you. Are you certain you can manage without him?"

Renee and I ordered a dish of sweet and sour nippet balls, a plate of vegetable fried rice, a plate of vegetable chow mien and five bottles of six ounce Cokes. "That should do us all nicely," Renee commented. "No leftovers this time." During the whole conversation Mary's husband remained silent. I discovered he was a stone mason who started out on his own in the construction business after he learned his craft. A native of Toronto he was called "Frank Sedgewick." He had attended Eastern Technical School and graduated in the late 1930's from the trowel trades course. He was a quiet man. His small company employed 12 tradesmen. He was currently working on a new shopping plaza in Scarborough.

At a predetermined time Mary Watson and her husband and some friends making up a party of five people began to make preparations to move Hugh from the small house on The Farm that Margaret and he shared for over 20 years. The furnishings in the small house were in good repair, clean and functional but nobody responded to the advertisements in the local papers when an attempt was made to sell off the contents of the house. The result was that the furnishings were donated to the Salvation Army who was happy to receive the goods. They also obtained the bedding, towels and cutlery and china. It was enough to furnish a house for a young couple just starting out. The Salvation Army, in Toronto, had helped many a beginning family. I however inspected the house before we sold the contents looking for miscellaneous treasures that might be given away. Such treasures as the mint state Canadian coins recklessly tossed away as playthings for tiny toddlers by the youngest daughter of Esther Perez. Esther's youngest daughter and her daughter's wasteful husband Benny Seltzer pitched away a small numismatic fortune. I found two paintings, small oil sketches, on the living room wall. These were signed "J. E. H. MacDonald." My instincts told me they were valuable. I took those for the large house. There were also two bound sketch books from the artist depicting various scenes around Northern Ontario. I had a sense these were valuable as well and placed them to the library of the big house. I would study them later. Hugh was not interested in the art work. When it was time for Hugh to leave his children packed him into the old de Soto. I had transferred the ownership of the vehicle to Hugh before the final move was made. Only his clothing and personal items accompanied him to his oldest daughter's home. He died seven months later! Renee and I never saw him again. His funeral service was followed by a cremation. When and where it was held was not told to us. Renee discovered information about Hugh's passing when she was reading the obituary notices in the Toronto Comet.

Strangely enough, Hugh left a fortune of $200 000 to be divided among his four children. This information came to me via Walter Abercromby. This was a great deal of money in 1957. This fortune caused a squabble amongst the four daughters. All of them felt entitled to a greater share than they were left, especially the oldest daughter Mary. Renee and I had the two paintings and sketch book appraised by a reputable art dealer. The paintings had been the original property of Alastair Duncan who loaned them to the Watsons for wall decorations. I discovered a statement on the back of each framed painting. It outlined where the paintings were purchased and the dates of purchase. I learned that these statements showed the art's "provenance," that is their history. The dealer offered $14 000 for the pair. I kept them. Renee and I decided not to contact the heirs of Hugh. That part of our lives was over.

CHAPTER 39

The Farm is sold

B ill Noble and his new wife Dorothy moved into The Farm late in the autumn of 1957. I had decided to ask him to live there until Renee and I could determine what to do with The Farm. We didn't have a clue. Then later, we opened a letter from Harwood Property Development. It was an offer to purchase The Farm. This was the second offer for The Farm. The first was from J. Baird Development a few years earlier. That offer was for $1 000 000! The new developers wanted The Farm acreage and the house. They outlined, in the letter, that they wanted to build a large subdivision on the land but keep the big Farm house. They were offering $2 000 000 for everything. I sent the letter to Walter Abercromby and asked him to look into it. I reminded Abercromby that I had turned down an offer from another developer a few years earlier. Now I appeared to have no need for The Farm because Renee and I were now anticipating living on Renee's and my new property in Norfolk County.

So a deal was negotiated with Harwood on behalf of Renee and me by Walter Abercromby and a friend of his; who was a successful retired land developer. The retired developer was called "Eduard Gautier," a bilingual Québécois, who retired to Florida. Gautier had developed a small subdivision and apartment building in Tampa Florida for retired Canadians from Quebec and Ontario. The large farm house on the property would remain untouched along with one acre of grounds surrounding it. Bill Noble and Dorothy would remain there for two years rent free paying only the utilities. The house would then revert to the ownership of the developers. Altogether Renee and I received a sum of $2 400 000 for the former Alastair Duncan property. A sum increased in magnitude of over 48 times what Alastair had originally invested to purchase The Farm and erect the large farm house and out buildings! Walter Abercromby informed Renee and me that Harwood Development was a highly reputable company and intended to build medium and small houses for rising young families that wished to move out of the now quickly saturating City of Toronto. The Township of North York, having been in existence since the mid 1920's had a population of about 40 000 right after World War II. It consisted mostly of farms little housing and a huge RCAF station called "Downsview."

Downsview would in time become a park and North York swell to a population of nearly 800 000 by the year 2010. It was now beginning to fill up with new housing. Streets were being widened. Bathurst Street, originally a two lane road just a few 100 meters north of St. Clair Avenue was widened to four lanes. The four lanes had reached Wilson Avenue by 1957. Former villages such as Emery and Armour Heights were absorbed by the sprawling region. Developers were looking for large areas to build on. My farm, which I inherited from Alastair Duncan, now filled that requirement. It was outside the Township of North York. Harwood was far sighted. They foresaw that Metropolitan Toronto would, in a few years fill up North York and additional population would spread beyond the City Limits of Metropolitan Toronto.

A chartered accountant engaged by the Abercromby Law firm went over the assets of Renee and me in late 1957. Renee and I were both at 24 years of age. We had a joint worth of $8 500 000! It was true that I had inherited more than $3 000 000 and Renee had earned nearly $1 500 000 after taxes from her concert tours and recordings. Our wealth had increased nearly $4 000 000! Working for a living was academic. Renee refused to make concert appearances and I found it harder and harder to maintain interest in my engineering studies. My grades fell off from the first class honors I achieved in my pre engineering and first two years of regular engineering studies to high second class honors in my third year and low second class honors in my fourth and fifth years. Renee and I were searching for the Truth of Life. I would do the minimum studying to pass my courses and would work at a cooperative assignment only to fulfill my university requirements. I was no longer the star at Waterville University I was in my first three years.

Gradually, The Farm library in Norfolk Country began to fill up with books from all sorts of authors. First there were books by Emmanuel Swedenborg, then a series of reissued publications such as the *Aquarius Bible*, and endless other books from different occult libraries and book stores. We wanted to purchase anything and everything which would lead us closer to the Light. Yet the Light seemed to be further away than ever.

My graduation date was moved ahead because the numbers of students in each year were rapidly dwindling due to excessive failures. I started with over 130 students in pre engineering. At the end of the first semester that figure had been reduced to less than 70. By the end of the first year, it was down to 43, the end of the second year to 31. There were not enough numbers to fill classes so the three classes, each running consecutively, were to be lumped together into one large class. My class was in the middle. There was a class that started three months earlier in engineering proper. My class and one that started in pre engineering behind me were now one large class. I would have to spend three of my work terms at school. This suited me well. I didn't care for the cooperative work assignments. They proved to be jobs unsuitable for smart young men. Unscrupulous companies were taking advantage of the new university's cooperative program to gain inexpensive employees. This combining of three different years into one single year was not expensive by my standards and it moved my graduation forward by six months and cost me three work terms. I completed my studies in May, 1959 and was awarded a B.A.Sc. degree in Engineering Physics at the convocation the following July. I decided not to look for employment but take some time off and think.

I was disappointed that Agnes did not show up at the graduation ceremony when I received my degree. I telephoned her at her Niagara apartment and offered to pay for the expenses of a limousine and driver to fetch her and bring her on the one and one half hour drive to

Waterville. After a "victory dinner" she would have been chauffeured home. It would have cost her nothing. It was too much of a journey to the "sticks."

"Why haven't you given me grandchildren by now?" Agnes would ask on the telephone when either Renee or me would call her." Bill was not her son by blood. He and Dorothy were expecting their first child. This child would not be a blood relative. Marion was completing secondary school and was planning a stage career. Eventually Marion would marry into an "Establishment May Flower Family" and have a daughter, by her husband Garnette Allen. Garnette was a Yale man. Garnette carried the genes of an alcoholic but he got hold of himself. He joined AA and went on the wagon. Garnette knew the head of every major publishing house on the East Coast. He was successful in getting Marion's first book published. After that she was on her way. Later on, I was to discover that Garnette was initiated into something called "The Skull and Bones Society" during his senior year at Yale. The Society was very secretive and Garnette never spoke of it too often. Renee and I were also at the age of 35 years were also initiated into a Society. This Society was known to its members as "The Activity." It was dedicated to bringing the Victory of The Permanent Golden Age into the World. It was also dedicated to bringing the Victory of the Permanent Golden Age into the world as fast as possible.

There is a great deal of talk in the World about courage. There is more courage displayed by a man and women serving in the Light than there is by an army of solders fighting in a war for some vague political motive that those solders do not really understand.

CHAPTER 40

The Entrepreneur

The library at The New Farm house began to fill up with occult literature quickly. While Renee and I were reading this stuff I decided to become an entrepreneur. While picking up some books from a specialty shop on Yonge Street I noticed a restaurant called "Mister Toby's" next door and dropped in. The eatery had about 75 seats and was finished somewhat like a shower room in a high class gymnasium. The place was painted in white with semi tiled walls also in white. It had white tables and table cloths. The place had an overall sterile glare to it. It was too antiseptic in appearance. I inquired as to what they did their cooking in. The counter girl grew edgy. She called the owner.

"This is Mr. McCaffrey," she said. McCaffrey was a dead ringer for Senator Joseph Raymond McCarthy, he of the "McCarthy -Army Hearings" shown on network TV in the States during the mid- 1950's. He even talked like him. I studied him carefully. I almost expected him to say, "point of order." Later I was to discover that McCaffrey's nickname was indeed "Senator Joe." Other people were also aware of his startling similarity to the Junior Senator from Wisconsin. I wondered where Roy Cohn was.

"What matter does it make what we cook in?" Senator Joe replied to my question to the counter girl. "We serve freshly made products!"

"I have dietary requirements," I answered. "If I were to eat something made in lard or beef fat I could get seriously ill; why I might even die on your floor." Senator Joe looked at me strangely.

"We can't have that," Joe answered. "Is there something on the menu you like?"

"Well," I answered, if your French fries are fresh cut and cooked in vegetable oil I would dearly love to have an order along with your spinach salad."

Senator Joe walked away from the table. He gave orders to the counter girl. I was left alone at the table. Senator Joe returned a few minutes later with a tray containing a spinach salad and a tub of fries. "Is this what you want?" Joe asked. I noticed he had a white apron attached to his blue pin striped suit.

"I'll try it out." I consumed the fries first and then the salad. Senator Joe delivered a 10 ounce drink, served in a paper cup, which looked like Coke, to the table.

"I have friends that have been trying to crack the formula for Coke for the last year. This isn't the real thing but you can't tell the difference." I tried the "coke." It tasted more like Pepsi but inferior to both colas. I made no comment about the "coke" to Senator Joe. "Tell me about your place here," I remarked to Joe.

Joe disappeared again and returned five minutes later with a bound booklet with the title, *Expansion plans for Mr. Toby's Restaurants* printed on the cover. "Study this document," Joe requested.

So both Renee and I looked over the 10 page document later that evening while in the library-study of The New Farm. "This looks okay," I commented looking up from my reading. I will be downtown tomorrow and I'll talk to Mr. McCaffrey again."

Two new occult books were waiting at the book store next to Mr. Toby's sterile, white emporium. I took delivery of them and stopped next to Mr. Toby's. Senator Joe was there dressed in a gray pinstriped suit with black shoes. He was entrenched behind the counter instructing a young lady, a different one from the one behind the counter when I was there last. They looked up and senator spotted me immediately. I ordered a tub of French fries and a "coke." It was a snack. "I forgot to pay you for yesterday's food," I told McCaffrey. "I would like to know more about investing in Mr. Toby's Restaurants. I have some spare cash."

"Boy have I got a deal for you!" McCaffrey exclaimed. McCaffrey sounded like Roy Rollins when making this remark. It was a remark that Rollins always made when dealing with a customer. Senator Joe quickly left the counter girl by herself and sat down beside me. I noticed a plump woman about 35 years of age, who joined him at the table. "This is Elizabeth Barrett, a noted author and antiques expert, especially Canadian antiques. She is my business associate." The plump lady smiled. I would too if I had the same name as the famous English Poet "Elizabeth Barrett Browning.

"Joseph is a brilliant operator!" Elizabeth said, turning an admiring eye to Senator Joe. He's the one who helped me get my book published. Elizabeth produced a large tome from her briefcase. It was titled, *Collecting Upper Canada's Antiquities*. I perused the book, which was about 50% composed of pictures. Elizabeth was smiling at me and secretly nodding to Senator Joe.

"To start out in Mr. Toby's a client has to put up $25 000. For that he will receive a 10% share in our new venture. This restaurant you are now sitting in has been franchised to another party. It is not available." Senator Joe shuffled some paper around on the table. The plump lady kept looking at him when he talked but never looked at me.

"What do I owe you for yesterday and today?"

"Why not a penny," Senator Joe replied. "All our investors enjoy eating here on the house." Senator Joe smiled at Elizabeth. Elizabeth placed her book back into her briefcase. Senator Joe carried on with his spiel. "I have owned seven successful restaurants before this one. They all made money and were sold for a profit. Why five Greeks from the old country bought two of my former businesses and have increased their sales. You know how good the Greeks are at running restaurants!" Then "senator" smiled and Elizabeth nodded looking at Joe with deep admiration in her eyes.

"When can we expect your investment?" Senator Joe asked. "The money goes into an escrow account until the venture goes ahead. Do you know what an escrow account is?" He directed this question at me.

"I do not," I replied.

Elizabeth broke into the conversation. "Why my dear," she said, "an escrow account is an account held by the Law Society of Upper Canada for the investors in a new business venture. When the venture starts up the money is used to develop it. If the project doesn't go ahead for any reason the money is returned to the investors by the lawyers. There is no interest paid to the original investor as that is kept by the Law Society of Upper Canada."

"Our lawyer, John Fisher has all the papers," remarked Senator Joe, as he handed me a business card. "My associate and I feel that any investor will recover his investment within one year. Then we can always use the gains to start another venture. Duplication is how these large chains got big" Joe McCaffrey smiled as he gave his spiel.

I decided to talk with Fisher the lawyer during that afternoon and called for an appointment if one was available. According to McCaffrey's spiel I would get 10% of the ownership of the new venture for a mere $25 000. Fisher's secretary told me to come by the office at 2:00 PM. I always carried a check book with me in case I wanted to make small purchases. I knew the household account only earned 1.5% annual interest but there was over $40 000 on deposit in it. All other accounts were locked into one or more yearly deposits drawing a much higher rate of interest. I walked into the Fisher's office located in an old building near Yonge and Carleton Streets. The secretary led me into the office. John Fisher was a thin man about 5'9" tall. He was stooped over. I estimated his age at 40 years. He wore granny glasses. I read some additional documents Fisher handed over to me. It stated that the $25 000 I was about to turn over to the lawyer was to be held in an escrow account until money was required to start the new venture which was planned to be located near Parliament and Carleton Streets. For my investment I would be entitled to 10% of the gross profits. The profits were estimated to be $230 000 for the first year. John Fisher was not interested in talking at any length. But he made some comments.

"I own the building this venture is to occupy," Fisher stated. I know landlord and tenant laws. I will get my rent." I felt strangely doubtful when that remark was made. Fisher handled the signed papers for a few seconds then gave them to his secretary along with the check. I was hastily moved out of his office. I made a collect telephone call to The New Farm. There was a receiver near the grand piano in the study.

Renee picked up the telephone. I told her I had picked up the biweekly supply of occult books and would be taking the 4:00 PM train to Simcoe from the Union Station. I would be at the rail station by 5:45 PM. Would she pick me up there? I had the shopping bag of books I had picked up at Miller's Book Store and some additional volumes purchased from a group called "British Israel." I rode the Yonge Subway down to the Union Station and purchased a non-commuter's ticket on the express train to Simcoe. The train only made four stops after it left the Union Station before it found its way to Simcoe. Four minutes after it arrived at the Union Station it departed. I opened the shopping bag of books and looked them over. I decided to peruse a book called the *Middle Eastern Roots of the Canadian and American Peoples.* It was a very interesting book.

The main thesis of the book had nothing to do with the modern state of Israel founded in 1948. This book stated that the ancient Hebrew People of the Exodus, the 12 Tribes of Israel, were not the modern Jews at all. These ancient folk developed in the Anglo-Saxons, Celts, Scandinavians, Norman French and other white western peoples of modern Europe and were the principal founding peoples of the British Commonwealth and the United States. Even the French Canadians descended from the ancient Hebrews. It claimed the modern Jewish people, at least 95% of them, were descended from the Khazer nation which thrived from about 600 AD to 1000 AD. These were a Turkish-Mongolian folk who converted to Judaism in order to unite their peoples. The nation of Khazers was pressed from many sides. The "Rus" or "Vikings" as they were commonly referred to were coming down from the North while the Islamic hordes were pushing the Khazers from the south. The royal family of the Khazers decided to organize a state religion which they hoped would unite their various peoples to help defend their kingdom. The "Kagan," as their king was called, invited emissaries from the principal religions of the world. Agents of Catholicism, Islam and Judaism visited his kingdom. The Kagan of the Khazers, opted for Judaism. The Kagan did not go for Catholicism because it would make him a vassal of the Pope. When Khazaria collapsed around 1000 AD many fled the Khazer nation and settled in Eastern Europe: in Poland, Hungary, and eventually as far west as Germany. Suddenly out of nowhere vast quantities of Jews sprang up in Eastern Europe. These Jews from Eastern Europe are known today as "Ashkenazim." The book backed up what Esther Perez de Leon Hombre Noble had told me on at least two occasions. The book was fascinating, so much so that I almost missed getting off the train at Simcoe.

Renee was waiting at the Simcoe station. A cab from the station to The New Farm was steep. I felt the $8.00 fare was exorbitant. It was avoided on this occasion because Renee brought the Chevy Nomad. It was a pleasant evening, cold but comfortable. I kissed Renee and we entered the nearly new 1957 Chevy Nomad and drove to The Farm.

"I purchased an interest in a new business," I told Renee.

"That is nice dear, she answered. "I hope it works out." The Nomad reached The New Farm in 20 minutes. Nothing was said about the new venture for days after that until three months had passed. Renee and I made a trip to Toronto to stop at two bookstores to retrieve telephone orders we placed for several books we wanted. Two titles intrigued each of Renee and me. One was a book about miracle cures at Lourdes and a second about some spiritual things by a woman called "Elizabeth Keubler Ross." We arranged to visit the second book store which was situated near Mr. Toby's Restaurant as a last stop. We picked up the volumes packed in two small shopping bags and went next door to the restaurant to snack on something. It was closed. The premises smelled strange as if something was burnt. We went back to the book store to enquire what had happened.

"They had a fire that started in the kitchen and spread into the dining room. The store is a total 'write off.' Luckily the fire department kept it from spreading to the other buildings. They were pretty fast to get here," the bookshop owner, "Felix Underling," commented.

Then Renee and I went to visit Fisher, the lawyer representing Senator Joe. His office was closed up and a "For Rent" sign hanging on the door. The manager of the office building where Fisher rented his office informed Renee and me that Fisher had his secretary stay an extra two weeks in the office even though the lawyer had moved his files out and had not showed up at the office once during those weeks.

The secretary had not been paid for two weeks nor was the lawyer seen. Renee and I dropped by the office of Walter Abercromby to inform him of the goings on with the Mr. Toby's Company.

"A young man with all your smarts would have visited me before venturing into such a scheme," Walter Abercromby commented. "As for Fisher, I believe he was thrown out of the legal profession two years ago. It was business fraud or cooking the company's books or something like that." I don't know much about this Joseph McCaffrey but I will put someone on it immediately. When will you be back in Toronto?"

Two weeks later Renee and I returned to Toronto to pick up more books. The former Mr. Toby's was still closed and not undergoing any renovations. We journeyed down to Abercromby's office to make a 2:30 PM appointment as previously set up. Walter Abercromby dumped the contents of a file folder on his desk. "What a schmuck this Joe McCaffrey is," Abercromby commented as he opened the file. "Listen to this. McCaffrey owned a 100 seat restaurant in East York 10 years ago. It was destroyed in a fire. Fortunately nobody was injured. Then he had a second place, the 'Potato Parlor' he called it. It ran, I might add, successfully for two years. Know what happened? It burned down. Four years ago he owned the 'Salmon Wharf.' It burned down a year after he opened it. He had the current place, Mr. Toby's for the last year. Know what, it burned down. Unfortunately, the elderly couple, who rented the flat above the restaurant were severely burned in the fire. The old lady died and the old man is in the hospital with severe burns all over. His prognosis is not too good." Walter Abercromby moved his head side to side. "As a result of this last fire the insurance company is holding up payment for losses. They have every reason to." Walter Abercromby crossed himself like a devout Catholic. "I want you to sue him and Elizabeth Barrett. The woman has two valuable properties she inherited from her father. As far as I know they are debt free. I know it costs money to sue, but if you win we can attach the houses. If we sell them we can put the money to good use. Best of all we can put McCaffrey out of business."

"Do it," I replied. "If I keep losing $25 000 each year in bad business ventures at that rate in 300 years or so I'll go broke. If I don't spend money on the necessities of life such as food and shelter it might take me 400 years to go broke!" Renee and I returned to The New Farm to read occult books. Renee never said a word about the lost $25 000. We noticed something strange about the house. It was filled with a new fragrance of roses. We noticed this was strongest in the new chapel we devoted a smaller room to. Each day we lived there the fragrance grew stronger. In time, it spread everywhere in the house and then started to be detected outside the house. One day Renee while dusting the chapel noticed a strange blue flower sitting on the small stand where fresh flowers were always kept. It looked like a rose but was of a pale blue color. Some of the petals had fallen off and were lying on the glass top covering the flower stand. The rose remained in the house for two weeks and then mysteriously disappeared, as if swallowed up by the Cosmos but the fragrance continue on.

Abercromby and his associates worked away on the case while two more months passed. Cold weather was now in progress and a chill was in the air. The legal process had caught up with "Senator Joe" McCaffrey. They found him staying at the Bridle Path mansion of Bud Buchanan, the wealthy Toronto financier. Buchanan and his alcoholic wife had departed the Bridle Path for Sarasota, Florida in mid-October, 1958. They wouldn't return until late April 1959. It seems that Bud Buchanan had taken an immediate liking to Senator Joe and his playmate Elizabeth Barrett when he first met them at Mr. Toby's. The saying says "like does attract like." Such was the arrogance of Buchanan that his chauffeur parked the Rolls Royce directly in front of the Yonge Street location of Mister Toby's. This usually occurred during rush hour. There was no parking in that area but the Police never ticketed him. The chauffeur remained inside the car while Bud Buchanan and his drunken wife would "slum it" at Mr. Toby's. While McCaffrey and Buchanan chatted together the two women, Elizabeth Barrett and Doris Buchanan discussed antiques.

In time, Bud Buchanan offered "Senator" Joe McCaffrey and Elisabeth Barrett the opportunity to "house sit" the Buchanan's Bridle Path mansion while Mr. and Mrs.Buchanan were in Florida for the winter.

"Joseph McCaffrey is such a charming man," Doris Buchanan commented. "If I had an older brother I wish he were like Joseph."

How Walter Abercromby and his staff found Senator Joe and Elizabeth residing on a January, 1959 day, shacked up inside the 10 000 square foot mansion, has always been a mystery to me but find them he did. They were detained, not by the police, but by professional body guards hired for just such contingencies by Walter Abercromby. It appears that Elizabeth and Senator Joe had been quietly looting the Bridle Path mansion selling off "valuable art" and clothing belonging to the migrating Buchanan couple and all sorts of other goodies. Of course some of the paintings Bud Buchanan had acquired were stolen "Canadian masterpieces." This was something Bud did not want discovered. When the Bud and his spouse were in Florida they were contacted by the Toronto Police. They were appalled to discover the extent of the pillaging performed by Senator Joe and Elizabeth Barrett. Years later some of the stolen antiquities appeared on the market. They were purchased by wealthy tycoons residing in the Toronto area in the 1970's. They thought they were getting a deal when all they bought were fakes. These fakes were authenticated as real by the "reputable" and famous auction houses with sales centers world-wide. I found out from Abercromby that two well-known Canadian artists, both members of the Royal Canadian Academy had stated they were bogus.

"But how did those artists know this?" I asked.

"Those artists told me that if they could paint a better picture on the subject matter that the supposed real artists did then they were fakes," Ambercromby answered.

The whole matter of Mr. Toby's Restaurants went to trial in a civil court about six months after Abercromby started action against Senator Joe and Elizabeth. Joe was found responsible for stealing the financial resources of 17 people. The police were given evidence of arson in seven cases in total. Various insurance companies had paid out nearly $2 000 000 in claims. Police were also investigating Joseph McCaffrey and Elizabeth Barrett for looting the Buchanan house. Renee and I received a settlement of $25 000 plus damages to the tune of $40 000 in total. Elizabeth Barrett's two houses came under the control of Abercromby.

The insurance companies then got involved in a battle with Abercromby trying to gain control of the settlement. Abercromby settled with the insurance companies for $100 000. The properties were worth nearly $500 000! McCaffrey and Barrett were liable for the court costs and legal fees. Renee and I kept the $25 000 but donated the remaining money to James Schmidt. He was the fellow who was harmed in the last fire that killed his wife and destroyed Mr. Toby's. He was now a widower because of Senator Joe. He needed money to survive and pay for nursing care.

I could not help reflecting on a comment Senator Joe made two times in front of me. Senator Joe found some minor fault in a paint job a contractor did in the washroom. The contractor offered to fix it. The job would have taken a few minutes. Instead Joe refused to pay up making an excuse that the work was shoddy which it was not. While the contractor and Joe were bickering Joe screamed out "Don't put your hands on me." The painter left the premises without his money. One of the teenage girls working the counter said: "it is wrong to cheat that man."

Senator Joe responded. "In business there is no right or wrong, only business."

When the court case was settled Walter Abercromby made me promise to consult him anytime I thought about investing in any business venture. He also gave the name of a Chartered Accountant I should consult.

"A Chartered Accountant is always a good bet to have available in any new business. Just as good as a lawyer," Abercromby remarked. "But not all bad came out of this affair. Your money helped a disabled man. You forced a dangerous criminal off the streets. And even though you don't know him personally you got back at Bud Buchanan. Now there is a thief if there ever was one. Do you know that he along with Irwin Carter and the rest of their cohorts looted the pension funds of Imperial Appliances when they bought that industrial enterprise. There was about $10 000 000 in surplus funds in the pension plan. Imperial Appliances was the company that rented 10 acres for a warehouse from the old Duncan estate. Mrs. Masters, the widow of the former owner said she was drugged and then forced to sign over her assets to Bud Buchanan and his pals. They ripped her off. After the looting the company was closed and its assets were sold, the buildings and mechanical gear being its most valuable assets. Of course they couldn't steal the land. You owned that. The 1000 former blue collars workers were left with almost worthless pensions. Imagine working for a company that touted how loyal it was to its employees, weekly deducting 10% of the gross wages of those employees and then putting those moneys in their pockets. In the final year the company was in business the deductions for income taxes and employment insurance were not reported to the Federal government or were pension deductions turned over to the pension administrators. After the plant was closed the Feds came after the former employees for back income taxes on the 10% of their salaries deducted for pensions but not reported. Those deductions reported as part of the gross employee's pay on the company's books! I can't stand a crook! Besides where were our Federal and Provincial governments when this happened? Bud Buchanan is a thief! Maybe there some truth in that expression: 'what goes around comes around.' Dear young friends, you seem to have a team of Divine Guardians about you whatever you do!"

Renee and I felt good after the little torrent of words from Walter Abercromby. That evening after a train ride back to Norfolk Country. We settled in for a lunch at the Norfolk Golf Club we paid for a taxi ride to The New Farm. We spent the evening studying occult literature.

"Well, once again the great man fails in a venture," I commented. "What do I do with myself? I am getting older but not wiser." I shuffled around in the recliner in the library-study. "I have tried everything you can imagine. I thought I could make it as a professional golfer, but my body let me down there. That was a failure. Then I became an observer in the RCAF, I couldn't last in that. Then I went to University, I started off well then declined. I couldn't engineer worth a damn. Obviously I am not cut out for any business. I've sat idly by at this Farm for almost a year. I have hit a few golf balls. I have read some books. What is to become of me?"

Renee looked at me with a funny look. Then she said, "You are to become an Angel. Our marriage was predestined. The simple truth is you are not a person who belongs in the Outer World unless your "Mighty I Am Presence" is in it is for the World's benefit. You never have been a failure. If you give yourself over to the Divine you will become what you were meant to be, a 'Grail Child.'"

I looked at her with a puzzled expression. "Can we give a prayer at bed time. Let us both together ask the Almighty what we should do. It says: "Ask in My Name what you should do and it will be answered." So that evening at 11:00 PM Renee and I stood in the library-study before a likeness of Jesus and said aloud: "In the name of God: 'I Am' what is it you want me to do?" The room filled immediately with the scent of sandalwood as a white light brilliant but short lived possessed the room. Renee and I had discovered "The I Am Presence." We would never let it go.

CHAPTER 41

A Couple in Hibernation

Renee and I were in hibernation for almost 12 months after the Mr. Toby's affair. Renee practiced her music four hours per day while I gave one hour per day to hitting golf shots. Occasionally I would visit the Western Golf Club where I held a membership. It was a hilly short track of 6500 yards with badly designed putting greens which sloped severely towards the golfers as they approached it from the fairway. The "wise acre" professional at the club was a fortyish man who had a problem with alcohol. At one time he was a superb player. His name was "Herbert Kelly." He usually began drinking at noon. Herbert had squandered his gift for golf. He played with me frequently.

"Why did you give up your playing career?" Herbert Kelly asked me. I explained about my lower back problem. I would usually play nine holes. I could not walk the 18 holes without getting seriously sore in the lower back. I posted my nine-hole scores in the pro shop. I played to a two handicap. My body didn't permit me to practice my short game: putting and chipping for a long enough time to make my scores lower. The maximum time was limited to 30 minutes. I long ago had mastered the changes Nelson Burns had taught me. If I exceeded 30 minutes of practice I could hardly walk. I couldn't practice for more than 30 minutes on putting and chipping or I wouldn't be able to stand up let alone leave the practice green. Besides how can one explain a karmic injury to an uninitiated man?

When I joined the hilly Western Golf Club I simply walked into the clubhouse and asked to see the club manager. They charged me a $500 initiation fee. The Club was looking for adult members. I purchased 20 shares of common stock in the club for $1000. I also purchased a membership for Renee but she had abandoned the game for which she once showed so much promise. So I swapped the membership for Renee for two junior memberships which I gave to two promising young players. Occasionally Renee would walk about the course with me but she declined to swing a club. Word got around the Western Golf Club that I was once a golf professional who actually competed for money. There were several male prima donnas anxious to try me out. I did my best to avoid them all. When I played on weekends I teed off after Noon. This allowed me to play alone in a golf cart while Renee accompanied me. Occasionally a prima donna would force his company on Renee and me.

"What are we going to play for?" was always the question asked.

"We are going to play for pleasure," I would always answer. I detested gambling. During one nine hole round I played with the "club champion." I pulled hooked my opening drive into the long right rough on the first hole. I pitched the ball back onto the fairway on the next shot and hit a short iron 30 feet from the hole on my third shot. I then took three putts for a double bogey six.

"Some touring pro," I heard the "club champion" say under his breath. That peeved me. My ego was bruised. My former competitive juices began to surge. I then proceeded to make birdies on each of the next five holes. I finished with pars on the final three holes and was two under for the nine. The club champion said nothing. The club champion after those nine holes always wanted strokes when he played with me even though he also held a two handicap! Eventually, over the course of a few months the "hotshot" amateurs stopped pestering me for a game and left me alone. There wasn't anybody in the Western Country Club that could beat me in a legitimate match!

I was the young man who had to master everything I attempted. I would never be satisfied with being just an excellent golfer, which I was. I had to be capable of beating anybody. But I did not have the physical tools to do so. It was hard for me to play casual golf. After all, my wife

Renee was not a casual pianist. She still practiced four hours per day and taught at the university.

After a year of hibernation I had to find some line of work. In August of 1960, I made enquiries at the University of Waterville as to the whereabouts Dr. Ralph Renton, B.Sc. M.A. Ph.D. Dr. Ralph was still teaching freshman Calculus. I often marveled at Ralph's ability to learn the names of the 100 or so students sitting in the lecture hall shortly after he began teaching his introductory first class. Ralph was proficient in Portuguese and German. He taught Calculus to students at the Catholic University of Rio for two years. He was a master communicator!

"Have you tried teaching?" Ralph asked me as he sipped on the black coffee in the University's Tuck Shop. Ralph always placed a clean napkin over the saucer and then mounted the filled cup on the napkin before he began to sip the coffee. Ralph was not an athletic man and a confirmed bachelor. His graduate students, well into scuba diving, said "he swam like a stone."

"You have great communications skills and are creative. These are the things most of the teaching professionals lack. There is only one drawback." Ralph paused and took a swig of coffee. He looked at me intently. "I don't think you will last long; maybe five years or so. You will never stand for the bullshit. You will be offered promotions but if you accept them woe betide you. The higher up you go the more miserable you will become. Teaching is something you will do well but it is not your life's work! After all, public schools are essentially government institutions. You don't want to be institutionalized do you?

I returned from the University of Waterville in the late afternoon. I stopped off at Willard's Cigar Store in Kitchener to purchase copies of the latest golf publications: *National Golf Digest and Golf National*. These were magazines only a golfer could love. There was a portrait of Nelson Burns on the front covers of both major magazines. I thought about Nelson Burns before I last saw him in April of 1951. I promised to correspond with him at least once a month. Nelson was now dead. I had ceased regular communication with him when I started at Waterville in the first year of engineering. Before that I wrote him once per month.

Now I only wrote a two or three page summary of events that took place in the previous year. Nelson usually sent a Christmas card once a year. There was always an open invitation to visit him at his Ranch in Florida. Nelson was suffering from a degenerative bone disease that started to take disastrous effects on him in his late 30's. Once a tall man about 6'2" he had shrunk to 5'9" by the time he was in his final year of embodiment. His game was gone when he reached 60 years of age and I was completing my studies at Waterville. He married Louise Turner when he was a young professional starting out in tournament golf. She was his care giver for the final remaining 10 years he would stay in embodiment after he quit golf. Nelson could no longer play golf to his standards in his early 60's so he took up painting in oils instead. His work was well received by collectors. "If only he had been formally trained he could have been an outstanding artist," they said in his obituaries in both major golf publications. So Nelson Burns, star professional golfer, winner of five major championships, devoutly spiritual man met his end at the hands of a debilitating bone disease. For the final 10 years of his embodiment he stopped playing golf. He occasionally tutored new young playing professionals but spent most of his time painting the "quiet places" of his central Florida ranch. After all, Nelson Burns was a quiet man!

I had not written to him more than once a year since my marriage to Renee some five years earlier in 1955. But Renee had recently consented to do a concert tour throughout the southern United States and I agreed to accompany her. Music promoters were interested in exploring how a nearly 10 year absence from the public stage had either developed her talent or diminished it. Renee had consented to the tour. Renee had lucrative recording contracts and after my graduation from the University of Waterville world famous musical artists with expertise in all instruments would visit The New Farm.

"Now Renee," they would often remark, "the world wants to hear you play. You owe it to them. Make a short tour once a year." Renee was more of an isolationist than even I had become. Our world now consisted of Norfolk County and The New Farm. I had gotten off my final letter to Nelson Burns about a month before his passing. I had not corresponded with him for a year. Renee and I were going to visit the Central Florida Region and give a two night stand in Orlando. The wife of Nelson Burns never answered my last letter. I sent no more letters. Yet fate was to take a strange twist. That twist would come in the month when the tour began. The first stop of the tour was Nashville, Tennessee where classical piano temporarily competed with country music. Both were successful tours. Then it was on to Atlanta, Georgia for another two day stand. Reviews of the concerts were outstanding.

> *Great talent comes out of hibernation. Isolationist concert pianist returns to the concert stage with an outstanding repertoire playing it in public after an absence of nearly ten years*

I began to assemble a scrapbook for Renee. I had compiled several from my pro golfing days. These were newspaper clippings from the small town papers in Florida where I competed as a professional for three months. They were now gathering dust on a remote shelf in the library of The New Farm. Finally, there was the two day stopover in Orlando, Florida. While Renee, and her manager Lewis Syme, were checking out the venue for the first evening, I made excuses to be absent. I wanted to visit Nelson's Ranch. Renee decided to accompany me. Renee and I engaged a limousine service. I had Nelson's telephone number. I called the Ranch. Louise Turner had invited us out that afternoon. We arrived by chauffeured limousine at 1:00 PM.

Louise Turner Burns was a beautiful elderly lady. She was as tall and as slim as Renee. "Welcome to my home," Louise said. "When I received your letter about one month ago and found out that you wanted to call here I was overjoyed. Nelson talked often of you. He was disappointed that you only wrote him once a year." He knew that you had to give up professional golf because of a spinal injury. Let me speak about Nelson Burns in a very special manner. My dear late husband was loath to define himself as a professional golfer. He felt that that was what he did for a living. He, in secret, defined himself as a 'God Being.' Nelson was a 'Light Seeker!' I must tell you he converted me into what he was - is."

Louise corrected herself when referring to Nelson. In her mind he never passed through the change called death. It was obvious to Renee and me that she did not consider him dead. He had just gone into another Octave of Life. Louise poured some lime-aid from a pitcher brought into the living room of the ranch house by an elderly black, male servant. Louise rose from the leather sofa and walked over to a wall cabinet. She removed a large carton and placed it on the end table in front of the couch where Renee and I were sitting.

"Would you examine the contents of this box?" Louise removed several medallions from the container. "These are Nelson's medals for many of his golfing accomplishments. They are now your property." I would keep these awards for two years. After Louise made the change I donated them to a golf museum in Florida.

Renee and I spent two hours at Louise Turner Burns' Ranch. The conversation shifted to Nelson's spiritual hunt for the Meaning of Life. I was part of that hunt; so was Renee and so was Louise Turner Burns. We left the Ranch at 4:00 PM and headed back to the hotel to ready ourselves for Renee's evening recital. It was a brilliant success. I added more raves to her scrapbook.

CHAPTER 42

Return to Isolationism

The tour lasted two weeks. Lewis Syme had prepared the way with his customary excellence. Every hotel was selected with great care. Luggage was always packed with diligence. No stone was left unturned. Rental cars were always available. Renee and I liked to explore the areas where we were temporarily billeted. We loved Alabama and I planned to visit Dothan and look up Abraham Warshawsky's oldest sister but the last address I had for her was no longer any good. She had moved away and could not be located. Ultimately Renee and I made our way by airliner back to Malton Airport with our abundant luggage. A hired limousine took us to The New Farm.

"I don't want to travel anymore," Renee said softly. "My concert tours are over. I wonder if I can prepare for recording sessions anymore. I can't tolerate the outer world the way it is now. It is too insane. Something has happened to me which I can't understand."

"I know we made money on this tour," I responded. "I somehow feel the way about what you called 'the outer world.' What the hell! Do we need the money?" I paused for a few seconds. "I went to see Dr. Ralph as the University just before we started this tour. We talked about my future. I told him I wasn't happy with engineering and couldn't work at it any longer; as if I work at it now. He suggested I go into teaching. It is now late August 1961. I have decided to take the one year secondary school teacher's training course at Eastern University starting this September. I will be done with it in May. They are short of maths and physics teachers. The Faculty of Education there considers me to be a ripe catch."

Renee nodded. "I suppose you have to do something. I am going to teach at the university again. So we will both be busy."

I had Doug Smith an associate of Walter Abercrombie handle had the paper work and the forwarding of transcripts to the Faculty of Education at Eastern University. By Early September 1961, I rented a small furnished apartment near the university and we took up temporarily residence once again, Renee teaching music at Eastern and me taking "instruction" on how to become a teacher. Boy! I was in for an awakening! There is an expression in schooling: "Those who can, do; those who can't do, teach; and those who can't teach; teach teachers." So with Renee and I temporarily, during the week, confined to an apartment, situated in a small Ontario city. I was apprenticing to learn my third trade: secondary school teacher.

CHAPTER 43

Teacher Training

There were 12 candidates in mathematics, six in physics and only two qualified to specialize in both. I was slated to become a specialist in both. When I finished my seven month course I would be awarded an *Interim Type A certificate* in mathematics and physics. After two years of successful classroom experience; if my teaching was sufficiently good according to Department of Education Inspectors; I would be granted a permanent *Ontario Specialist's Certificate in Mathematics and Physics*. This required a "5" rating or higher from a Department of Education Inspector.

I had two weeks of instruction in the lecture rooms of Eastern University's Faculty of Education. The man in charge of mathematics instruction was a Gerald MacLaren DSO, M.A. B.Sc. During World War II he worked with British Army Intelligence on loan from the Canadian Forces, as an intelligence officer. This interrupted his teaching career which began in 1935. He was now in his twilight years and recruited by the Faculty of Education of Eastern University to train teachers. He was 5'5" tall and pudgy. It was September 1961.

"Don't let them migrate," MacLaren would often say. "You are not selling Grey Cup Tickets." I was at a loss to understand him. I observed my instructors and could not help noticing how much they seemed to lack basic communications skills! They didn't appear to know how to direct a guest in their homes to the washroom. I could not abide muddled instruction and yet the myriad of "master teachers," seemed to be muddled at all times.

After several days of pedagogical theory I was dispatched to "practice teach" for a week at Middlesex Central Secondary School. My "Critic Teacher" was "A. Lawson Dewer B.A." a teacher in Ontario's Secondary Schools for 25 years! The name was pronounced "doo were" but I called him "de ware" stressing the first syllable. When I was introduced to him the critic teacher nearly had apoplexy. After all, his surname was mispronounced. He was a man about 47 years old. His posture was poor. He had a squeaky voice. His clothes were scruffy. Dewer had a "gigolo" moustache which gave him an unctuous appearance. I was to observe him for one day then teach some of his classes and Dewer was to make comments on my performance.

Dewer began his lesson in Grade 12 mathematics on the quadratic formula. This is the formula for solving the general quadratic equation: $ax^2 + bx + c = 0$. The formula and its development can be taught from scratch by a good teacher to an above average class. To an average class it can be given to the class as a tool, without illustration of how the formula was developed and to be used to solve quadratic equations. The contents of the day's lesson for that class were never written on the chalk board. Dewer "communicated" all information orally. At the conclusion of the lesson Dewer informed the class that there would be a brief quiz on the "quadratic formula" on Thursday, the day after my first lesson to them. Dewer talked to the chalk board rather than the class. He was, in one word, "incompetent." I had been instructed in mathematics and vectors and some physics in the RCAF and by superb officers and at Waterville by master teachers such as Dr. Ralph in mathematics. Dewer was none of these. True, he taught for 25 years. But those were 25 repetitions of one year's experience. One of the cardinal sins I committed was to sit in an easy chair in the staff room. This chair had no reservation sign on it and I took it. This was Mr. Dewer's special chair. Instead of confronting me face on to demand his chair he went to the Union branch president. The union president then told me I had offended Mr. Dewer and warned me not to sit in that chair again. I later discovered the furniture in the staff room was owned entirely by the Board. From that point on I made a special, point of sitting in that particular chair on every occasional I had a chance to.

The following day I took over Dewer's morning three classes. Dewer was kind enough to inform me of the topics. The first period was Grade 12 math and the quadratic formula was to be reviewed. I stayed in the apartment that evening totally ignoring Renee and planned the three lessons I was to teach the next morning. I planned to put an outline of the lesson in the left side of the chalk board at the front of the room.

The next day came and I placed the Outline of the lesson on the Board. I saw an elderly gentleman about 50 years of age enter the room and sit down in the back of the classroom. It was the principal of the school: Watford Watt. Unusually, Watt had also served during WW II with the RCAF. He retired from the RCAF in September 1945 and resumed his teaching career. His final rank was Squadron Leader. He received the ED for his superb WWII Service as well as an M.B.E. An incredible coincidence it was, but the former Squadron Leader Watt was also a navigation instructor! He never got oversees during the War. In his early 40's at the time of his enlistment; the RCAF drooled at the prospects of getting a mathematic and sciences graduate of a reputable Canadian University and a highly esteemed teacher as well. Watford Watt and I shared a common experience of being navigation instructors with about 4.5 years of military service. Watt had read my resume in his office and had to see me in action. Watt carried an RCAF moustache on his face. I still didn't have the nerve to grow one. I knew this second visitor was someone important but I pretended to ignore him. I placed the Outline on the chalk board. It looked like this.

Outline
Review Quadratic Formula
Take up HW. Page 56, Questions 1 to 23
Test Tomorrow.

Watt scribbled on a note pad. Dewer seemed to be in some sort of pain. I began to question the class. I had Dewer's seating plan in hand.

"In the last class Mr. Dewer gave you the quadratic formula. Let us review the formula, and understand what the symbols represent and try it out on a few of the questions from your homework assignment." I walked over to the chalkboard and pointed to the "outline" written on the board. I continued: "This outline will tell you what we are going to do today, where we have been and what we are going to accomplish by the end of this class." I pointed to the chalkboard and showed where I had indicated my name. "Mr. Noble" was printed on the board. "I will be addressed as 'Mr. Noble' or 'Sir.' I am in no way your friend. I am your teacher. Now let's get on with the lesson."

I looked at the class. "What is the formula for solving the general quadratic equation: $ax^2 + bx + c = 0$? Several hands went up. I paused for a few seconds and selected a girl from the middle of the room. "Would you stand up to answer the question young lady," I said. The young lady rose and replied correctly. I wrote on the chalkboard the formula:

$$x = \frac{-b \pm \sqrt{b^2 - 4ac}}{2a}$$

From then on it was question and answer. The class, with my help, drilled on the previous homework which all but a minority of the class could handle. After 20 minutes of instruction everyone started seat work. I had a student write his solution to question 10 using the quadratic formula on the chalk board. For the remainder of the class the homework was placed, after short intervals, on the chalk board by other students. I made corrections on the board work with yellow chalk. The time dwindled on. I noticed Dewer in the back corner of the room writing furiously in a coiled note book. He looked angry. I dismissed the class when the bell sounded.

The remaining two classes were grades 9 and 10 mathematics. Dewer's instructions for handling the lessons for these classes were vague. I kept them in my files. I went to lunch in the teachers' lunch room. Dewer sat alone at a table. No other teacher in the lunch room would sit with him. Watford Watt entered the room. Several of the staff looked up. Watt walked to my table.

"May I sit here?" Mr. Noble. Watt sat across from met. "Where did you learn to teach like that, young man?"

"I was a navigation instructor in the RCAF," I replied. "Instructors in the Air Force have to be competent. Accidents result when they are not." I was very careful to make certain that Watt would know that I served with the RCAF as a navigation instructor. I began again. "I went to the University of Waterville after my Short Service Commission was up."

Watt looked at me. "How old are you now?"

I answered: "I will be 29 years old on December 1, 1961 - this year." We both started to eat our lunch. It was Italian penne with vegetable sauce. For cafeteria food it was excellent.

"While you are training to be a teacher you are going to see all types of teaching, most of it: piss poor!" Watt said. "What did you think of Mr. Dewer's lessons?" This was a dangerous question for me to answer truthfully. It was considered by the Ontario Federation of Teacher's as "unprofessional." I remained silent. "Dewer is a classroom 'klutz,' Watt continued. There is order in his class, that's about it. I think the order comes from having put them to sleep. He is the head of the mathematics department here. Look, Mr. Noble, you already know the score. People like Dewer should never have been promoted, hell they should never have been teachers. They have absolutely no communication skills! That klutz actually complained to me that you took his seat in the staff room, as if it were his personal property."

"Then why is he still here?" I asked.

"Oh God, do you know how I have wanted to trash him? Since I have been principal of this school I wanted him out. I have worked with him on preparing his lessons, class rapport and God know what else. He is beyond hope."

"Then why is he a critic teacher?" I asked.

"He is a classic example of what I hope a young man or lady starting out in this line of work should never develop into. Let his assessment of you go in one ear and out the other. When it comes to your written evaluation I will see that you get a proper rating. When it comes time for you to obtain a position would you see me first of all. It is difficult to get good competent teachers to settle here. They think the opportunities are in the big cities like Toronto. You know the living costs are much easier here."

So I spent five classroom days watching Dewer's performance. Dewer as I discovered was "non-dismissible." His brother was on the Board of Education. His family was wealthy. They owned half of Suffolk County. Dewer was hopeless at running any part of the family enterprises. He was a good student in high school, and average in mathematics and sciences at Eastern University. After a below average performance at the Faculty of Education at Eastern University he headed into the classrooms of the Ontario Secondary School System. He was sub average there. Because of a shortage of university trained science and mathematics graduates he was granted a permanent teaching endorsement after two years. He also earned a specialist in Mathematics and Science. It was a very serious mistake. When a position as head of mathematics became available he was the only qualified candidate, on paper, for the job. It was difficult to get promising beginners to teach in Suffolk County. For the position of math head that Dewer received several more able candidates were turned away without an interview. Mr. Dewer became the head of maths in a school, of over 1000 students, while at least two other more capable teachers situated with that school were denied the job over paper technicalities.

I was pleased to find I had an excellent written report from Watford Watt to MacLaren at the Faculty of Education. There was no mention of Dewer or any of his opinions in the report. Dewer had written that I was an insubordinate student teacher because I wouldn't put into effect his suggestions. He failed me! Watford Watt tore up the report to the Faculty of Education. "A man like Dewer;" he was heard to comment to his secretary; "writes 'bum wipe.'" So it was for me back to the Faculty of Education for more pronouncements on teaching. At the faculty, MacLaren demonstrated the "discovery" method of teaching. This was the latest philosophical crap to come down the line from the gurus of education: the chowder heads and nonsense pundits that felt that they knew best how to run a school. Most of these gurus had never taught in a classroom. Why if they had their way the current sorry state of the World would disappear instantly. Their answer to the World's problems was a "one world government." Perhaps this delusion was why the vast majority of teachers working in Ontario's Public Schools were ardent socialists if not out and out reds! I had a chance to listen to their palaver in the staff rooms of many schools. An election was brewing in 1962 and the history teachers and other types were campaigning vigorously on behalf of the CCF.

In one school, a teacher approached me with a hand full of pamphlets. "Who are you voting for?" the middle aged woman asked. She did not know who I was! I looked deeper into the *Toronto Conservative News and Report* I was reading. "Who are you voting for?" There was a pause of several seconds.

"That is none of your business," I replied. The older woman was becoming impatient.

"You are surely not voting against the CCF?" she asked. "Those other parties are anti-education. It's your duty as a teacher to vote for the CCF." So there you have it! A secret, endorsed ballot cast in all federal elections didn't count. The teachers of Ontario had to vote for a socialist ticket. It was their duty!

"What is that magazine you are reading? Is that a copy of the *Conservative News and Report*? I am going to the principal. You have no right to bring a copy of that Fascist rag into my staff room. I've gone to the principal before. I will not tolerate right wing fascist bullshit in my school." By this time the elderly woman was screaming at the top of her voice. I was to find out the elderly teacher's name was Irene O'Dell. She was a spinster. She hated being called "a spinster." She preferred the title "bachelor lady." Nobody ever could determine if she had any male friends at all. She was always by herself in the staff room. She was the head of the English department.

I found out this "lady" was constantly indoctrinating her students, especially those in the higher grades to vote for the CCF. Miss O'Dell, on my third day at the school, suggested in the staff room to all present there that it might be a wonderful idea if she invited a CCF candidate to visit the class and give a speech. I enquired if the other candidates would also be invited. Irene O'Dell practically had a fit. "That would hardly be fair to my students," she commented. "After all, those Liberals and Conservatives might poison the minds of my students! I want them to get a clear picture of things."

Irene O'Dell bullied all the staff members. "Why I could throw a cup of coffee at you," she told a small young man who dared to disagree on some topic in the staff room. Watford Watt, possibly the only conservative on the staff of that school, started compiling a file on Irene's complaints, many of which she put in writing, dated and signed. It was a very large mistake. It would result in her receiving a chastisement from the Board. After that came her "voluntary" resignation from it.

On my final day at the school I went to the staff dining room to try the lunch. It was egg salad sandwich on white or brown bread with a garden salad. Whatever else was wrong in the school its cafeteria seemed to put out decent food. I selected an empty table, placed my tray on it and opened my copy of *Air Force Monthly*. This was a publication examining the military affairs of both the USAF and the RCAF.

When she saw me reading my magazine Irene O'Dell reacted. "How dare you bring a subversive thing like that into 'my dining room,'" Irene O'Dell commented. I wondered how this woman took possession of everything. With Dewer it was only his chair. With O'Dell it was everything in the school. It was "her school, her staff room, her students," and so on. Irene O'Dell picked up a cup of coffee from the table where two male teachers were eating. She walked over to my table and threw it at me. It landed on my tan custom tailored business suit, an expensive item. The scene was witnessed by more than 20 people in the room including Watford Watt. Irene O'Dell was doomed. She had committed an unprovoked assault on a visitor to the school. Usually when this happened on previous occasions there were only five or so people who witnessed the entire scene. Every time it happened nobody would complain and no supervisory person was among the witnesses. Irene's "right" to dictate the reading matter of her fellow staff and how her students should persuade their parents to vote was challenged. Her reaction was one of pure uncontrolled hatred. She lost control of her veneer of integrity and that would force her out of the teaching profession.

I calmly wiped the excess liquid off the suit. I wasn't scheduled to teach that Friday afternoon. I was requested to report to Watford Watt's office. "How are you going to handle this," Watt asked?

"I am going to file a charge of assault with the police against Miss O'Dell!"

"I saw what happened," Watt commented. "Now I don't have to beg the other witnesses to come forth. She had too many 'friends' ready to tell the truth, her version of the truth. This time I can take stronger action."

So the police were called into the school and Miss O'Dell was summoned to Watford Watt's office after the police departed. The branch president of the Teachers' Union was present. So were me and five other witnesses. Also present was the superintendent of education of Watt's district. Miss O'Dell was shocked when she entered the office.

"Sit here," Watford Watt gestured to the woman and pointed to the large visitor's chair in his oversized office. "Charges have been laid against you with the police for willful assault on a visitor to our school. That visitor was Mr. Noble, a student teacher with us. He has taken time off from his courses at the Faculty of Education to make an additional trip here to be present at this meeting. It is written in this statement that you threw a cup of hot coffee at the gentleman without provocation ruining a new business suit he was wearing at the time of the said incident. You may answer these allegations."

"It is true that I threw coffee at Mr. Noble but he was reading offensive material in my lunch room. He shouldn't be doing that. My God, he was reading war monger magazines. I can't tolerate such behavior." Oddly, Irene O'Dell proclaimed herself to be an advocate against censorship. The meeting went on for 30 minutes. Miss O'Dell knew she was in serious trouble but didn't seem to grasp the reasons why. Finally the inquisition seemed to be exhausted when the superintendent turned to me.

"Have you any suggestions as to what to do Mr. Noble?"

I thought for a few seconds. "I would like Miss O'Dell to pay for the cost of a new suit and replace the shirt I was wearing during the day of the assault. She must also compensate me to the sum of $100 for the time lost while replacing my damaged clothing and my expenses to travel here today. It is on her account I was forced to come here. Then I would like a written apology from her that will be read aloud at a staff meeting then placed in her personnel file. If she doesn't want to do this then I will leave her fate up to the Board and to the police. After that request from me the meeting disbanded. I went back to my afternoon classes at Eastern University and nothing further was heard for about two weeks. Then one evening I received a telephone call from Watford Watt at The New Farm.

"Robert, this is Watford Watt, calling. Miss O'Dell has resigned her position. She said she would rather retire than make a public apology. She remarked that 'you are a rotten young man.' She has reluctantly agreed that you should purchase a new suit and shirt to replace the ones ruined by coffee. She consented to pay for these and that you should be awarded $100 for damages but she will not apologize in front of the staff for her actions. She claims you provoked her. You could have talked your differences over with her. She said: 'you went behind her back to the authorities!' My Robert, "You are a nasty bag of goods." She said 'I would rather resign than apologize to the likes of you.'"

I did not want to pursue the incident any further "I am going to send her a telegraph message."

What's it going to say?" Watt asked.

"Congratulations on your retirement; you have rendered a great service to education." I could hear Watt laughing on the other end of the line.

So my training went on until the mid-spring of 1962. I was released from custody and attended the "cattle auction" in several Toronto hotels about two days before the termination of courses at Eastern I received two telephone calls from Watford Watt asking me to take a purely mathematics teaching position at his school. I telephoned him back saying I would consider working for Watt's employer's Board but have to have a situation where I was closer to the relatively new home I had just completed in Norfolk County. My grades at the Faculty of

Education were excellent and with a temporary or interim certificate in Physics, Mathematics and Science I could pick my spot. So I attended the cattle auction at the Wellington Hotel in May 1962. The hotel was also located in Toronto and I secured an invitation to attend an interview concerning a position with a secondary school on the extreme south eastern boundaries of Watt's school district and only a 20 minute drive from The New Farm. The new School was called "Suffolk District Composite School." I was going to teach grade 9 advanced mathematics, grade 11 general mathematics and grade 13 mathematics A which included some calculus. This grade 13 course was meant for students going onto engineering, maths or science courses at university. I was invited to visit the school for a week's indoctrination in late May 1962. I would be paid supply teacher rates for my attendance. As a test drive I drove to Suffolk District Composite School leaving The New Farm at 7:00 AM on a busy Friday to time my drive. It took about 25 minutes. The traffic on the roads was sparse.

The principal of Suffolk was "Richard O. Buck." I recalled that Buck had taught music at Parkside Collegiate Institute while I served time there in the Autumn of 1945. I had taken music from him. Buck was a tall man, well over six feet. He was also associated and related to other people called Buck who were heavily into the Labor movement. He was a devout CCFer. Another teacher in the school was "Charlie Buck," a cousin of Richard and also a devout socialist. "Best not to be dragged into any political talks with these two," I thought. I realized fully that socialist teachers and administrators were never to be challenged. Their assessment of a teacher could be biased if conservative view points were expressed. I did not want another Miss O'Dell incident. When the Liberal government of Canada was upended in the late 1950's and replaced with a Conservative one; a diehard socialist teacher I knew because he was a neighbor of my brother Bill threw a tantrum. Bill's wife Dorothy had this teacher over to their home which was now the old Duncan house. Renee and I were visiting. It was 10 PM when the election results were coming across on television.

"What is wrong with the voters?" the teacher asked. "By voting for the Tories they are dooming themselves." He then spewed out profanity

galore. Then he said "If you can't vote for the CCF then for God's sake
vote for the Liberals." This teacher's name, long forgotten, did not know
Bill and Dorothy were Conservatives. The socialist went on: "If they
can't vote properly they should lose their right to vote!" Better nobody
votes who might oppose socialism. This is how elections are conducted
in the USSR!

So I, Robert MacAlpine Noble Air Force Cross, AFC, B.A.Sc.
a newly acquired staff member, began my teaching career at Suffolk
District Composite School. I was determined to establish discipline
in my classes immediately. I adopted a no nonsense attitude. The vice-
principal of the school was Harold FitzSimmons, a former lacrosse
player about 5'11" tall and 190 pounds. He had been promoted to
vice-principal with less than 10 years teaching experience. He was
formally a phys. ed. and maths teacher. The students respected him. A
second hobby was golf. After about one month on the job; "Fitz" as they
referred to the vice-principal, came in to my grade 9 class. He sat down
quietly at the back of the room. The lesson was on "integers." An integer
line representing the integers was drawn on the black board. The line
was vertical. Most teachers used a horizontal line. Far fewer pupils could
relate to it. Fitz was evaluating me. Buck preferred Fitz do this because
Buck was a music teacher. He was almost a mathematical illiterate.
When I reflected backward to my short time at Parkside Collegiate I
felt Buck was an adequate teacher.

I was flattered when I studied Fitz's report. "Am I that good?" I
asked.

"I only write down what I observe," Fitz answered. You know the
Ministry Inspector is a former principal with this board. His name is
Watford Watt! He will visit you later this year." Thus I had made a good
impression, at least on Fitz. I bumped into Watt after the New Year
started. We talked briefly in the hall about the usual stuff, "Would I be
interested in pursuing a M.Ed. Degree in school administration? OISP
(the Ontario Institute for Studies in Pedagogy) was offering a program.
You never know," Watt said, "Boards are looking for principals. You
wouldn't be a mediocre one." Just then Mr. Buck approached us.

"Oh how are you sir?" he pandered. "Mr. Noble, this is the inspector,

'Mr. Wadford Wilt?'" Why he introduced me to a man that I was already talking to amazed me. From this greeting I knew Mr. Buck was scared shitless in the presence of Watt. Mr. Buck could offer no voluntary opinion on any teacher in the school. Usually the provincial inspector only called at his office as a formality. This was to avoid the principal biasing the report of the inspector.

Mr. Buck spent his time locked away in his office doing paper work or standing in the halls inspecting student traffic when classes changed. I would be in that school for two school years. Buck seldom spoke to me never mind visiting my classroom. With the summer break coming up I went to OISP (The Ontario Institute for Studies in Pedagogy) and enquired about entering the M.Ed. Program. There the dean of the faculty told me I must take six undergraduate courses to meet the entrance requirements. The dean was an "artsy fartsy" man! The dean considered anybody who studied mathematics and physics could not possibly manage an M.Ed, program. I thought he was absurd. I went to Dr. Ralph at Waterville University.

"This is crap," Dr. Ralph responded. "A bright young man with above average results in Engineering Physics is to be put through almost two years of part time study so he can satisfy some "rectal orifice's" inane requirements to enter his graduate program. You know there is a M.Ed. Program starting here this summer. Dr. Cramer, who by the way is a mathematician, is the Dean. Let me see what I can do."

So one week later I was admitted to the graduate M. Ed. Program at Waterville. I would spend eight weeks in residency. During each summer vacation one term of residency of four weeks would be required for the course. I could take two courses during each academic year. The program could be completed in 21 months. So in the first week of July 1962, I start working toward my M.Ed. in school administration. During the entire M.Ed. program never was a word mentioned about private schooling or other alternatives to public schools. It was all about the public system. Nothing else was viable in the professors' minds. Private education did not exist.

Near the end of my second year of teaching a ministry inspector visited my classroom to evaluate me for my Secondary Specialist's

Certificate in Mathematics and Physics. Incredibly, it was Watford Watt. Mr. Buck offered his evaluation of me when Watt stopped at Buck's office. I never could determine what the remarks were. I didn't have to.

"I stopped by Mr. Buck's office before I came here." These were the words of Watt. There was another slightly younger man with Watt. "This is Mr. Segal. Mr. Segal has just become an inspector. He is going to sit in with me today and watch your class. We will discuss our evaluation after this class."

Watt's visit was a day earlier than announced. The lesson was on exponents and the class was grade 9 advanced mathematics. It went off well, very well. "Mr. Noble, when I first observed you when you were at the Faculty of Education I thought you would make an outstanding classroom teacher. Today I am sure of it. I am certainly recommending you for your permanent certificate. I would evaluate you at 6.0 but I will not give you that grade just yet. I will make it 5.8. A 6.0 rating would make you look like some favorite of mine. Mr. Segal is also of the same opinion.

CHAPTER 44

A More Responsible Position

One advertisement in the newspaper section of positions intrigued me. It was for a department head of mathematics at a school built in a small town in Suffolk County. The school had been amalgamated into Middle March Board of Education. It was called the Southern Middle March District Secondary School. The School Board consisted of seven secondary schools and many more elementary schools. Walter Lippman was the principal there for the last five years. He was past 55 years of age. He offered me the position three days after the interview which was held in London, Ontario on a Saturday afternoon. I attended the interview armed with Watford Watt's official evaluation of me when I was recommended for a Specialist's Certificate. Lippman was impressed with the 5.8 rating. Lippman had phoned Watt to check, on my resume and references.

"Nobody is that good!" Lippman told me when he contacted me at The New Farm on Monday evening. He forwarded an agreement to my current school. I sent it back to Lippman by the Board courier. It was all set. I was now a department head of mathematics with five and one half regular staff working in my department.

In late May, 1963, I had an invitation to sit in on several classes in my new school. One class I observed was in "general level" grade 12 mathematics. The teacher was Warren Wallace. He was a young man of about 30 years with seven years "teaching experience." He was younger than me. I sat at an empty desk at the back of the room. Half the pupils were already seated when I had entered the room. The remainder of the class came into the room after I did. There was a din in the room. Warren Wallace started to address the class while they were talking. No body stopped their talk. It would have been more effective if Mr. Wallace had just stood at the front of the class silently or written the lesson outline at the chalk board. He did neither. Twice more Wallace asked for attention from the class and twice more the class ignored him. Finally, about five minutes after the start of class the students quieted down and the lesson began.

The lesson had no beginning, no middle and no end. It had something to do with compound interest. A topic not understood by many Canadians. The problem Mr. Wallace stated orally to the class was this: "a man goes into an automobile dealer to buy a new Buick Fleet Master Sedan. The car lists at $8500. It features "dynaflow" automatic transmission, power steering, a fancy radio and all types of extras. The manufacturer is offering to finance the car at 12% annual interest compounded monthly. Other charges are taxes at $500 which go to the government and a $500 allowance for a 10 years old trade in. If the purchase is financed over three years what is the monthly payment?" Warren Wallace was about to discuss a problem of extreme value to his class of 17 and 18 year olds. Their attention grew. All teenagers want to know about buying "wheels."

Warren Wallace finally asked a question. "How do we determine the monthly payment?"

"We divide the $8500 by 36 months," a student in the back of the class answered. Wallace was getting flustered. He posed the question to the class without personally understanding the problem and its solution. With a pained look on his face Warren Wallace walked over to my desk, stooped down and whispered "Can you cover for me for about five minutes?" he asked. "I need to take a crap. Would you help me out?" He gave the chalk to me and left the room. After Wallace left the room I did not see him again for a long time. Not until I started my new assignment at the new school year after Labor Day in September. The problem was in the text book under the "C" exercises meaning it was intended as a challenging question. I noticed the principal, Mr. Lippman sitting at the back of the class. "Where is Warren Wallace?" Lippman asked.

"He went to have a dump. I haven't seen him since. He left 10 minutes ago." Mr. Lippman looked angry. He remained in the room and observed the remainder of the lesson. I went to the head of the classroom. I grabbed Wallace's seating plan on the desk. "You have to subtract the trade in allowance from the list price otherwise you as a customer will be paying tax on something you are selling to the dealer. It is the buyer that pays sales tax. This is what you are going to finance with equal payments. On what money do we pay the tax?" Some hands went up in the back.

A young girl raised her hand. I looked at the seating plan. Her name was Ann Lind. I called on her. "I guess about $8000." I wrote her answer on the chalk board and a table of data began to appear as each subsequent question was answered.

List Price of a new Car = 8500
Trade in = 500
tax = 500
Net Purchase Price = 8500

Without interest the monthly payment would be simple to figure out. Now the main problem is to determine the interest. Obviously, the longer it takes to make all the payments the greater is the interest on the balance owing if the rate of interest remains the same. All the students were interested. I used the payment factor in the automotive salesman's book I happened to have with me. I placed the relevant page of the salesman's payment book on the overhead projector. I had the class look up the payment factor for 36 months at 12% annual rate compounded monthly. "What is the payment factor listed in the book for 12% annually compounded monthly really come to as an annual rate? Remember this is 1% per month. I let it go after that. Try these homework problems this afternoon or evening and we look at them in class tomorrow." With that, I dismissed the class. This problem is discussed thoroughly in **Appendix 3.**

CHAPTER 45

The Picket Line

In my third year of Teaching was approached by some older staff members to run for president of my union branch at Middle March Secondary School. Obviously those teachers did not know I was a conservative. I was interested in seeing what the job was like so I accepted the nomination. I had prior knowledge of what union people were like but I wanted to know what dealing with Principals and higher ups was to entail. With a staff of 46 teachers at my school including the principal and vice-principal; as president of my branch I would have to mediate disputes between labor and management. The residing branch president was a man in his 50's named "Herman Hicks."

Hicks, the technical department head, who was in a word "incompetent" at his jobs of technical director and union branch president. The collective agreement with his Board called for a maximum of 40 students in a class, and no more unless the teacher signed an agreement with the principal allowing an extra student. Hicks, in order to placate the staff was always urging the teachers to cooperate with the collective agreement but Hicks always put the wishes of the administration ahead of his obligations as branch president. In Hicks' mind all teachers had to obey, implicitly, the higher administration. He felt his job was not to enforce the collective agreement but ensure "harmony" within the school. So it was that a classroom teacher could be cajoled into accepting an overload by being bullied. The principal Mr. Buck, himself a member of the union branch often remarked:

"Now you are not going to allow the collective agreement to hinder you from doing your professional duty are you?" Yet Buck, a devout socialist, disregarded the collective agreement the entire secondary teaching staff of the Board agreed to if it pleased his superiors. I disdained Buck's hypocrisy. It was one of the more puzzling enigmas of the teaching federation that management and labor were coagulated into the same union.

I couldn't believe the federation bigwigs of the school asked me to run. Did they not know I was not a diehard union man? If they did they would never have wanted me. Mr. Hicks, a man nearing retirement age held the position for the last five years. The teaching staff was not pleased with his performance. They made the mistake of pushing me for the job. I would do my best to uphold the collective agreement even if I didn't like some of the things in it. I would have to enforce if I agreed to accept the nomination. My only opponent was Mr. Herman Hicks. At a staff meeting after school hours a closed ballot election was held. The results were Robert Noble 34 votes and Herman Hicks 4. Hicks was so upset with this result he demanded a recount! This all happened during mid- September. So I was now the new head of Mathematics and was also now also the branch president of my school teachers' federation. I was in for an awakening.

My classes were all filled with the maximum of 40 pupils when Mr. Buck asked me to come to his office one October day after school hours. "I am placing two more students in your Grade 9 general level class. Sign this document." The document stated that I agreed to this thing Buck was proposing. I was stunned.

"That gives me 42 students," I explained. "That is two over the limit. That's a violation of the collective agreement."

"You realize that resisting me will reflect badly on your evaluation as a department head, don't you? I thought you were a sensible young man. Come on now sign this and I will forget everything that just happened. You're not going to let the collective agreement get in the way of your career."

I could not believe what I was hearing. Did Buck rise to become principal by kissing ass this much? I did not sign the statement and

Buck could not legally place additional students in his class. Buck was seething. He went ahead and scheduled them in my class anyways. I accepted the students and filed a grievance with the District Office. The two students were quietly withdrawn one week later. Then an additional two students added again two days after the original two were removed. Buck kept placing the two students back in my class and I kept notifying the district office. If I failed to notify the union higher ups the Board could then violate the collective agreement claiming it was a fair thing to do because of "past practice." Buck could do this with impunity. Ultimately lawyers were to get involved. The lawyers for the teachers' were busy along with the lawyer for the Board. Know what? The board had to back down. Nevertheless Mr. Buck was a staunch socialist! And so as the proper letters were signed and a few weeks passed Buck started to overload the class rooms again. Some people never learn. Finally the top honcho of the board ordered Buck to stop this. I did the right thing and made an enemy of Buck.

The officers of the union however loved the action I took. People from the head office in Toronto visited the school. "You did a fine job with Buck," one commented. Two months later a grievance arose between Buck and Herman Hicks. Both were ardent socialists and bragged about being devout union members. It seemed that technical studies were being downgraded at the school for the coming year. There was auto shop, machine shop and drafting left. The electrical shop was to go, the instructor was retiring. The electronics shop was to be closed. Woodworking was also going. Hicks drafting classes were cut in half and he was assigned two math classes under my supervision. Hicks did not like this one iota. Not only that but technical studies no longer counted as a major department but a minor one and Herman Hicks was due for a salary cut. Not a big one, but that was not what bothered him. It was the bruise to his ego. So Herman Hicks, Mr. Buck and I had to resolve this problem. So that spring we three sat down in Buck's office. Now can you possibly imagine how the teachers' federation was going to resolve a problem when two staff members, both department heads and the other the principal of the school all belonged to the same union. It was going to be resolved justly as far as I was concerned.

I was pushing for fair treatment of Hicks. He could have remained at his school for another two years with his current wage package and title until he retired but it was not offered to him. I felt Hicks was a fair teacher. He was adequate in communication skills but was a total loss at classroom management. The better teachers at his school referred to his classes as "chaotic." As a result of trying to win fair results for Hicks I created another enemy. That enemy was Hicks himself. Hicks would take an early retirement and was gone at the end of June. It had occurred to me that Buck was interested in satisfying the Board even at the expense of his teachers. Buck lacked scruples.

Things quieted down for the remainder of the year and I was re-elected as Branch President for the following year. In November of that year the head office of the union decided they would strike for two weeks because the Board was not dealing with the teachers fairly. The union members considered the Board unprincipled. The teachers had a collective agreement with the Board and a strike would violate Ontario Labor Laws. No strike could happen if the employees had a contract. A wildcat strike was called and at my school they approached and asked for council from me.

"This proposed strike is illegal," I said. "You cannot strike if you have a signed contract. If you call an illegal strike I will resign as president. I am not going to break the labor laws of Ontario. So a strike was called for two weeks in late November. I resigned as union president and a location was chosen where all scabs were to attend. Things got interesting. One particular member of the union was Ralph Morgan. Ralph was a technical director at another secondary school in my Board. This school was not the one I had to report to. Morgan and a gang of five others, loyal unionists, were picketing on the public sidewalk of the Osgood Primary School where the scabs were to be housed.

Renee was driving me to work. "Can you go in through a side door?" Renee asked. "Those idiots look rough."

"Drive right into the principal's parking space," I commanded. Renee did that. I left the car and walked through the main door of the building. When I entered the building I turned around and saw the six member gang hassling Renee. Two strikers were trying to open the locked car doors.

"Scab," they shouted, then began to shake the car. I turned to the OPP cop on duty inside the building. He was quietly observing the assault on the car and smoking a cigarette. I looked at the cop and the cop smiled.

"You have to stop them. They can't come on private property." I was writing the officer's badge number in a small notebook I always carried with me. "Put a stop to it." I entered the parking lot from the building with the cop following me. The gang was still hassling Renee. I went outside the building. I walked quickly over to the gang. I approached Ralph Morgan. The others five members of his gang quickly fled the scene. Morgan was left alone to face me. "Stop what you are doing and get off this lot or you'll regret it. And don't bother my wife." I slapped him on the face. Morgan started to cry. The bullies always cry when they perceived victims face them down.

"He assaulted me," Morgan said, as he turned to the cop who was now outside the school standing beside behind me. "What are you going to do about it?"

The cop said, "I didn't see anything." Morgan left without saying another word. "What the hell kind of man are you?' the cop asked. "You sure showed me how to do my duty."

When the strike passed I never heard a word of criticism from another staff member. The strike was called to show the board that they, the board employees, didn't agree with some obscure policy the board had that many of the teachers did not even understand. They lost three week's pay during the strike. The obscure policy remained on the board's bylaws.

CHAPTER 46

Agnes Finds True Love

About 22 years after Lem's death Agnes' older sister Bertie died. This left Jack Haynes, the husband of Bertie, a widower. Jack began to visit Agnes in her Niagara Village Apartment. Jack was a meticulous housekeeper and looked after the luxury two bedroom condominium he and Bertie purchased in the early 1950's when he became a vice president of his railway. At the time of Bertie's passing it was paid for. The man who started out as a baggage clerk at 15 years of age had nearly risen to the top of his profession. The only higher position available was to become president. This was not destined to happen. He would ultimately retire as vice president at 55 years of age. The five years he served as vice president enabled him to receive a maximum pension based on his best five years earnings. He had worked for the railroad for 40 years!

Jack began to call on Agnes two months after the funeral of Bertie. Jack and Bertie had no children. "I have always really loved you," he confessed to Agnes. "I married Bertie because you weren't available. I settled for Bertie because I thought it would be the same as being with you. It wasn't."

Agnes was dazzled by the advances Jack made. They began to date regularly. Jack was now 55 years old and Agnes nearly 54. It was 1964. Suddenly a marriage was coming up in June. As a wedding gift Renee and I decided to offer the New Farm as a Wedding venue. A few guests were invited and 14 people attended the private ceremony held in the living room of The New Farm. This was a catered affair. The Reverend Latticomb was engaged and agreed to perform the ceremony. Bill and Dorothy came, Marion came with her Skull and Bones husband Walter. Renee and I, Agnes and Jack Haynes, a friend of Jack who I didn't know and was not introduced to, and four poker playing cronies of Agnes also came. I sprang for a limousine to chauffeur the couple from Toronto to Norfolk County. Renee and I also paid for all the expenses at The New Farm. We also put up the money for accommodation for Jack and Agnes in Toronto at the Royal York Hotel later in the evening when the reception at the New Farm was over.

Things went well and Reverend Latticomb during the ceremony talked for a moments about Agnes being a descendent of "The Holy Grail Family." This of course went over the head of everybody in the large living room except the Reverend, Renee and me. Agnes was a member of the Grail and did not know it. I would never discuss this with her for I feared she might ridicule this idea as Lem surely would have, even though he also was a Grail child. I was still puzzled by how he could be born a Grail Child but was a very evil man. After the wedding reception Agnes approached Renee for a one on one talk. I noticed this while I was talking with Jack. The last time the two spoke Agnes informed Renee that the basis of a sound marriage was good connubial relations. Since that time I would seldom contact her. I resented her interference.

Eventually Renee came over to me. "Your mother," she said. "She is different. You can almost have a talk with her. When she's with her new husband she's nice."

"Well Jack is a gentleman. He always has been. To enter the University of Waterville I had him complete one of the required reference forms. I wasn't supposed to do that but I cheated. No relatives even in laws were permitted to give references. My other reference was from an Air-Vice Marshall, my commanding officer's boss in the RCAF. I never knew what he said in that form he completed. Listen," I added, "Jack must be great to marry two Posnanskis."

So Agnes Posnanski Noble Haynes and her husband Jack settled down in their 1800 square foot Bellevue Place luxury condominium in midtown Toronto. Agnes was fastidious in maintaining the place in apple pie order. This was totally unlike her previous residences. Renee and I spent a few weekends with Jack and with her. They were not altogether dull times. About 18 months after the wedding Jack began to complain about pains in his groin area. He went to a physician when the pains became too severe to shrug off. The news was not good. The physician sent Jack for a biopsy and the worst was confirmed. It was cancer in the testicular region. A man six feet tall and 180 pounds was slated to undergo emasculation. I shuddered when I heard the news. The operation was performed but it did not help. The dreaded disease has infiltrated his whole body. Renee and I went to visit Jack about two months after the castration and were appalled at his appearance. He was down to 140 pounds and looked deathly pale. I always felt that cancer doctors with their vile treatments never really helped their clients. They didn't help Margaret Williams or Jack Haynes or did they ever help me.

I shook my head in the corridor as I talked with Renee. "He won't last the week out," I remarked. The next morning he was dead. Renee and I decided to rent rooms at the South Hampton Hotel in Toronto two blocks from Agnes' condominium. When Lem died Agnes was already separated from him. She never saw him again. His funeral was a closed casket affair. I felt that Agnes did not care a hoot when Lem died. She had support from the Alistair Duncan estate. We called on Agnes until the funeral was to take place and then chauffeured her to the Mount Pleasant Cemetery where Jack was to be buried. About 100 people attended. No Posnanskis were there except Agnes. There was no hypocrisy spoken as there was at Lem's burial where he was referred to as "a loving husband and father."

From that point on Agnes became a devoted grandmother to Bill's three children even though they were not her blood. When Marion had a daughter she finally had a grandchild of her own blood. Agnes would die in 1992 at 82 years of age. She was cremated and her ashes placed in Mount Peasant Cemetery. A small plaque stood over grave site honoring her life. The plaque stated her age and birthplace and the time of her death. It also said: "I am sitting on a full house." The knowledge I discovered about her roots remained unknown to her.

As an interesting codicil to her life Marion, who was her mother's executor opened her safety deposit box, the largest one available and discovered 300 gold Kruger Rands which were South African one ounce 99.9% fine gold coins laying there. As well as rolls and rolls of Canadian pre-1968 ten and 25 cents pieces. They were stored in a second safety deposit box. They were not collectors' coins but what was called "junk silver." They were ultimately converted to paper money at 13 times their face value. Agnes had acquired them at face value during her years with Jack. The condominium was well maintained and sold in eight days for triple the price Jack Haynes purchased it for. The estate went to her four grandchildren. It amounted to nearly $400 000. Marion received an executor's fee and inherited some jewelry and a mink coat. In my mind Agnes had come a long way in redeeming herself.

CHAPTER 47

Yet another Career Begins

In September 1963, I started my job in a secondary school even closer to my home at The New Farm. At the opening staff meeting held the Tuesday before classes were to begin I had a chance to see who was on my staff. I noticed one of my teachers was Warren Wallace, he of the loose bowel. Wallace's timetable was 66% mathematics and 33% guidance. Then there was Mrs. Dunhill, a tiny Scots lady who taught secondary school in Scotland. She was barely five feet tall but an exceptional disciplinarian and above average as a teacher. She entered teaching in Ontario after doing it for 10 years in Glasgow. After raising her family she returned to the classroom. She was assistant head of mathematics. There was Fred Sharpe a young second year teacher. Leah Wilson, who attended the Faculty of Education with me, and was now entering her third year of teaching. Roy Preston and Ron Short rounded out the staff. Ron Short, I discovered, went to the Board to complain when I received the appointment as head of math. Short felt that he deserved the promotion. After all he was in that school for 19 years when the position of head of mathematics became available. He was an obese man of nearly six feet in height and weighed 250 pounds. As I began to review the teaching practices of my department members I would discover incompetence on a grand scale. This incompetency was very noticeable in the staff members who deluded themselves into believing they were good.

Warren Wallace, I knew was a slacker. Qualifying in guidance for him was one way out of the classroom. Another was administration and the usual steps followed were to become a vice-principal then a principal. In those positions you deal with fewer kids. I would take two visits to the classroom of Wallace. After each visit I would offer written advice as to how to spruce up Wallace's classes. This advice went unheeded. I would enjoy Mrs. Dunhill's classes. There was no bad behavior. She was in charge. Short's classes were a disaster. Short always seemed to weasel senior classes to teach. His grade 12 class of "gifted" mathematics students was being shortchanged on grades because Short graded them harder than the ordinary class. This result had them achieving lower grades than they would have achieved had they taken regular classes. I had a hard time convincing him of the folly of this fact. The principal and I had to alter Short's grades on the curve. The inspector, Watford Watt visited my school twice that year. He made a thorough inspection of all classes. Warren Wallace was conveniently sick that day. The inspector had to give notice he was going to visit well in advance. This is so the teacher he was visiting would not prepare a test or field trip. The inspector wanted to see a lesson. Wallace presented a doctor's medical note to explain his absence. Wallace had no desire to rise as a mathematics teacher. He wanted to be a principal.

Mr. Short would always score exactly "5" on his inspections. He knew enough about inspections to pull a con on the inspector. He would always have half the class working on the chalk boards and would walk about the room correcting the students' work. Since Short had relatives who were prominent in the area it wasn't easy to dismiss him. It wasn't easy to dismiss any teacher who had a permanent contract. Short was heard to comment in the staff room about how I should never have been given the position of mathematics head. "He doesn't have the experience I have" he would often say. You hear about "experience" when a good new candidate runs for political office. "He's not experienced in that job," his opponents usually say. Well Lincoln was not experienced when he was elected to that job in 1860. Ron Short had one year's experience many times. The other teachers taught physical education and shop classes. They were assigned junior grade mathematics classes. I discovered I had some say in the assignment of classes so I made it a point of assigning grade nine and ten general level classes to Ron Short. Surely they would benefit from his "experience." I divided the schedule of senior classes among Mrs. Dunhill, Leah Wilson, and myself. The other classes I taught were general level. Ron Short protested the assignment of his "Relations and Functions" course to Mrs. Dunhill. He barged into my mathematics office.

"How dare you take away my Functions and Relations class. I've taught that course since it began." Ron Short was beside himself. "Some kid with no experience walks into my school and gets the prime position over other teachers with much more experience."

I replied: "With your teaching load for this year your experience will be of prime benefit to those general level students. Your teaching expertise and classroom management will help them. You're wasted teaching advanced students. It's time we employed you properly." I enjoyed spelling out in person Short's new assignment. In fact, I was not unfair to Short. I simply assigned an even allotment of general and advanced level classes to all my staff, even Wallace and Short.

My fourth year in teaching was spent satisfying the needs of Wallace and Short. Wallace left the school after my fourth year and succeeded in obtaining a headship in Guidance at another school in a neighboring board. This meant a pay raise and having to deal with fewer students. It struck me that people like Wallace proved a principle about public schooling that I was forming: "the further a person distances himself from a classroom and the less young people he interacts with; the higher his paycheck goes." Warren Wallace, now safely lodged in a neighboring school Board was now dealing with students one on one. No more classrooms for him. Eventually Wallace attended the Principals' Course and wormed his way into an appointment from yet a third board as a vice-principal. It was in a school that was to be a model of classroom discipline! It was especially started by that other Board to answer the endless complaints from parents about lack of order in the schools of that Board. Warren Wallace was to be their new "enforcer." I wondered about the sanity of the World.

At the end of June during my fourth year of teaching and second as a department head I completed the eight courses for my M.Ed. No thesis was required. I had done the work in 21 months. Waterville University was becoming world renowned. It was the last academic degree I would be patient enough to earn. As I was completing my fifth year of teaching I was approached by Robinson Davis, the chairman and director of the Board of Education.

"The Middle March Board of Education has been allotted two positions for suitable candidates to attend the Principals' Program. The Board would like to send you. The course will take up a few weeks of your summer vacation but we would like you to go. Would you think it over and give us an answer by the end of next week." That evening at dinner I discussed the matter with Renee.

"I have a chance to take the Principals' Course, part I, this summer. The Board asked me to give them an answer by next Friday." Renee seemed agreeable. Renee and I were not the vacationing or traveling types. Expenses were not a problem.

"If you think you can improve the public school system from that position I think you should take the course! Where will you be taking it.?"

I replied: "at MacMaster University." I was 35 years old. I felt I might give administration a whirl. On Friday morning I left a message with the Board secretary that I would accept the offer.

The first part of the Principals' program seemed to spin around constructing a timetable for the students and teachers. Weeks of time were spent diddling about with this assignment and it was a time waster. One day in the not too distant future computers would handle this chore. Little was discussed about school management and teaching. I offered no comments during the weeks of July and August that were spent traveling from The New Farm to McMaster. Over one hour of travel each way was required. Fortunately it did not last forever. There was a lecture given by a Superintendent in which he displayed the organization chart for a midsized Board. The chart was ridiculous. It showed the position of Director of Education, it showed the various superintendents and it showed principals and vice-principals. Each rank was encased in a text block. The blocks were progressively smaller as the position got lower. There were no blocks on the chart for teachers and students. I suppose the block for students would have to be so small a microscope would be needed to examine it.

"Our school system would be ideal if it wasn't for the damned kids;" I heard one instructor say as he talked with another. I received my endorsement from the Ministry of Education in late August. I was qualified to be a vice-principal. I would never return to the school I held a department headship at. About a week prior to starting the Director of the Board called me at The New Farm.

"This is Robinson Davis," the voice on the other end said. Can you take over starting next week as the vice-principal at Cosgrove Composite School? The Board of Education approves of this move." I, in a daze, agreed. "Who would you like to replace you at Suffolk?"

"Mrs. Dunhill would be my choice."

"You will be working with Harry FitzSimmons. He just received the appointment to be principal. I think he will be great in the job." I visited the new school mainly to time the drive from The New Farm. It took five more minutes than the drive to my old school. The route was different. I noticed vehicles parked in the teachers' lot and went inside the building. The main office door was open so I went in and saw Fitz standing and talking with one of the school secretaries. It was Barbara Kirkland, the head secretary. Fitz saw me approaching the counter.

"This is Robert MacAlpine Noble, our new vice-principal." We two men had a private discussion behind closed door exchanging ideas on how the school was to be run.

"I will be happy to execute any policies you want to initiate," I told Fitz. Fitz handed me a book of procedures he drafted up after he received his appointment. Fitz's wife entered the office.

"Are we going out for lunch at the golf course?" she asked. "Some company is there that wants us to eat with us, 'Fitz.'"

"So it is true after all," I remarked.

"What is true?" Fitz remarked.

"I once heard two grade 12 students in the hallway where you were a vice-principal when I practice taught there. One student remarked to the other. "All the students call him 'Fitz' and all the teachers. I'll bet his wife calls him 'Fitz'"

CHAPTER 48

The Executive Officer

On the first day of school I was introduced to the assembly of students in the auditorium by Fitz. I was also scheduled to teach one period of grade 9 general level math. Even Fitz had to instruct one class a day. Most principals complained about teaching. They considered that task something only teachers should do. Yet they constantly referred to themselves as "educators." Teaching was a job beneath the level of an administrator. Fitz enjoyed the classroom and often expressed regrets about giving up his job as the head of the Phys. Ed. Department and part time mathematics teacher and accepting a VP's assignment. Fitz, now almost 50 years old had spent 10 years has a VP. Intrigues at the Board level worked against him. He was too rigid as a disciplinarian for the liberals on the Board and it was the Board that determined who was to be appointed principal and vice-principal. It was the Board who appointed superintendents and higher Board officers. But Fitz too had friends on the Board and they lobbied for his elevation to principal. Fitz would have moved over to another Board if he were denied a principalship one more time. The sane members of the Board knew this and convinced their left-leaning colleagues of his value and they caved. I now had a chance to work with a principal I respected.

About two months into my new assignment I was in his office. I had spent the day doing inspections of the science and math teachers. I had visited five classes: three math classes and one chemistry and physics class. I was waiting for typed evaluations to be prepared by

Mrs. Barb Kirkland. Fitz had only the head secretary handle this choir. The evaluations were for the eyes of Fitz, me and the teachers who were being evaluated.

Ministry inspectors were phased out at the end of 1967 and so were Ministry Grade 13 exams. It was now up to the principal, vice-principals and supervisory officers from the Board to evaluate a school's staff. I didn't like this move but could live with it. I was now approaching my 35th birthday and still had all my hair. It wasn't as curly as it was when I once was 12 years old. My posture was erect and I walked like a large tiger. Fitz kept me busy with inspections. Eventually I would inspect every staff member at least twice. My new head of math was Ron Short. I thought his appointment to math head was a blasphemy. He had applied for the position of math head to succeed the retiring Jack Fletcher who after 35 years decided to pack it in. Fletcher was very able at his job. The principal then was Ray Hall. Ray had to find a replacement from the general staff of qualified candidates. With a great error in judgment he chose Ron Short based on his 23 years of "service" to the Board and his "5" rating from the ministry inspector. One of the most incompetent people I had ever encountered was finally the head of a major department of a secondary school. It should never have occurred.

Fitz succeeded Ray Hall when Hall had a stroke during summer vacation. Hall's health went downhill rapidly. He needed constant care. Fitz received the appointment from the Board to succeed Hall. It was too late to change the appointment of Mr. Short. Fitz's and I were saddled with a loser. Walter Lippman had never been consulted as to the ability of Ron Short nor had I. Hall passed away in October my first year as a VP! Lippman was overjoyed to get rid of Short but he passed his problem on down the road. Ron Short was one of the first staff members I visited. Short's communications skills were worse than they were when I was the Math head at Suffolk. Short felt he had "made it." He wanted to take principal's qualifications. Fitz said no. The Board was considering it. The left-leaners on the Board and friends of Short's prosperous family said "yes."

Mrs. Dunhill was appointed the new head of mathematics. She

replaced me. She would serve in that capacity for five years then retire. Things were not to go well for Short. The first thing he did was con the Board into believing that he needed to teach no more than four periods per day while the regular teacher taught six. He had to help his teachers improve their skills and administer his department. The job seemed to make him fatter. Already obese at 250 pounds when I first encountered him he now ballooned up to 300 pounds by the Christmas holiday. He became a walking walrus. He considered himself a jock and would frequent the boys' gym after school hours "coaching" the kids in basketball. He looked like the antithesis of fitness rolling around the gym in his shorts and tee shirt. His corpulence bulged from all his clothes. His breasts were more ample than that of Jane Russell, a1940's star in the movies. Russell had appeared in a Howard Hughes movie called "The Outlaw. It was the first bosom movie. He offered to coach the senior boys' basketball team. Oddly enough they won their league championship that season!

I revolved the thought in my mind that if they could make the worst mathematics teacher I had ever encountered a department head; then in their great wisdom the Board could someday appoint him a principal. But my duties as VP kept me out of the math department except for mandatory visits. Otherwise things went well while Fitz and I ran the school. Fitz however in his zeal to make good in his first assignment as a principal was overdoing it. He wasn't willing to take it easy during his off duty hours and was over stressing himself. Near the end of my first full year as a vice-principal Fitz had a massive heart attack. The Board director, Robinson Davis, did not appoint me as principal. I needed to finish the second part of the Principals' course. With permission from the Ministry of Education however, I was allowed to assume the duties of Fitz for the final three weeks of school. There were no classes but some final examinations and administrative duties to perform. Fitz had been training me showing me where to obtain the necessary information on how to make difficult choices. I carried on the work of Fitz competently.

CHAPTER 49

The New Principal

I completed part 2 of the Principal's program during the summer holidays. I stopped off at the Western Ontario General Hospital in London, Ontario to visit the recovering Fitz. I was appalled at Fitz's appearance. From a nearly six feet tall husky 190 pounder he had diminished in mass to below 160 pounds. He had not been allowed to return to work by his doctors. He had used up 60 days of his accumulated sick leave and was now on long term disability. He would need at least six months to heal fully. He eventually came back to the Middle March Board administering a different school. A year later he died on the job. He was barely 50 years old. I visited him earlier when he was recovering in the hospital.

"How are you doing Orangeman?" I asked Fitz.

"I heard you took over for me while I was in here," he told me. "For once the Board did right. No wait a minute, twice they did right, they made you my VP. I told Robinson Davies that you could replace me for the next 12 months till I get back. You would be wise to accept the appointment."

"What appointment?" I looked bewildered. "Don't they have other candidates that can take your place?

Two days later I got a telephone call from Robinson Davies. "Would you accept a one year appointment as Principal?" he asked.

"I will," I answered. I was required to meet the Board members at a special interview held in late August. The encounter felt like an inquisition.

CHAPTER 50

My Final year in Teaching

I started preparing for my first official term as a fully qualified Principal. I was stunned to discover my vice-principal would be Ron Short! The Board, in its infinite infallible wisdom, had selected the worst possible candidate to fill a vital slot. I thought: "does the Board hate me?" That appointment, for Ron Short, was to be his end. The newly acquired power went to his head. He was now the victim of complete self-delusion.

"I am responsible for this school," I told Short, in a one on one meeting in my office. "The students come first, the staff second and you last. You screw up on this job and I will take it out of your hide, and believe me there is a lot to take out but if you do well I will be your greatest asset. That is all." Short waddled out of my office.

I evaluated the new teachers on my staff first. Bose Baker, a young Nigerian, was the assistant head of mathematics. He was authoritarian without over doing it. He needed polishing in his teaching technique. Another year under his belt and I felt you could send him to any school as a head and he would do a good job. Sandra Grimes, a young married woman of 25 years was directly out of the Faculty of Education of Waterville. She was engaged as a half time teacher but taught a two thirds schedule while Ron Short's successor, Anthony LeBlanc, came from outside the Board where he had been an assistant head of mathematics. He was a capable teacher highly endorsed by his previous

285

employer. Fitz had hired all three of them in April of the previous year before his cardiac event. They would all improve over the coming year.

In time, I would visit all of the staff. They were all competent. Ron Short was in charge of getting substitute teachers from a Board List if any regular staff were indisposed. After one or two visits to the school the female substitute teachers refused assignments at our school. I wanted to know why. I wanted to talk with the supply teachers but administrative duties forestalled that. The school year dragged on. Just prior to the Spring Break I found a young lady, a supply teacher, crying in the staff room. The lady was alone when I came in to get a bottle of Orange Juice from the vending machine. I noticed the almost inaudible sobbing in a corner of the room. I walked over to the young woman.

"Is there something wrong?" I asked.

"I have been assaulted in the vice-principal's office," she said, in a low voice. "I was informed if I told anyone, I would not be allowed to supply with any school in this Board. I don't know why I am telling you this. I need this job." I had the unusual property of being able to get the most unlikely people to confess their problems to me.

"I am the Principal of this school. I am ultimately responsible for all staff, including the vice-principal. This is a serious allegation. Will you come to my office and we will discuss it further." I was careful to discuss the allegation with Miss Rains, the supply teacher, in my office; the door fully open, and the head secretary sitting at a desk near the door but out of sight. I also had a small tape recorder in plain sight on my desk. I liked to record testimony and the allegation I was about to witness was serious. Miss Rains began to spill the beans. I recorded our talk with her permission. It seems that Ron Short had pulled off several sexual assaults on the young female supply teachers and none of them had been reported. If it was true Short would not only lose his position but word would get out. He could never teach in Ontario again. His teaching certification would be cancelled. In fact, a jail term might ensue. But one female complainant was not enough. Short had friends on the Board. They procured his appointment. I thought about bringing in the police on my own. It was my duty to do so according to Ontario regulations.

My mind reflected back a year earlier when I was Fitz's vice-principal. During my tenure at that school a "student" brought a 22 caliber pistol into the school. The weapon traveled from classroom to classroom throughout the day. It was observed by at least five teachers. In the English department the assistant head of English, a teacher with four years' experience was Ken Leaver. This young man who graduated from the Royal Queen's Military University was inept. After graduation he began to serve his three years compulsory military service. He was posted as a lieutenant to the Prince George Regiment. He was sent to far western Canada to serve. The precise location was Edmonton.

"That is the asshole of the world!" he commented frequently to the other staff. I also noticed his other comments. About classroom management he said: "I have no discipline problems in my classes because I have no discipline."

I was amazed at these comments. I was particularly amazed about Leaver's comments on discipline. I wondered: "How did you get though Military University?" I asked him one day.

"I rolled with the punches," Leaver answered.

The gun made its way from class to class during the day. Then the inevitable happened. It was discharged. This had occurred in Leaver's final period of a General Level grade 12 English lesson. Leaver was offended. A comedy of errors started. After earlier examining the weapon and showing it to the class he returned it to the student. The student was Jacques Tremblay. Jacques had one overwhelming ambition: he wanted to become a cop. Tremblay had no sense at all. He was the school lout. Leaver went to the PA system. He paged down to the office.

"Can you send Mr. FitzSimmon up here, immediately. There is a serious emergency.

"Mr. FitzSimmon cannot be disturbed. He is in a meeting!!" This is what I heard from the head secretary while I was in the office. Again Leaver called down. "For God's sake, send up Mr. FitzSimmon. Someone in my class has a pistol."

I left the office pronto and marched double pace to Leaver's classroom. The door was wide open. I entered his classroom. The room was silent. The pistol was still loose in the class. The situation was made worse by Leaver's failure to keep the weapon and the secretary's silliness

"I wasn't aiming at Mr. Leaver," Jacques Tremblay commented. "It just went off," he recited to me. Fitz wanted to dismiss Leaver from his position. Fitz also wanted the police brought in. I ultimately called the police. As a result of this action Fitz and I were summoned to a special Board meeting. The Board convened the meeting with Seymour Beale presiding. He was the Area Superintendent for my district and a man I thoroughly could not abide. Both Fitz and I attended this meeting during school hours.

"You just can't bring the Police into Board matters anytime you have an incident in a school." This comment was made by senior superintendent Seymour Beale. "Think of the image we show to the public! You both will keep your mouths shut and not talk to any of the media. If you value your careers mind what I say." It was obvious to both Fitz and I that image was more important to Seymour Beale than the safety of the students and staff of our school. Fitz was seething with anger. The superintendent, a former principal, was mediocre at every position he held once he was promoted beyond a classroom instructor. Because of a shortage of principals he was promoted rapidly so he ultimately could become incompetent at much higher levels. Whether Beale understood Ontario Law or not he was obliged to report criminal wrong doings to the police but preferred in this instance to cover up a criminal act.

"The man's a penis head," Fitz commented. If you want to go high in this business I suppose you have to be one. Forget this bullshit Bobby. One day schools will be run by the competent."

"Is that why they held you back?" I asked. Fitz did not respond.

CHAPTER 51

The Last Straw

I was on notice to bring all serious incidents to Superintendent Beale before taking any action. Beale would handle the liaison with the police if he felt it was necessary. I decided against dealing with Mr. Seymour Beale. Nobody was going to cover up the seven sexual assaults Ron Short had committed that I was aware of. Almost every unsavory event that came to my attention was always covered up by Beale.

"We have to consider the Board's image," Beale would respond when I informed him of the sexual adventures of Ron Short. What happened in my mind was as serious or perhaps more so than the Leaver gun incident. I was determined to send Ron Short up for what he did. After few days investigating the allegations on my own I turned my thick file over to Inspector Halliday of the Suffolk Regional Police. Part of the information was a description of the requests the higher brass on the Board who forced me to agree to the cover up. I would sign a statement agreeing to take no action without consulting Seymour Beale on any wrong doing by a Board's employee under my supervision. News of Short's doings never reached the media until after the authorities arrested him. I was suspended from my position without pay immediately after Beale discovered what I had done. Beale went to my office with a written letter of suspension for me from my duties. Guess who took my place? It was Ron Short! This was a wise decision in the mind of the elected Board members! It was willingly carried out by Superintendent Beale. The Board's image was intact. It was apparent to me that the Board thought Beale's crimes would reflect on them if word of them leaked out.

One evening while under suspension I was sitting in my study at the New Farm the Phone rang. I answered the call. It was from Inspector Halliday. "Mr. Noble," the inspector began." I have a special treat for you. I want you to come to your former school. Mr. Short thinks there is going to be a meeting in his office about what action there is to be taken about the complaints of sexual misconduct. Mr. Beale and Mr. Short think I am inviting you to this meeting as a witness. I really want you there for quite another reason. Show up a little before 10.00 A.M.

Ron Short's position had lasted four weeks. The Police arrested him right in his office. I had the privilege of standing outside that office as Inspector Halliday and a police constable putt the cuffs on Short. The cover up was uncovered. He was paraded in handcuffs through the corridors of the school. It was obvious to me that Inspector Halliday despised Ron Short. Two newspaper reporters were also on hand. Short, while on his way to the parking lot and ultimately to the police car was forced to pass me waiting in the hallway right outside his door after he was handcuffed.

"You really must hate me," Short commented to me. Why didn't we talk this over like two responsible people.

"You are not worth hating," I answered and the police went on about their business. Seymour Beale was hiding in the principal's office during this encounter. Only three victims of the seven assaults were willing to testify but it was enough. The Board refused to reinstate me acting on Beale's advice. I called Walter Abercromby's office. Walter was seriously ill but William Butler his senior associate was in charge of the office. Walter Abercromby's Law Firm loved dealing with injustice. They sued the Board for having a policy illegal in the eyes of the Laws of the Province of Ontario. Any settlement would go in favor of me but the money would come from the pockets of the taxpayers. I did not like this. I wanted the payments of all settlements to come out of the pockets of Beale, Short and the idiots that ran the Board of Education. I would get my way. I also wanted Beale dismissed from his position. Beale would have to retire two years short of the 90 factor. He was rewarded with a fairly decent pension for 33 years of incompetence. He and Ron Short never returned to teaching. Short was raped repeatedly in the Provincial Reformatory where he was confined. He was, in fact, ultimately segregated from the general prison population for his own safety. The other unknown victims of Short's misadventures began to come out of the woodwork. But the case was over. They received nothing in compensation because they didn't want to testify in a court of law. It cost them.

I wanted written references from the Board. They didn't want to issue them. "Why just have those people telephone us," Arnold Decker, superintendent of human resources pronounced. Decker, another misfit was Beale's friend. "They will receive a fair reference from us." I reported this declaration from Decker to Walter Abercromby's firm. The Board felt that I breached a written request and brought the Police into a Board matter. By this time I trusted no one. I telephoned Walter Abercromby and Associates and they arranged for a legitimate inquiry into the status that I had. This was eventually referred to Decker. The enquiry was from Stanley Lowe, a director of education from a similar sized Board near Toronto. Lowe was a friend of Abercromby. Decker led with his chin. The telephone conversation was witnessed by two associates listening in on telephone extensions in Abercromby's office and transcribed later in shorthand by a stenographer. Goodbye Decker as well.

Early retirement is not that bad even if you fall short of the "90 factor." I got written letters of reference from the Director of Education and two area superintendents. They couldn't refuse. "Enough," one superintendent heard from the Director. "Let it drop." Of course I also got Beale tossed. Beale was in a job at least three levels over his head! Beale would do anything to cover for his employer. Beale was heard to remark, "Why didn't that young man come to me. We could have discussed this entire police business like two gentlemen?"

"So it all comes down to this," I thought, "I do the right thing and I become the victim of an injustice. What kind of asshole world do I live in?"

Fitz was barely 52 years old when he died on the job. His condition grew worse from day to day. His heart was damaged and he should have gone on long term disability until his teacher's pension kicked in. He would never work on a long term basis again but he tried to. He made the change a year after the cardiac incident. I inquired discretely about his widow's financial resources. Her house was paid up and she had no pressing financial needs. Mrs. Fitz would receive a survivor's pension. It was 60% of Fitz's best five years of salary. I left teaching at the end of the academic year. Beale's orders that I be suspended without pay were still in effect months after the police arrested Short. They were rescinded after Beale's dismissal. I would never return to my job. I received some settlement from the civil suits launched against the Board. Those I donated to the victims of Short.

Robinson Davis, the Director, did not want me to resign. "For God's sake," he said to me. "Can't you roll with this shit?"

To which I replied: "I can roll with the bullshit but I will not lie down in it!" It was now obvious to me that Dr. Ralph's prediction given over eight years earlier had now come true.

Davis and I had a private one on one in the Director's office. Davis had the letter of resignation on his desk. "You can't pay your bills with principles.

"As long as 'primo rectal orifices' such as Seymour Beale and Gerald Decker,' I answered, "are permitted to run things here public education will be in a sorry state. I am in a position to do what is right, and what is right is to get rid of the Seymour Beales! Gerald Decker was a bonus."

The Board had a difficult time covering up the mess Seymour Beale and Ron Short had created. In this matter, Inspector Halliday was a great help. Beale moved out of Suffolk County right after he retired. The Board confiscated Beale's sick leave gratuity to cover payments made to Abercromby on behalf of me. Investigations by a forensic accountant showed that Seymour used his Board credit card for furnishing his private residence. The Trustees of the Board insisted he repay all the money. Beale refused and hired a lawyer. This cost him thousands of dollars. It was money wasted. The Board would not back down. Criminal charges were talked about. Nothing was ever heard about Beale after that.

CHAPTER 52

Total Commitment
to the Light

An accounting of our resources done by a Chartered Accountant in July 1975 indicated that Renee and I had assets worth $14 000 000 in land, bank accounts, and royalties. There was enough income from bank interest alone to support us indefinitely. Working to earn a living was academic. I finally decided against further ventures into the outer world. I felt that too many trips into the outer world would drive me insane! Of course then I would fit right in. Strangely, Renee also felt this way. I was now closer to 40 years old than to 30. Running The New Farm was taking up several hours per day. Renee and I purchased a 30% share of two new condominium projects going up in Simcoe. These sold out six months after their completion. Tobacco in Norfolk County was beginning to slide. The Canadian cigarette manufacturers were purchasing cheaper Virginia leaf from the United States. The buyers of tobacco were demanding larger bulk deliveries and the smaller growers could not make the financial outlays for bigger and more expensive equipment necessary to stay in business. The governments were overtaxing the finished product. Smaller tobacco farmers were selling off their quota and converting their farms into other crops. Norfolk County was being purified. The incoming Golden Age of Earth was in a cosmic sense right around the corner. Renee and I leased out 90% of the arable land on The New Farm. We spent a great many hours contemplating our "Mighty I Am Presence." We began to be noticed as that strange couple who kept to themselves, didn't party and attend any local church but everyone in the 63 000 peopled region seemed to know us. They just couldn't get close to us. One day Renee and I were shopping at the Superstore market located in Simcoe. It was a weekday afternoon near 3:00 PM. It was in the summer of 1975. I, Robert MacAlpine Noble AFC, M.Ed., B.A.Sc. felt a tap on my shoulder. I turned about and looked at a Canadian Air Force officer, a major who was standing behind me. The man looked familiar. He was accompanied by woman of about 50 years.

"Excuse me sir," the officer said, "are you Flying Officer Noble?"

I did not immediately recognize the man. I studied the officer's decorations. There was the DFM and the CD along with several WW II decorations. But why was the officer wearing a DFM? Officers earned the DFC. Then I recognized a face. It was the former flight sergeant Fraser, at least he was a flight sergeant 25 years earlier.

"Major Fraser?" I asked.

"Indeed it is me!" Fraser extended his hand. Then he turned to the woman beside him. "Meg this is Flying Officer Noble. He was one of the first flight cadets I ever recruited when I was posted to the recruiting station in Toronto. That was in 1950. Mr. Noble what have you done with yourself since you left the RCAF?"

"Did you by chance get a classified commission sir?" I asked.

"Indeed I did," Fraser answered. "I am retiring from the Service next month. Did you know that I own the old Hunter dairy farm a mile down the road from where your place is I have been lucky in that I inherited it from an uncle. We don't work it ourselves but lease everything out. We live in the old farm house. This is Meg my wife. I thought I spotted you in this store about a week ago. I assume the red headed lady is your wife."

I handed out my business card to Major Fraser. The RCAF adopted the rank names used by the army when they integrated with the army, navy and air forces. Major Fraser would have been Squadron Leader Fraser under the old designations. "I thought you were going to get out after 20 years. By my estimation you have been in service for over 32 years. Is that true?"

'"My war service counts double," Fraser answered. "Meg and I are packing it in. My two boys have both graduated from university. One is a pharmacist and one a civil engineer I have been lucky." Major Fraser handed me a card with his contact information. "May I contact you later?" he asked. I agreed. With that we parted company. Renee was loading the four doors Jeep she used to do marketing.

"Who was that couple you were talking with just a while ago?" she asked.

I said, "Someone I haven't seen for nearly 25 years. Unbelievable, they are neighbors of ours. We are going to have them visit us shortly."

So the Frasers came to visit Renee and me at The New Farm. They were the first "outsiders" Renee and I ever admitted to our property that did not work for us.

"I have searched all my life for the real reason I am here," Fraser confessed to me while we were having tea in the living room of The New Farm. "There must be a Divine Reason why we all live. I believe we come back again and again until we get it right. What do you two think?" Major Fraser directed his question to Renee and me.

I answered him. "I now believe there is a Heavenly Father," I replied. "I will search for Him and find Him or I will die trying! I also believe that you two will do the same. A life stream reincarnates many times. He has to because he has to get it right before he can join the Ascended Beings in the Higher Octaves. I have only been informed about one past embodiment. Even though everyone considers that a great life time I did not make the Ascension. Here I am back again. This time I will make it. I have searched for the Holy Grail since - forever. Is it here? Perhaps this vocation is the Grail? Is it under this coffee table? Is it hidden in this corner, or is it across the street?"

"Have you found it?" Major Fraser asked.

"I Am part of it," I replied. "The Holy Grail is the family of Jesus the Christ. They are his children.

CHAPTER 53

Robert and Renee are Old People

Renee and I have lived nearly 40 years apart from the World. Although we are in it we are not part of it. Both of us have enjoyed good health and have kept active. I was now 80 years of age. One day while playing golf I became winded after three holes and had to rest a while. I collared a player coming down the 9th fairway and asked him to send a golf cart to pick me up while I went to sit on the bench beside the 4th tee. I wasn't in pain but had a difficult time catching my breath. This shortness of breath was becoming a common occurrence. The cart arrived and I returned to the clubhouse. I stored my clubs in the Jeep Liberty I used for my personal transport and went back to The New Farm. It was the first and hopefully the last time I would ever abort a round after three holes. When I arrived at the farm house I thought about my regular bimonthly visit that I last had with Dr. Weaver, my family physician. True, I was on high blood pressure medication but that seemed to bring the condition under control. There had been other attacks causing me to be windless but nothing compared to this last one. I simply wanted to lie down but first I wanted to call Dr. Weaver's office and have him make an appointment with the local cardiologist for a more comprehensive examination. Weaver had suggested this at an earlier visit.

"I would like you to have an angiogram," Dr. March stated. "My testing has shown there may have been a heart attack recently. Did you have any serious pain recently?" I didn't recall any pain but I consented to the treatment. So three days later Renee and I arrived at the Hamilton Institute of Cardiology at 10.00 AM. The Doctor supervising the procedure decided to insert the needle in the right wrist rather than the groin. Some sort of dye was inserted which would illumine the arteries. The entire job took about 15 minutes. I waited in the lobby of the Cardiologist's office. He came out to talk with me in 20 minutes. Renee was also there.

My name is Dr. George. You are going to need a triple bypass operation immediately. I have consulted with a colleague. Stents might have helped a year or two ago but in your case a bypass is the answer. One of your arteries is almost completely clogged, a second is 80% clogged and another 50% clogged. If you consent to this surgery we can start tomorrow at 3 PM. I was stunned. My last visit to the family physician showed no heart problems. I went to Dr. March our physician because I wondered why I was weak and winded easily. A simple walk around a downtown Simcoe block was tiresome. Frequently I had to stop and rest and lean against an electrical pole. I knew I had some type of defect but I didn't consider it that serious. I decided right then to have the operation.

So one and one half days later I checked into the Hamilton Cardiac Institute. The nurse assigned to me took my clothes and I was dressed in a hospital gown. The nurse shaved me in the areas that were to be operated on. I went to surgery at 6 PM. I came to at 10.30 PM. The intensive care unit was noisy and most of it came from the nurses stationed there. I looked at clock. I noticed the catheter inserted in my penis. I detested this procedure and had told the physicians and nurses not to do this. The last time it was done for a minor operation of 20 minutes the catheter had damaged my urinary track. I had to stay in the hospital for two extra days having catheters inserted in and taken out of my penis. This was done in order to get the urinary system working again. The doctors told me it was the use of catheters that caused the urinary system to go weak in the first place. Why did they do the same thing that caused the problem to make it work? It didn't work so I went home against the advice of the urologist. I "stole" a urinal from that hospital to measure my piss. After about three months my urination returned to normal. Now the quacks had put the catheter back into my penis after I specifically told the surgeon not to do it. They agreed not to. Their word meant nothing and they considered their judgment infallible.

I spent 11 days in the cardiac ward. I met several younger men and in their 50s who also had bypass operations. I then went home with Renee and a neighbor who volunteered to drive us. When I arrived beside the farm house I had to pee badly. So I discharged what must have been a liter of fluid on the lawn. I had no urinary problems after that. I went upstairs to the bedroom and fell asleep instantly. It was 2 PM.

I awoke about 3 AM. There was a very tall man standing about two feet from the right side of the bed. I knew this being was an Ascended Master. Then I noticed a feminine being standing on the left side of the room. This being was not as tall as the male. It was time for me to pass through the change called "death" and I fully knew it.

"I want to stay on until the Permanent Golden Age is fully anchored in this world," I thought as I directed my desire towards the male being. The tall Being did not answer. He stood near the bed silent. I knew the Being as Jesus but could not determine the identity of the feminine being. I was later to determine the other being was "Ruth" who had been Jesus' teacher when he was in Egypt. There were other parts of the discussion between me and Jesus. These were always done in The Silence. As the days passed I regained my strength rapidly. The tendency to become winded after brief exercise disappeared in three months and after six months I was walking about The New Farm. Renee had gained 20 pounds during my recovery which she never could lose. She remarked to me: "You are very courageous." So it is with all Students of the Light. It takes courage to follow the Light. I never told any other human being about this experience.

CHAPTER 54

Alumni Reunion, the Same Old Shit

W hile Renee and I were recovering from my triple bypass we received a telephone call from the Alumni Office of the University of Waterville. It was a request for me to attend a 50th anniversary reunion. I was, after all, an original graduate in 1959 from the first ever engineering class and from the defunct course of Engineering Physics. I requested not to attend because I was still in recovery but was talked into attending by my former classmate, Jack Lennox for at least the secret ceremony of the "Sons of Martha."

I could not recognize the campus after an absence of almost 50 years. I finally flagged down an engineering student in his third year of studies and asked him to drive Renee and I in our Jeep Liberty to the meeting area. The young man obliged us. Renee was getting antsy. I tipped the young student with a $20 dollar bill.

"Let's stay for the important things," she said. Then we will leave. The Jeep Liberty was parked outside the banquet hall and Renee and I entered at 7.00 PM. A hostess escorted us to the small dining room where the ceremonies were to take place. I was to sit at a special table. The kitchen served Renee and me a meat dinner which I did not eat. This happened even though I requested through the alumni office for a total vegetarian meal with no alcoholic drinks to be served. The spread cost us $200 and there was absolutely nothing we could eat or drink. A request to the kitchen staff had the unsatisfactory dishes replaced with two wilted salads and some glasses of flat coca cola. An exorbitant price was paid for this. After a few short talks and the Iron Ring ceremony three big wigs got up and gave short ceremonial speeches on the current mess the world was in.

"We need a one world government," the first speaker said. That is the only movement which will allow us to achieve world peace.

"This world needs a world currency and world central bank. It will stabilize our economy and bring prosperity. It is the movement some of us favor." This was said by a second speaker.

"We need a world religion. That movement will stop bickering between different members of different creeds," a third speaker said. Then I was asked to say a few words. I declined but the Dean of engineering and other big wigs persuaded me to give the audience some of my thoughts. After all, I was a wealthy man. So I rose. I examined the distinguished attendees and then I said, "There has been a lot of talk about movements tonight. While these movements seem to be important I will tell you about the most important one. Do you know what that is? It is the bowel movement."

This is a story of two People in the Light. They cast no shadows because the Light casts no shadows.

GLOSSARY OF
CANADIAN TERMS

Aircraft Monthly - A fictitious magazine modeled on *Soldier of Fortune*.

Air Force Cross - A medal rewarded to officers of the RCAF for gallantry exhibited while not in combat. The initials are AFC.

Ashkenazi - A Jew who is a descendent of the ancient Khazer nation that existed from about 700 AD to 1000 AD. The Khazer royal family converted to Judaism under their King to solidify their nation which was being threatened from two sides. One threat came from the Rus (ancient Vikings) while the other threat was from Islam. Eventually, most of the ordinary people of Khazaria also converted. With the collapse of the Khazer Kingdom, (circa 1000AD) suddenly hundreds of thousands of Jews appeared in the nations of Eastern Europe such as Poland, Russia and Hungary. They are not descendants of any of the 12 tribes mentioned in Exodus. For an authentic discussion of this read Arthur Koestler's book the *Thirteenth Tribe*.

BC - British Columbia, the Westernmost Province of Canada, Japanese Canadians were interned there during the War from 1942 to 1945.

B. Ed. - Bachelor of Education. A degree granted to an aspiring teacher in Ontario by any faculty of education connected to any university in Ontario.

Bathurst Street - A north south road running from Lake Ontario to far north of Metropolitan Toronto's upper boundary

Bay Street – This is the financial artery of Metropolitan Toronto. It runs north from the waterfront at Lake Ontario for about three miles.

Bf109C – This was a pre-1940 Messerschmidt fighter aircraft; a precursor of the Bf109E-2 which opposed the Royal Air Force during the Battle of Britain.

Beer parlor – This is a tavern where only beer or ale is served. A spit and saw dust emporium.

Boiler room – This is an office with several desks and telephones. This term would now represent an office used by several telemarketers.

Borough of York - A large township separate from the original City of Toronto. It is situated north of the city. In the mid 1920's part of York Township withdrew from the original township in a squabble over how tax money was used and become the Township of North York. The other townships making up Metropolitan Toronto are: Etobicoke on the western side of the city, Scarborough on the eastern side, East York on the east and central part of the city. York township is now located on the north central side of the original city. With the absorption of these townships and the expansion of the populations after World War II the population of metro Toronto is about 3 000 000 in 2011. It recently passed Chicago in population making it the 3rd largest English speaking city in North America.

Boston - A Toronto word for the American game of pocket billiards. The game is also referred to as "bang ball."

Bridle Path - A fancy area located north of the original Toronto and located near and east of Yonge Street. The lots containing these houses can be measured in acres.

British Commonwealth Air Training Plan – A plan instituted in 1940 to train Allied air crews. During the War there were seven aircrew trades: pilots, observers, navigators, air gunners, wireless air gunners, flight engineers and air bombers. It was abandoned in March 1945. In peacetime only pilots and observers were trained as air crew.

Cattle Auction – This was the wholesale recruitment of teachers for work in the Ontario Secondary School System. This was caused because the school system was growing faster than the faculties of education could train teachers. It usually took place in the spring time and featured a newspaper section of advertisements in the Toronto Globe and Mail. It lasted till about 1971 and disappeared. New job openings had become scarce.

CCF - The initials of the Cooperative Commonwealth Federation. This was the precursor of the NDP (New Democratic Party), a socialist Mecca. It once formed the Government of Ontario in the 1990's. During their tenure the provincial debt more than tripled!

Chipmunk - A totally aerobatic training aircraft manufactured by the de Havilland Aircraft Company and in service in the RAF and RCAF immediately after World War II. It is said that Princes Phillip and Charles of the British Royal family trained on this plane.

Class A golf professional - A rank granted to a golf professional who has completed an apprenticeship in Canada lasting at least four years. The candidate must demonstrate some playing ability.

Classified Commission - A senior NCO in the Canadian Armed Forces would retire in his 40's. However he could be commissioned from the ranks as he neared retirement. For example, a junior NCO could be commissioned as a lieutenant in the army, spend a few years in that rank and be promoted to a captain for his final five years to maximize his pension. A senior NCO could be promoted to Captain and finish his career as a major. This benefitted both parties. The service kept a competent service man longer and the serviceman increased his retirement benefits.

Cruiser - A 1940's name for a Toronto police patrol car.

Danforth Avenue - An East-West street starting east of the Don River in Toronto and running to Scarborough. It was famous for many used car lots. There is a sizeable Greek community living there.

Director of Education - What they call a superintendent in the USA. This is the highest administrative officer of the board. It is an appointed position.

DFC - Distinguished Flying Cross; a decoration awarded to Canadian Airmen for gallantry during World War II. They held officer rank.

DFM - Distinguished Flying Medal; a decoration awarded to airmen who were not officers during World War II.

ED - The Efficiency Decoration giving to middle ranking officers during World War II.

Family Compact – This was a clique of white Anglo-Saxons, northern Irish Protestants and Scots who was the established rulers of Upper Canada and Toronto in the 1800's. Most Canadian conspiracy theory addicts think they still rule today.

First Form – This is now Grade 9 in modern language. Obviously second form was grade 10 and so on.

Flight Lieutenant - Royal Canadian Air Force rank equivalent to Captain in the USAF

Flying Officer - Royal Canadian Air Force rank equivalent to Lieutenant in the USAF

Glen Echo Loop - The terminal point of the Yonge Street Car line located at the northernmost boundary of the Old City of Toronto. North of Glen Echo was North York. In 1945, North York had about 40 000 people. In 2011 it had about 800 000.

Goy - A derogatory term to describe a non-Jew, usually a white person. The plural is "goyim." The word is used by Ashkenazis.

Gray Coach - A bus company started by the TTC, in the 1920's to provide inter urban transport.

Grey Cup Tickets - Tickets for the championship football game of the Canadian Football League. They are hard to come by.

Junior Matriculation - Graduation from grade 12 or fourth form.

Knish - Pronounced with the "k". A patty of dough stuffed with liver or beef. Essentially scrape the kitchen. Sephardic Jews don't eat these.

Kasha - A form of buck wheat.

KBE - British Decoration, meaning Knight Commander of the British Empire. Not accepted by Canadians any longer. In fact, the Canadian government forbids it.

KC - King's Councillor, a right granted to successful lawyers in Canada. Applicable as long as the reigning British monarch is a man.

King George V – The British Monarch reigning from 1911 to 1935. He was succeeded by his son King Edward VIII in 1935. Edward VIII reigned for about one year. This is the future King who abdicated because he could not carry on as King without the help of the woman he loved. He saw that the munitions makers and financiers were planning a war in Europe and tried to stop it. It cost him his throne.

King George VI - British Monarch from 1936 to 1952 who was a chronic smoker and father of Queen Elizabeth II of England, also Queen Elizabeth I of Great Britain. The original Good Queen Bess of the 16th century was not a queen of Great Britain. The current Queen Elizabeth cannot be Elizabeth II of Great Britain! There was never a Queen Elizabeth II of Great Britain.

Leslieville - A village absorbed by Toronto along Lake Ontario in the east.

Maple Leaf Stadium - Built in the mid 1920's and demolished in the 1960's. Formerly this was the home baseball stadium for the Triple A, International League Toronto Maple Leafs. Oddly enough, it was torn down right after the Toronto Maple Leafs won the Little World Series in 1967.

MC - Military Cross: A Decoration for gallantry awarded to officers serving with the Canadian Forces in World War II.

Melekas – Portuguese for caked snot in one's nose

Mensch – A Yiddish word which means "man."

Muskoka - A vacation area north of Toronto. Goldie Hahn and Kurt Russell have a cottage there.

Newfoundland Screech – This is a very cheap wine. It was the staple drink of a rubbydubs living in Toronto. It cost less than $1:00 to buy a quart in 1945.

Niagara Village – This is a community bounded by Queen Street, Bathurst Street and Niagara Street in Toronto.

999 Queen Street West - The Toronto Insane Asylum built in the mid-1800s. Conservationists fought to preserve this creepy and large building which was a grim reminder of how the mentally ill were treated in former times. A place of bad experiences.

Ontario High School Entrance Exams - Some unfortunate grade 8 students had to write these tests if their teacher did not recommend them for acceptance to a secondary school.

Orangeman - A Protestant Irish man usually from Ulster living in Toronto. Also he belonged in many instances to the Orange Order. No person, for many years, could be mayor or chief of police in Toronto unless he was an Orangeman. He also had to be a high ranking Mason. This barrier was breeched in the 1960's when Nathan Phillips, a candidate of Jewish background was elected mayor.

PCC Streetcar – This was The Presidents Conference Committee car; the first of a truly modern streetcar design. It originated in the USA to save the dying street railways of many large cities. The original design originated in the USA. These cars were produced by the St. Louis Car Company and Pullman Standard. Toronto, at one time, operated about 750 cars. This was the largest fleet of any city in the world.

Peter Witt Streetcar - The TTC's first new steel streetcar built by three companies: Canadian Car and Foundry, the Ottawa Car Company and Brill. These cars lasted more than 42 years in service.

Pilot Officer - A rank equal to that of 2nd lieutenant in the USAF.

Principals' Course - A teacher with five years of good experience could be recommended by his employer to take the principals' course. It was mandatory to have both parts of this program to become as principal or superintendent. Boards, depending on their size were allotted so many positions on the course.

QC - Queen's Counsel, an honorary title to a recognized lawyer granted when the reigning British monarch is a woman.

QEW - The Queen Elizabeth Way, a four lane road running from the western limits of the original city of Toronto to Niagara Falls, Ontario. Portions of it have been expanded to six lanes. It has controlled access. It was one of the first expressways built in the World. The road was named after Queen Elizabeth II's mother, the former wife of George VI. It opened in 1939.

Queen Street - An east-west street running from the western limits of the City of Toronto to the eastern Limits. A National Geographic article, published in the 2000's featured the Queen Street Car Route.

RAF - Royal Air Force, started after WWI in the 1920's.

RCAF Enlisted Ranks:

AC 2nd Class, equal to E1 in the US Army
AC 1st Class, equal to E2 in the US Army
LAC, leading aircraftsman equal to E3 in the US Army
Corporal, equal to E4 in the US Army
Sergeant, equal to E5 in the US Army
Flight Sergeant, equal to E6 in the US Army
WO2, Warrant Officer 2nd Class, equal to E7 in the US Army
WO1, Warrant Officer 1st Class, equal to E8 in the US Army

RBC – This is completely fictitious broadcasting company. The initials mean Royal Broadcasting Corporation.

RCAF - Royal Canadian Air Force started after WWI and continues at time of publication as part of the Canadian Forces. It is now referred to as the Canadian Air Force.

Rehab School – This was formerly an institution for training WW II veterans of the Canadian Forces returning to civilian life. It is now the site of Ryerson University in Toronto.

Rosedale – This is an upscale region of Toronto where old money resides.

Royal Conservatory of Music – This is a music school located in Toronto. The famous Canadian pianist Glenn Gould trained there.

Rubbydub - A Toronto slang expression for a hopeless alcoholic.

Sapper - A Canadian and British slang word for military engineer.

Schmuck - A derogatory Yiddish expression used to describe a nasty person or sometimes the male sexual member.

Senior Matriculation - During the great Depression in the 1930's the Ontario Government decided to include an extra year of public schooling called fifth form or grade 13. What was taught was supposed to be equivalent to year one of university. When completed successfully it was called a Senior Matriculation.

Sephardic - A Jew descending from the Holy Land ancestry. About 4% or less of the modern Jews descend from ancient Israel. These people mostly settled, after leaving the Holy Land, in what is now Spain, Portugal or the British Isles. They came to America in the 1600's or perhaps earlier. They were among the first settlers in North America coming from Spanish Territories. In modern Israel, founded in 1948, the Sephardic are treated as third class citizens. Eastern European Jews are first, then American Jews second. The Arabs are the lowest class even if they are citizens.

Shiksa - Yiddish term denoting a non-Jewish female, usually white.

Szchlub – This is the actual Yiddish name for slob. It is amazing how Yiddish words have been absorbed into Modern English. I recently overheard a new immigrant from Scotland refer to himself as a "klutz" after he spilled soup during a luncheon on his trousers while visiting with the author.

Squadron Leader - Royal Canadian Air Force rank equivalent to a major in the USAF.

St. Clair Avenue - An east to west road running from the western city limit of Toronto City to near the eastern limit.

Superintendent - In Ontario, this is usually the next rank under the Director of Education.

Teachers' Ratings - If a teacher was rated 1 or 2 by a provincial inspector dismissal was eminent. A rating of 3 meant he was keeping his job. If he had a 4 rating he was considered good. If he had a 5 rating very good. A 6 rating was excellent. The inspectors decimalized the ratings, for example 5.8.

Toronto Comet – There is no such daily.

Toronto Telegraph - A fictional daily.

TTC - The Toronto Transportation Commission started operations in September 1921 taken over from the Toronto Railway Company, a privately owned street railway which in its latter years of operation provided unsatisfactory service. The TTC restored track work, established additional routes into newer parts of the city, and funded the purchase of new street cars. Some of the older but serviceable cars used by its predecessor were modified and upgraded by the TTC and saw service until as late as March 1951. The TTC still operates the transit of Toronto to this date. The author finds it eerie that certain people now want to privatize the TTC so it will be more efficiently operated!

United Empire Loyalist - After the War for American Independence (1775 to 1783) some people residing in the new United States of America decided to venture north into Canada and receive land grants offered by the British Government. Seizing the opportunity they left the USA and moved, usually via the Niagara Frontier, into Upper Canada (now

Ontario) these settlers didn't move because they were necessarily loyal to King George III but because they sensed the opportunity.

Upper Canada - The name the Province of Ontario had before Canada came into being on July 4, 1867. It was also called "Canada West."

Upper Canada College - Probably the premier private school situated in Ontario, at least in the opinion of its alumni. It was started in the mid 1800's.

Virginia Ovals - A Canadian cigarette which was rolled in manufacturing process to be oval in cross section rather than round. The author recalls that the actress Tallulah Bankhead smoked these.

VP – This refers to the vice-principal otherwise known as an assistant principal in the USA.

YMHA - Young Men's' Hebrew Association, usually used exclusively by Ashkenazi

Yonge Street - Main north-south Street in Toronto. In 1796, when Lieutenant Governor of Upper Canada; John Graves Simcoe landed on the future site of Toronto; he called the location's name "York." Simcoe wanted access to the northern regions of Upper Canada and gave land grants to the new settlers if they could clear a new road running from the waterfront to the northern regions. This road became Yonge Street. Toronto folk brag that it is recognized as the longest street in the World by the *Guinness Book of Records*.

Zombie - A derogatory name applied to all Canadian Servicemen who were drafted into the armed forces during WWII.

APPENDIX 1

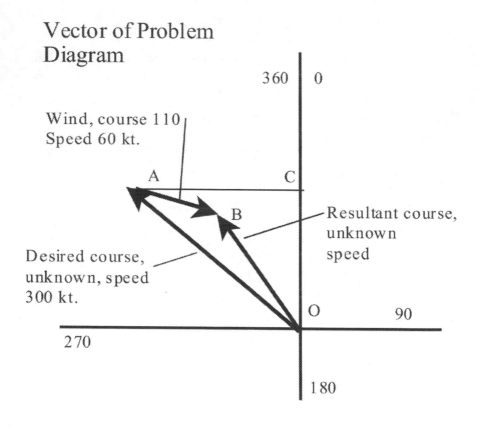

Vector of Problem Diagram

360 | 0

Wind, course 110
Speed 60 kt.

A   C

B   Resultant course,
unknown
speed

Desired course,
unknown, speed
300 kt.

O   90

270

180

1. Construct a wind vector diagram as shown.
Representing the aircraft's final speed and
course is the vector $\overrightarrow{OB}$. Representing the wind
is vector $\overrightarrow{AB}$. And the vector representing the
path that the aircraft must take to finish on
the correct course is $\overrightarrow{OA}$.

2. Draw a $\perp$ line to the north-south axis from A to C.
Examine the quadrilateral ACOB.

3. The angles of quadrilateral ACOB add to 360°.
$\angle ABO$ can be determined by subtracting from 360°
as follows: $360° - (\angle CAB + \angle BOC + \angle ACO) = 220°$.
This gives $\angle ABO$ the reflex angle as 140°.

4. Use the law of sines in $\triangle AOB$ to determine $\angle AOB$.
$\dfrac{\sin \angle AOB}{60} = \dfrac{\sin 140°}{300}$ which solves and gives
$\text{Sin} \angle AOB = 0.129$, hence $\angle AOB = 7.30°$.

5. Take 7.30° off the desired course. This $330 - 7 = 307$.
This is the desired course.

6. We now must determine the resultant speed. Using
the sine law we will determine the size of OB.

7. $\dfrac{OB}{\text{Sin} 33°} = \dfrac{300}{\sin 140°}$

This solves for OB = 251kt.

8. Using the Law of Cosines this can be checked.
We have $OA^2 = OB^2 + AB^2 - 2OA \times AB \times \text{Cos} 140°$
Using numbers we have $OA^2 = 251^2 + 60^2 - 251 \times 60 \times \cos 140°$
This gives OA = 300 kt. approximately.

9. A symbol like $\overrightarrow{AB}$ is a classical math representation
of a vector. It has both direction and magnitude. AB
represents the size alone. Volume which has no diection is
called a scalar. Some times the magnitude of $\overrightarrow{AB}$ may be
signifed as just AB.

APPENDIX 2 – THE
HOUSE OF JESUS

With the Advent of Dr. David Hawkins Books, especially *Power versus Force*, in 1995 (see Suggested Reading) a new method of determining Truth as opposed to Falsehood had come on the scene. As a person always seeking Truth had I realized in the early 1960's how to determine Truth I could have saved myself many distressing events that cost me tens of thousands of dollars of hard acquired funds from being unwisely invested in bad business ventures. Knowing the Truth from falsehood would have also pointed me in the right direction in my search for Enlightenment. Knowing how to determine Truth from falsehood would have led me to avoid encounters with many unsavory characters whose main concern was to advance themselves no matter what the cost would be to others.

I learned of the arm test used in kinesiology in the early 1960's yet gave it little attention. "An interesting phenomenon," I thought. "How could I possibly use such a thing for anything other than the adjustment of the physical body?" Then in 1983, I met an interesting gentleman, possibly in his early 50's. "Mr. Nobleman," he commented to me. "You should check out your ancestry. You have a tremendous amount of Royal Blood, especially from the Scottish Line."

"Indeed," I thought. "So how do I go about doing this checking?" As far as I understood my ancestors on my father's side originated in what is now Spain but was then called Leon. They had to flee from that troubled land in 1492. Two of them sailed with Columbus to the New World on his First Voyage. Why, for them to avoid persecution from the Roman Catholic Church and its Inquisition. This was the story related to me by Esther Perez my paternal grandmother who kept an oral history of her family. It is the female genes through which important things are passed down. Little did I realize many years later, when I was consulting Irene Yaychuck Ph.D., a supreme practitioner of Kinesiology that I started to probe my roots. What came out about my Scottish roots and my Ancient Spanish origins was far from fiction. It was absolutely true!

The use of Educational Kinesiology, or EK, to balance the physical body is wonderful. But it is not the only use for it. It is far superior to investigating yellowed old papers with dubious family trees; it is far simpler to pose simple questions about one's origins and test whether they are true. On testing my mother's roots I discovered that she had 56% Scottish roots and was a direct lineal descendant of King Kenneth MacAlpine (circa 850 AD). King Kenneth was himself a descendent of Princess Tea Tempi (circa 580 BC) who was taken from the Holy Land by the Prophet Jeremiah when the Babylonians invaded. King Kenneth was the son of Alpin, King of Scots who married the daughter of the King of Picts. This marriage succeeded in merging the Picts and Scots into one nation. Apparently, the Blood of Jesus himself filtered into this line, making it indeed a part of the Sangreal. When this came to light I felt extremely privileged. "Did Jesus' genes present me with some special quality? Perhaps. My mother was essentially a MacAlpine.

And what about the father, a man with the man who descended from Columbus? Well he was a descendent of King David also. He was also a descendent of Charlemagne (circa 800 AD) He was also a descendent of Jesus. Yet he spent his lifetime in many unsavory pursuits. Because of probing into my father's line I discovered my many relationships. Third and fourth cousins existed on both sides dating back 200 years and more in the Americas. Indeed our roots are so interesting I feel like boasting to Canadian and American establishment families that my family was here first. I am even a cousin of the British Royal Family.

The fecal matter hit the fan in the early 1980's when *Holy Blood, Holy Grail* came out. Most religious leaders had a fit. "Not true," they screamed, "of all the nonsense." Now, at this time, 28 June 2016 there are many books about Jesus and his children. Why such anger over a book? The anger comes from the realization that the descendent of Jesus, and there about 8600 of them at this time are members of the most powerful Royal Family on the Earth. The religious authorities think: "God forbid anything so audacious should come out. What if the ordinary man suddenly discovered this? Where would our power go? "The descendants of Jesus are the "Sangreal or the true Holy Grail!

I know personally that about 4900 of them are working to hasten the Permanent Golden Age of Mankind. I have worked with them for 45 some years. I suspect that the vast numbers are ignorant of their Royal Genes. This Permanent Golden Age has already arrived and has been with us for about a year. No attempt to form a world government, a North American Union, or anything leading up to a global slave state will ever succeed. Planet Earth is not destined to be governed by the dark side any longer. It is this insidious group of players on the dark side of life who can't abide Freedom and Prosperity in the world. At this time a wave of freedom is sweeping the Middle East. It will spread over the World. Canadians and Americans are being woken up.

Mankind does not need a king or dictator who suffers, no doubt, from the worst traits a human being can fall into. What is the worst of these: messianic megalomaniacal narcissism. God must be king over every soul. All men have their own Mighty I AM Presence. The World's Spiritual Energy is now constantly growing. Every time it jumps up in comes the darkness to try to quash it. The darkness is running out of time.

APPENDIX 3 -CAR
PAYMENT PROBLEM

The formula for computing monthly car payment is

$$P = \frac{iA}{1 - \dfrac{1}{(1+i)^n}}$$

In this formula **i** represents the interest charged over the payment interval, in this case one month. N will represent the numbers of years during which the payments are made.

n will represent the total number of payments and **A** is the loan amount. We will let **P** represent the equal payment.

In this case N = 3 years

Since the payments are monthly n = 12 (months) ✕ 3 (years) = 36 payments

The annual interest rate is 12% so the monthly rate = 12/12 = 1% per month, so i = 0.01

The amount borrowed A is $8500.

$$P = \frac{0.01 \times 8500}{(1 - \dfrac{1}{(1+0.01)^{36}})}$$

This can be computed easily on a scientific calculator. The numerator will become 85. Next determine $(1.01)^{36}$. Use the exponent key on the calculator usually designated y^x Enter the number 1.01 on the calculated. Push the y^x key and enter 36, now push the = key. The value of $(1.01)^{36}$ = 1.43077. Now you have:

$$P = \frac{85}{1 - \dfrac{1}{1.43077}}$$

Now enter: 1-1÷1.43077=0.30108

Divide 85 by 0.30108 and you get 282.32. You calculate $282.32 as your monthly payment.

As a check 36 payments will come to 36 X 282.32 = $10163.56.
The interest you will pay will be $10163.56 -$8500 = $1653.66
A 1% interest rate doesn't sound small anymore.

SELECTED READING

The followings books should be read by any person seeking the Spiritual Way.

1. The Magdalen Legacy,
Laurence Gardner,
Harper-Element Publishers
77-85 Fulham Palace Road,
Hammersmith, London W6 8JB

2. Bloodline of the Holy Grail,
Laurence Gardner
Harper-Element 77-85 Fulham Palace Road,
Hammersmith, London W6 8JB

3.Holy Blood, Holy Grail
Michael Baigent; Richard Leigh, and Henry Lincoln,
Jonathan Cape, Ltd. 30 Bedford Square
London, WC1

4. Jesus, Last of the Pharaohs
Ralph Ellis,
Adventures Unlimited,
PO Box 74,
Kempton, Illinois 60946

5. Power versus Force,
David Hawkins, MD, Ph.D.
Veritas Publishing,
PO Box 3516,
W. Sedona, Arizona 86340, USA

6. The Eye of the I: From which Nothing is Hidden,
David Hawkins, MD, Ph.D.
Veritas Publishing,
PO Box 3516,
W. Sedona, Arizona 86340, USA

7. Discovering the Presence of God, Devotional Non Duality,
David Hawkins, MD, Ph.D.
Veritas Publishing,
PO Box 3516,
W. Sedona, Arizona 86340, USA

8. Reality and Subjectivity
David Hawkins, MD, Ph.D.
Veritas Publishing,
PO Box 3516,
W. Sedona, Arizona 86340, USA

9. Truth vs. Falsehood, How to tell the Difference,
David Hawkins, MD, Ph.D.
Veritas Publishing,
PO Box 3516,
W. Sedona, Arizona 86340, USA

10. Unveiled Mysteries,
Guy Warren Ballard (Godfrey Ray King)
Saint Germain Press,
1120 Stonehedge Drive,
Schaumburg, Illinois, 60194, USA

11. The Magic Presence,
Guy Warren Ballard (Godfrey Ray King)
Saint Germain Press,
1120 Stonehedge Drive,
Schaumburg, Illinois, 60194, USA

12. The Two Marys,
Sylvia Brown,
New American Library, Penguin Group (USA)
375 Hudson Street, New York, New York,10014, USA

13. The Thirteenth Tribe - The Khazer Empire and its Heritage
Arthur Koestler, Hutchinson
& Co. 1976

14. Lost Horizon
James Hilton,
MacMillan Publishers

ABOUT THE AUTHOR

Leonard Comyn Nobleman was born in Toronto on December 1, 1935. He likes to say he grew up in the slums. After being educated in the "choicest" of Toronto elementary and secondary institutions he attended the University of Waterloo from January 1958 until graduating with a B.A.Sc. in Engineering Physics in July 1962. His engineering career was a failure and he quit that profession and took teacher training. While acting as a teacher of mathematics and physics he obtained an M. Ed. in school administration from Queen's University at Kingston in 1973. He also tried his hand as a professional golfer. While it was fun there is no living to be earned except for the elite players.

He has been a Spiritual Seeker from childhood. He considers that his full time career. He is married to Renee, a trained social worker from Rio de Janeiro and New York City. He considers himself fortunate to have another Spiritual Seeker as his wife.

In the late 1990's Len Nobleman discovered the Work of Doctor David Hawkins M.D., Ph.D. Using Kinesiology he tested for the spiritual energy of his parents. He found that his mother vibrated between 20 and 150. So also did his father. Yet his brother and sister vibrated between the lower to higher 400's. Perhaps these children were born with the parents they were blessed with not to be helped by them but the other way around.

In 1983 he left Toronto never to take up residence there again and settled in Norfolk County. He no longer can reside in a populated area so he dwells in a house built in the 19th century but modernized on a large lot in the country. Very few people seeking the Light can tolerate a large city.

Printed in the United States
By Bookmasters